D0385717

Voices from the
BATTLE OF
THE BULGE

Voices from the
BATTLE OF
THE BULGE

Nigel de Lee

David & Charles

A DAVID & CHARLES BOOK

David & Charles is a subsidiary of F+W (UK) Ltd.,
an F+W Publications Inc. company

First published in the UK in 2004

Copyright © David & Charles 2004

Distributed in North America
by F+W Publications, Inc.
4700 East Galbraith Road
Cincinnati, OH 45236
1-800-289-0963

All rights reserved. No part of this publication may be reproduced, stored in
a retrieval system, or transmitted, in any form or by any means, electronic or
mechanical, by photocopying, recording or otherwise, without prior permission
in writing from the publisher.

Every reasonable effort has been made to contact the copyright holders,
but if there are any errors or omissions, David & Charles will be pleased
to correct these in any subsequent printing.

A catalogue record for this book is available from the British Library.

ISBN 0 7153 1920 5 hardback

Printed in Great Britain by Antony Rowe Ltd
for David & Charles
Brunel House   Newton Abbot   Devon

Commissioning Editor   Ruth Binney
Head of Design   Ali Myer
Desk Editor   Lewis Birchon
Production Controller   Jennifer Campbell

Visit our website at www.davidandcharles.co.uk
A catalogue record for this book is available from the British Library.

David & Charles books are available from all good bookshops;
alternatively you can contact our Orderline on (0)1626 334555
or write to us at FREEPOST EX2 110, David & Charles Direct,
Newton Abbot, TQ12 4ZZ (no stamp required UK mainland).

CONTENTS

OBJECTIVES OF THE BATTLE

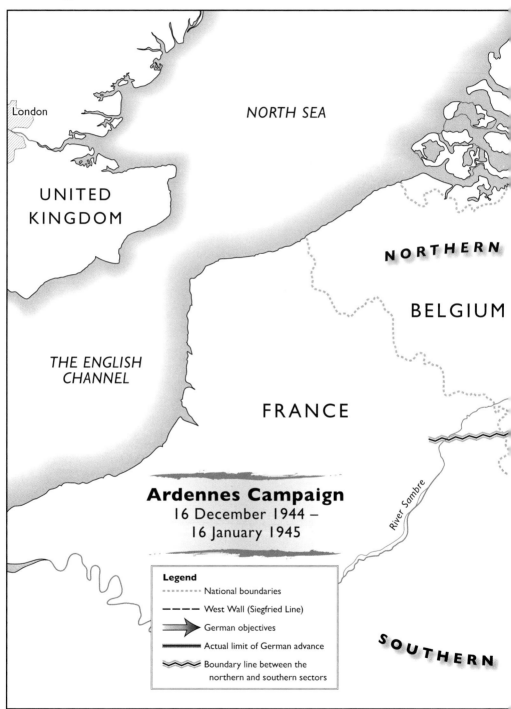

London

NORTH SEA

UNITED
KINGDOM

N O R T H E R N

BELGIUM

*THE ENGLISH
CHANNEL*

FRANCE

Ardennes Campaign
16 December 1944 –
16 January 1945

River Sambre

Legend
`··········` National boundaries
`— — —` West Wall (Siegfried Line)
➤ German objectives
`▮▮▮▮▮▮` Actual limit of German advance
〰〰 Boundary line between the
northern and southern sectors

S O U T H E R N

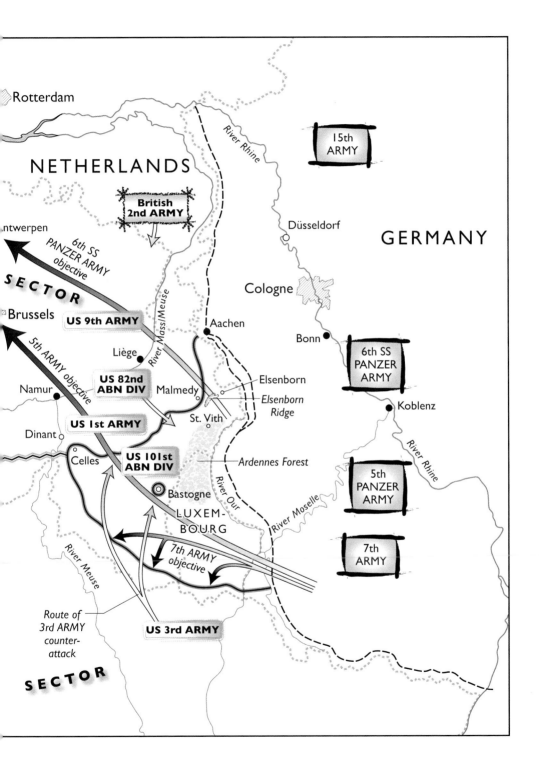

Rotterdam

NETHERLANDS

15th
ARMY

British
2nd ARMY

Düsseldorf

GERMANY

6th SS
PANZER ARMY
objective

Cologne

SECTOR

Brussels

US 9th ARMY

Aachen

Bonn

6th SS
PANZER
ARMY

5th ARMY objective

Liège

Elsenborn

Koblenz

Namur

US 82nd
ABN DIV

Malmedy

Elsenborn
Ridge

US 1st ARMY

St. Vith

Dinant

Celles

US 101st
ABN DIV

Ardennes Forest

5th
PANZER
ARMY

Bastogne

LUXEM-
BOURG

River Our

River Moselle

7th
ARMY

River Meuse

7th ARMY
objective

Route of
3rd ARMY
counter-
attack

US 3rd ARMY

SECTOR

River Mass/Meuse

River Rhine

River Rhine

FOREWORD

By the autumn of 1944 Hitler knew that he had no hope of successfully defending his Greater German Reich against both the Western Allies and the Red Army. He resolved therefore that before turning his full fury on the Russians, he would take one last desperate gamble by launching a major offensive in the west. The fact that he was committing Germany's last reserves in men and resources gave the operation an air of finality – even he predicted that the outcome of this offensive would bring life or death for the German nation.

Hitler's plan called for three armies to break through the weak American front in the Ardennes and Luxembourg and then to cross the Meuse river and exploit to the great port of Antwerp. This would cut off the First Canadian, Second British and Ninth US Armies, deprive the Allies of their most important port and hopefully cause mass surrenders. Indeed, Hitler saw it as the basis of another 'Dunkirk'.

The 'Battle of the Bulge', as it became known, was the largest land battle ever fought by the US Army. It began early on 16 December with a barrage by over 1,900 German guns and rocket launchers, following which a total of seven Panzer, two Parachute and 11 Volks-Grenadier Divisions were unleashed on a 90-mile front against just five American divisions. The Germans pitted some 200,000 men, 700 tanks and armoured assault guns against an initial 83,000 Americans who had just over 400 tanks and tank destroyers.

By the tenth day of Hitler's offensive the Germans had penetrated about 60 miles; but the average width of the 'Bulge' had already been reduced to 30 miles and its tip measured no more than 5 miles across. The Americans had poured in reinforcements, notably two airborne divisions and the bulk of George Patton's 3rd Army and as Chester Wilmot put it: 'the [Nazi] spearhead . . . lay broken in the snow. The Germans had looked upon the Meuse for the last time.'

By the end of January 1945 the 'Bulge' had been eliminated. The costs to the Americans and Germans were roughly the same – about 80,000 men and 700 tanks. There was, however, a vital difference – the Germans had reached the limits of their strength, while the Americans had not. Hitler's chance of saving himself and the Third Reich had vanished.

This book is not a history of the battle as such. Rather it is the raw material from which history is made – a collection of memories of what it was like to be involved in the conflict. These memories are extremely varied because, in such dramatic and exciting events as these, experience and recollection cover a wide range, from the tedium and misery of sitting in a foxhole in freezing cold to the intense mixture of terror and elation of being in action. By reading these vivid accounts it becomes possible to imagine what it was really like to take part in, and to witness first hand, the decisive battle that put an end to Hitler's hopes of avoiding defeat in the West.

Major General Michael Reynolds
(Author of three books on 'The Battle of the Bulge'
The Devil's Adjutant, Men of Steel and *Sons of the Reich*.)

1
HITLER'S LAST GAMBLE

According to his devoted followers Adolf Hitler was an infallible military genius. His critics and enemies regarded him as a reckless adventurer, lacking the professional training and prudence of the true strategist. With hindsight we can say he was a gifted amateur who was lucky in the early stages of his career as supreme commander of the German armed forces. But by autumn 1944 his luck was running out. Germany's military situation was desperate. In the east the Red Army was rolling across Poland towards Berlin. In the south the Allied armies in Italy were advancing towards the alpine frontier of Austria. In the west the American and British armies were closing on the Rhine.

The Ardennes offensive of December 1944 was the gambler's last throw of the dice. The competent professionals in the German High Command never believed that the plan for *Wacht am Rhein* had a chance of success, but were unable to persuade Hitler to give it up. On 3 November 1944, Field Marshal Hasso von Manteuffel attended a conference at the HQ of Army Group B at which Colonel General Alfred Jodl, Chief of Staff at Oberkommando der Werhmacht (OKW – Supreme Command of the Armed Forces), produced a draft plan, together with sketch maps for 'a decisive offensive' to be launched against the Western Allies.

The aims of the plan were ambitious: to push two Panzer armies through the wooded hills in the middle of winter, then move on to take Antwerp, the greatest port in Europe and vital to the supply of the Allied armies. This bold thrust would separate the British 2nd Army from the American armies, cut it off, and force another evacuation by sea – a second Dunkirk. Such a disaster would demoralize the war-weary British people. If this did not force Churchill to negotiate a compromise peace it would at least gain time for the V-2 and other 'miracle weapons' to sap the will of the British to

Field Marshal Walter Model, a dutiful and committed Nazi and Hitler's personal choice as commander of the attack, was at odds with the Führer throughout, constantly seeking permission for the best military solutions but regularly having his plans rejected or changed.

carry on. As for the Americans, Hitler's racial prejudices led him to believe that they were morally weak and would collapse if caught unawares by a surprise attack.

Field Marshal Gerd von Runstedt, the overall commander in the West, felt that the plan was not a practical operation and tried to persuade Hitler to accept a 'small solution' in which the aim of the offensive would be to gain the banks of the River Meuse running along the western side of the Ardennes. He argued that a successful advance to the Meuse would have a similar shock effect but at much lower cost and risk.

When von Runstedt declared that he was tired of the argument and would take no responsibility for the projected offensive Hitler appointed Field

Marshal Walter Model to command the attack. Model was a committed Nazi who believed that he had a strict duty to obey his Führer, although he felt that the plan he was to carry out was unsound. He allowed ideological loyalty to overrule professional judgement. Model's senior subordinates also lacked confidence in the plan. Josef 'Sepp' Dietrich, commander of the 6th Panzer Army in the north, was an old comrade of Hitler driven by personal loyalty. Field Marshal von Manteuffel, commander of 5th Panzer Army to the south, was a personal favourite of Hitler, and was held in thrall by his personality. General Erich Brandenburger, commander of the 7th Army on the southern flank, felt that he had no choice but to obey his orders in solidarity with the commanders to the north. All these senior officers felt that they would be lucky to reach the River Meuse because of both the balance of forces in the theatre and their own lack of the necessary resources. But they also felt a sense of duty to do their best to make the offensive succeed.

TROOP POSITIONS

For the Allied forces, December 1944 had brought a confident and offensive mood. The US 12th Army Group of the 9th, 1st and 3rd Armies was deployed between Geilenkichen and the Saar, engaged in offensive actions or preparing to mount attacks in the near future. North of 12th Army Group the 21st Army Group was making ready to advance to the Rhine as part of the planned final assault on the western defences of Germany. But in the Ardennes the Allies were not planning any major operations on the grounds that the terrain made any large-scale activity too difficult. Between Geilenkirchen and Monschau, on the northern edge of the Ardennes, there were 16 American divisions on a front of around 25 miles; in the Saar sector 10 American divisions held about 40 miles. In contrast in the Ardennes five divisions occupied a line of around 63 miles. Four of these divisions were in the VIII Corps, one in the V Corps. The VIII Corps divisions were the 28th and 4th, which were seasoned by experience of combat in Normandy, but were tired and depleted, especially the 28th which had suffered grievous losses in the Hurtgen Forest. The other divisions, the 106th and the 9th Armoured Division, were green and untried in battle. The American troops in the Ardennes were confidently expecting to enjoy a period of rest and quiet until the time came to move on Germany in the spring. They had deployed a thin screen of outposts forward to watch the German lines, but most of them were well to the rear, lodged in warm billets for the winter.

Although they had been retreating since their defeat in Normandy in August, by December the Germans were also intent on offensive action in a desperate attempt to gain time to improve German defences and for the V-weapons to take effect. The High Command decided to concentrate the main effort in the Ardennes, but planned supporting offensives to the north in the sector of the 15th Army and also in Lorraine, in order to distract the American forces to the south of the decisive blow. Three armies were to attack through the Ardennes. In the north the 6th Panzer Army, consisting of two SS panzer corps and an infantry corps, was to advance on a front of 15½ miles. The LXVII Corps was to assault the American V Corps positions around Monschau and Butgenbach in order to secure the right flank of the Army. In support, a scratch force of 10,000 paratroopers was to drop into the high ground north of Malmedy, behind the American lines, to open up routes from Elsenborn to Eupen. To the south of the LXVII Corps the I SS Panzer Corps would advance westwards via Butgenbach, Malmedy and Stavelot to cross the Meuse on both sides of Liège, then motor on to the strategic objective of the whole offensive, Antwerp.

The II SS Panzer Corps was in reserve, earmarked to follow on and exploit opportunities and deal with Allied counter-attacks as required. The two panzer corps could not be deployed abreast because their sector offered too few roads for them to get forward and the heavily wooded steep ridges running to the south-west made movement off the roads impractical for tanks. The 5th Panzer Army was to advance in the centre with the LXVI Corps, LVII SS Panzer Corps and XLVII Panzer Corps in line on a front of 28 miles across more open and undulating country where movement off the roads was easier. The infantry corps in the north of the sector was to envelop the American 106th Division in the Schnee Eiffel (eastern extension of the Ardennes) and then move on to take the town of St Vith, a centre of road communications vital to the advance of the 6th Panzer Army. The two panzer corps were to cross the Our then move west as quickly as possible via Houffalize and Bastogne. They would then move on across the Meuse at Dinant and Namur, en route to Brussels, to cover the left flank of the advance by the 6th Panzer Army.

On the left the 7th Army was to send four infantry divisions west and south to form a protective line north of Luxembourg and Arlon. The Luftwaffe was to provide air support as needed when the weather permitted.

Herman Göering had promised to devote 2,000 aircraft to this mission, but even Hitler expected only half this number to appear. Special Forces were also to act; in Operation GREIF troops commanded by Otto Skorzeny, using American uniforms and equipment, were to undertake covert operations to seize the bridges over the Meuse and to conduct deception and disruption activities.

The German plan depended heavily on the use of rapid movement to surprise and shock the Allies, using the paralysing effect to counteract the imbalance of forces in the theatre. Because of this, Field Marshal Model realized that control of the road network was of critical importance.

Without free passage along the roads the German mechanized forces would never be able to keep to their schedule, and their shortage of fuel would become a crippling handicap. This meant that the road centres of Bastogne and St Vith had to be secured early. Even if they were, Model believed that it would take his leading elements at least four days to reach the Meuse rather than the two days reckoned by Hitler. In the northern sector the 6th Panzer Army would have to count on good luck to find enough clear routes forward, threading along the sides of the ridges and across the rivers through many sites ideally suited to demolitions, ambushes and blocking actions. They relied on the human factors of audacity and flexibility to make the most of their chances. Also significant was the fact that Hitler ignored the logistic realities of his forces' position far from sources of fuel, and expected his soldiers to capture necessary supplies from their enemies. He believed that the attack would be so unexpected that it could succeed by shock alone, and was influenced by superstition to think that because the German Army had been lucky in the Ardennes in 1940 it would be lucky again in 1944.

INTO THE ATTACK

The attack began at 05.30 on 16 December with an artillery barrage delivered by 2,000 guns all along the front from Monschau to Echternach. On the northern shoulder the planned parachute drop had to be postponed because there was no fuel available to transport the paratroops to their airfield. When they did jump, the next day, strong winds scattered them so badly that they were not able to assemble in sufficient numbers to be effective. The LXVII Corps attacked with the 326th and 272nd Volksgrenadier Divisions but stout defence by the V Corps meant that they failed to take Monschau and Butgenbach, even when reinforced by 12th SS Panzer Division.

The 1st SS Panzer Division did better, pushing along the boundary of V and VIII Corps, but was delayed by traffic congestion and bad roads, and was behind schedule by the end of the day. The 5th Panzer Army had more success, partly because each division had sent a 'storm' battalion to infiltrate behind the American outpost positions during the night to isolate them by cutting their telephone wires and attacking them from the rear at first light. These actions disrupted and confused the defence. In the north of the area the 106th Division was encircled; by the morning of the 17th two regiments had been wiped out and 8,000 troops had been captured. South of the Eiffel the panzer corps infantry and sappers swiftly seized and improved crossings over the Our and the tanks rolled forward through the startled 28th Division. But although the 5th Panzer Army did better than the 6th it was also falling behind schedule; in particular the LXVI Corps had failed to secure St Vith. Further south the 7th Army was also late, held up by a lack of trained sappers and a resolute defence by the 4th Division.

At first the Allied senior commanders did not appreciate the scale of the offensive. On the 16th, General Hodges, commanding the 1st Army, refused to reinforce the V Corps. When Eisenhower and Bradley ordered the 7th Armoured Division from 9th Army and the 10th Armoured Division from 3rd Army to move to the Ardennes, Patton questioned the need. But on the 17th, as the German armies continued to advance, they took a more serious view. In the north the 99th and 2nd Divisions held on at Monschau and Butgenbach, but KampfGruppe Peiper, the leading element of 1st SS Panzer Division, moved 20 miles into Belgium and threatened the 1st Army HQ at Spa. In the area of 5th Panzer Army the 2nd Panzer Division crossed the Clerf, followed up by 26th VolksGrenadier Division.

However, the German commanders were already apprehensive that things were going wrong. Skorzeny observed that his Special Forces teams could not get forward because the roads were jammed. The American 7th Armoured Division had begun to arrive and deploy in a horseshoe position east of St Vith, and until this town was taken the 6th Panzer Army would be confined to a front of advance of a mere five miles. Model ordered the FührerBegleit Panzer Brigade to reinforce the attack on the 18th, but it did not get into action until the 20th. In response to the evidence of a major German attack, which was still unclear but increasingly convincing,

Eisenhower ordered the 82nd and 101st Airborne Divisions to move to the Ardennes. Montgomery, acting on his own initiative, ordered the British XXX Corps to move to a position covering the approaches to Brussels just in case the Germans were able to cross the Meuse. The Guards Armoured Division, three extra armoured brigades and the 43rd, 51st and 53rd Infantry Divisions began to roll south from Holland. They were delayed by wintry conditions, but not as much as their enemies were in the rough terrain of the Ardennes.

As the American 7th Armoured Division and various stragglers continued to hang on around St Vith the two German panzer armies were unable to co-ordinate their actions and were in effect fighting separate battles. Before the offensive began they had not had the opportunity to reconcile their views and plans, nor to overcome the bad effects of the increasingly bitter distrust and rivalry developing between the Army and the SS. The 5th Panzer Army's failure to clear St Vith meant that the I SS Panzer Corps had only one road open to it heading in the right direction, winding along the banks of the Ambleve. The lead was taken by KampfGruppe Peiper consisting of about 4,000 men with 70 main battle tanks, including 20 of the huge, cumbersome and underpowered Tigers that were a hindrance to the rapid movement required for the attack on the Americans. This powerful column was often only able to advance on a one-tank front as it dashed forward towards the vital bridges over the Ambleve, Salm and Meuse. Peiper had been frustrated by delays due to a variety of reasons, such as the presence of 'friendly' minefields and horse-drawn transport belonging to other formations from the start of his advance to contact on the 16th. Once moving he soon got far ahead of the 12th VolksGrenadier Division infantry who were supposed to follow up to secure his flanks and lines of communication. His advance was impeded by the skirmishing of the American 14th Cavalry Group and by small parties of American soldiers carrying out demolitions and ambushes along the route. These actions did little physical damage but robbed Peiper of time, the most precious commodity of all in the circumstances.

On the evening of the 17th a party of the 291 Engineers set up an improvised roadblock, with a few mines covered by bazookas and light machine-guns, on the road just east of Stavelot; it checked Peiper's advance and persuaded him to halt for the night. During the night a handful of American anti-tank guns and some infantry moved into Stavelot.

An essential element of the German plans was to make use of existing Allied installations, including bridges such as this one, as well as their dumps of fuel. The roads, many of which were unsuitably narrow for tanks, would prove a key element in the battle to come.

Early on the morning of the 18th they were overwhelmed by artillery firing in support of Peiper. The KampfGruppe pushed through the town, taking a side road to evade contact with an anti-tank gun in the square, firing at all the windows en route to discourage snipers. They pressed on down the road to Trois Ponts without bothering to clear the town, so that it was passed but not actually captured. A flank recce force explored the road towards Francorchamps to the north but turned back before finding the American fuel dump.

As Peiper was making the most progress of any in the 1st SS Panzer Division another KampfGruppe, 'Knittel', was sent to follow and reinforce him. Knittel traversed Stavelot at 19.00 on the 18th; by 20.00 a battalion of the US 30th Division had taken possession of the town and placed artillery and tank destroyers to cover the bridge. This severed the line of communication for Peiper and Knittel. On the 19th Knittel attacked Stavelot from the west whilst another KampfGruppe, 'Sandig', based on a battalion of SS Panzer-Grenadiers with Mk IV and Mk VI tanks in support, assaulted the bridge from the south-east. The Americans in the town beat off both these attacks.

Before dawn on the 20th Sandig's infantry waded the river in an attempt to storm the town but were spotted in the light from flares and burning buildings and driven back. At 05.00 combat engineers blew the bridge and ruined all hope of restoring the line of supply to Peiper and Knittel. Meanwhile, on the 18th, Peiper had forced his way through Trois Ponts, but two of the bridges were blown, which prevented him from crossing to the south side of the Ambleve. Attempts to ford the river failed because the water was too deep. A bridge over the Ambleve at Petit Spai collapsed under the weight of a self-propelled anti-tank gun and engineers trying to repair the span were stopped by artillery fire.

Peiper explored other routes to the west and north but was blocked in all directions as bridges were blown or his recce troops ran into Task Forces of American infantry mixed with tanks from the 30th Division and 82nd Airborne Division. Both these divisions were highly experienced, having seen intense fighting in Normandy. In this battle they showed great skill and flexibility as well as a powerful military spirit. As he was running short of fuel and engineer stores Peiper was progressively hemmed in around Stoumont and La Gleize. His land line of supply was cut. On the 22nd the Luftwaffe made a supply drop but only 10 per cent of the goods fell in the right area. Attempts to float supplies down the river failed. Task forces of the XVIII Airborne Corps with infantry from the 82nd and tanks of the 3rd Armoured Division fought their way forward to confine Peiper to a pocket at La Gleize. Although his force could not be re-supplied nor relieved, he was denied permission to break out and make for the rear until 17.00 on the 23rd, by which time there was no fuel to move the vehicles. At 02.00 on the 24th Peiper led 800 of his men out, swimming the icy Salm and creeping through the forest back to the German lines at Wanne.

Peiper's adventure illustrates the impracticality of the whole plan of 6th Panzer Army which depended on unrealistic rates of movement in the difficult winter conditions and on the idea of capturing vital supplies from the enemy. In some areas the advancing troops were fortunate enough to capture American fuel and food, or seize supplies from the civilian economy, but in other areas their tanks and transport were stranded and the soldiers starved. Their misery and weakness were made worse as the temperature dropped and snow fell.

In addition, while some American troops obliged by panicking and running away, many did not, and did what they could to delay the Germans. After the first few days these guerrilla actions were reinforced by more substantial improvised counter-attacks as the 1st Army fed in reinforcements from 9th Army and the SHAEF reserve. These operations denied ground and access routes temporarily or permanently and so prevented the I SS Panzer Corps from carrying out its plan to attack by rapid manoeuvre.

By 19 December, Model had realized that the 6th Army had been checked and was unlikely to succeed. He proposed that the 6th Panzer Army should send five divisions to exploit better opportunities in the 5th Panzer Army area. Hitler rejected this idea; for ideological reasons he was intent on ensuring greater success for the SS than for the Army. He was also considering an operation to attack the American line at Aachen, north of the Ardennes. He gave categorical orders that the II SS Panzer Corps must advance in the northern sector, even though there was no room to deploy it, but also agreed to allow Model to send a panzer and a panzer-grenadier division to the 5th Panzer Army.

THE ALLIES REACH BASTOGNE

The 5th Panzer Army was still held by the 7th Armoured Division east of St Vith but had advanced further west to the south. In effect, XLVII Panzer Corps was now in a race for Bastogne, which it narrowly lost. The corps, particularly the Panzer Lehr Division, was held up by bad roads on the 18th. On that day Bastogne could have been taken easily; the only American troops in the town were the HQ of VIII Corps and some disorganized elements of the 28th Division. Combat Command B of the 10th Armoured Division, sent up by 3rd Army, was 40 miles away in Luxembourg. The 101st Airborne Division was 100 miles off at Rheims, moving up in trucks.

Late in the evening of the 18th, Panzer Lehr was within five miles of the town but was persuaded by local civilians to take a 'short cut' which led the tanks into a mire from which they could not be recovered until the morning of the 19th. On the approaches to Bastogne, Panzer Lehr met ad hoc task forces of CCB and the 28th, picketing the villages on all the roads into the town. During the fighting the American task forces suffered heavy losses but gained time for the 101st Airborne to arrive and deploy inside the town and beyond in an inner perimeter of villages, thus giving defence in depth. These developments presented von Luttwitz, Commander of the Panzer Corps, with a difficult question: should he commit all his formations to make certain of seizing Bastogne? Or should he use his 26th VolksGrenadier Division to mask and then attack the town, and send his two panzer divisions to by-pass it and push on swiftly to the Meuse?

In the event he decided on a compromise: 2nd Panzer Division was to take Noville, a village north of Bastogne on the road to Houffalize, go round the north of Bastogne on minor roads and motor on westwards, while the VolksGrenadiers attacked Bastogne from the north and Panzer Lehr wheeled round to drive in from the east. The disadvantages of this plan were that neither the force moving west to the Meuse nor the one assaulting Bastogne was strong enough for its mission, and that the condition of the minor roads, complicated by artillery fire from the American garrison, prevented rapid movement. But von Luttwitz was under great pressure both to take Bastogne in order to secure efficient lines of communication for 5th Panzer Army on its march to and beyond the Meuse, and also to capture intact bridges over that river as soon as possible, before the Allies could either guard or demolish them. On that day the British 29th Armoured Brigade was ordered to move to defend the bridges from Dinant to Namur. The Household Cavalry Regiment sent armoured car patrols across the river on reconnaissance and the Special Air Service went into the Ardennes on covert surveillance missions to give early warning of a German approach.

STRATEGY AND TACTICS

The Allied commanders had received the first reports of the German attacks in the Ardennes without much concern on the 16th, became alarmed by the lack of reliable intelligence and the signs of a major offensive on the 17th, and started to feed in whatever reinforcements were available on the 18th, with a vague idea of attempting a general containment of the enemy. Failures of signals, the disruption activities of Skorzeny's troops and the rumours that always emerge in times of crisis deprived them of the sort of information that they needed in order to make a considered response. The Germans were fighting separate battles in the two panzer army sectors and the Allies were sending in extra troops piecemeal and blind. The 101st Airborne Division had been sent to Bastogne only because the town was at the centre of the road network in the southern Ardennes and so a good location from which to be deployed elsewhere. The 82nd Airborne had originally been ordered to concentrate at Bastogne but was diverted en route to block the advance of KampfGruppe Peiper.

On 19 December, Eisenhower held a conference at Verdun at which a concerted strategy and coherent concepts of operations were formed. Bradley, Patton and Deevers, Commander of the US 6th Army Group which was deployed south of 12th Army Group, were present. Eisenhower opened the discussion by remarking that the German attack must be treated as an opportunity and not a serious threat to the Allies, since he doubted that the enemy had the resources to sustain this effort for much longer. Patton agreed and proposed a high-risk/high-gain strategy. He wanted to allow the Germans to advance as far to the west as they could before launching counter-attacks from north and south simultaneously – from the eastern-most positions of the 1st Army and his own 3rd Army – so inflicting the maximum possible loss on the enemy.

Eisenhower favoured a less aggressive and more cautious strategy. He insisted that the Allies must, in any circumstance, hold the line of the Meuse, and particularly the crossings at Liège and Namur. The northern flank held by the 1st Army must stand firm just in case the German intent was to swing north against the Aachen salient. The main counter-stroke was to be delivered from the south by the 3rd Army making a methodical series of attacks via Bastogne. In order to provide the resources for this move he wanted Deevers' Army group to take over from the 3rd Army in the Saar, withdrawing from Strasbourg and the eastern Vosges if this was necessary. This latter proposal was vigorously opposed by the French who insisted there must be no sacrifice of recently recovered French territory.

By the afternoon of the 19th the situation as the American commanders at Verdun understood it was as follows: the northern and southern flanks of the 'Bulge' were holding; the position at St Vith was obscure, but the Germans had gone past the town to the north and south, so the American

Like other Allied leaders, General Omar Bradley was taken by surprise by the German offensive in the Ardennes. As he himself admitted: 'The weakest link in our front was the Ardennes sector . . . we did not then consider it an unusually dangerous area.'

defenders must be outflanked; Houffalize had fallen to the enemy and Bastogne was about to be surrounded; there was a 20-mile gap between Bastogne and Werbomont which could be used by at least six panzer and panzer-grenadier divisions to exploit to the west; and the enemy were moving on Namur, Givet and Dinant with leading units 15 miles from Liège in the northern sector and 15 miles west of Bastogne in the southern. For the Allies, 3rd Army had sent two divisions northwards and would be able to send four more by the 22nd, 12th Army Group would need two or three days to move additional divisions from the Roer area into the Ardennes' northern shoulder and four British divisions were on the way to deploy as a back-stop along the Meuse.

Another significant fact that emerged was that 12th Army Group had been split by the German advance, with the troops north of the 'Bulge' being effectively isolated from Bradley's HQ in Luxembourg. Bradley could still communicate with Hodges by radio but could not actually visit the HQ of 1st Army without making a long journey via western Belgium which was not practical in the circumstances. It was for this reason that on the 20th Eisenhower decided to give Montgomery command of all Allied forces north of the Ardennes, an arrangement that made co-ordination much faster and simpler. Eisenhower himself supervised and controlled the overall strategic action by all the Allied Armies involved in meeting the German offensive.

Montgomery was already in touch with Hodges and differences of opinion soon emerged about what the enemy intentions were and how best to defeat them. Hodges felt that the 6th Panzer Army objective was to envelop and take Liège, and that he must hold a line from Monschau to Stavelot from which he could mount a mobile attack via Werbomont through Vielsalm to Houffalize. This would cut into the enemy flank and relieve the 7th Armoured Division at St Vith. He and his corps commanders were anxious to go on the offensive immediately and also to yield no more ground to the Germans.

Montgomery thought that the 6th Panzer Army was heading for Antwerp and that the primary aim must be to divert them from their direct route in that direction. He felt that the Germans would move from Houffalize to the north-west astride the Our, aiming to cross the Meuse at Huy and Namur. He advised that 1st Army should bring in 9th Army to the Roer, give up its positions in the north-east and shift to form a front from Stavelot to Marche in order to block the way to Antwerp. Then the Army should assemble a powerful force under the VII Corps, led by 'Lightning Joe' Collins, the most aggressive of the corps commanders, to attack once the Germans were fully committed and running out of energy. Hodges insisted that he must not withdraw and must push forward to shorten his line of defence in order to maintain morale. Montgomery was persuaded by this argument, although he calculated that the XVIII Airborne Corps, which had only the 82nd Airborne Division, and a combat command of 3rd Armoured Division was too weak to attack across the Salm and advance to the line Malmedy–St Vith–Houffalize and relieve Bastogne as Hodges intended.

ATTACKS ON THE GROUND

On the ground in the Ardennes both sides were attacking on 20 December. In the 5th Panzer Army area the 2nd Panzer Division took Noville and Foy, then moved rapidly west to cross the Ourthe at Ourtheville. Panzer Lehr closed in on Bastogne from the north-east, taking Bixory, but the 26th VolksGrenadiers were stopped at Mont, another of the village outpost positions.

Late on the 20th the 82nd Airborne advanced across the Salm to begin the encirclement of Peiper and made tenuous contact with the 7th Armoured north of St Vith. But on the 21st the 116th Panzer Division attacked along the Ourthe via Hotton to gain a position 30 miles west of St Vith, while the 2nd and 9th SS Panzer Divisions swung north-west to attack the southern flank of the 82nd Airborne in the bridgehead over the Salm. The American forces lacked the strength necessary to sustain this scale of attack; the 82nd Airborne fell back and the 7th Armoured, now deeply outflanked on both sides, gave up St Vith to avoid annihilation.

Meanwhile, in the 5th Panzer Army area, Bastogne was surrounded – but the garrison showed no sign of weakening. The German commanders were nervous at the prospect of an assault, aware that they were short of artillery ammunition. The German leaders in both panzer armies were also anxious because their tanks were running out of fuel with no certainty of replenishment, and also alarmed by improvements in the weather that brought Allied tactical aircraft into play over the battlefield.

The Germans remembered that earlier, in Normandy, following the Allied invasion of France, their logistics and movements had been paralysed by Allied airpower. But the progress on the ground had given some hope for success, so on the 22nd and 23rd they carried on attacking where and when they could.

In 6th Panzer Army area the Germans made desperate attempts to break the line of defence of 1st Army from Monschau to Malmedy and failed. Further south they managed to clear roads forward from St Vith via Houffalize to St Hubert and via Vielsalm to La Roche. Panzer Lehr took St Hubert, 2nd Panzer broke the defence line from Rochefort to Marche and moved west to reach the ridge five miles east of Dinant where it ran out of fuel on the 23rd. 116th Panzer followed up the 2nd but could not get as far. There were no forces available to support and exploit this advance.

THE PRESSURE BUILDS

To the south of the push by 2nd and 116th Panzer Divisions the Americans seized the initiative. Leading elements of the armoured formations sent north by Patton made contact with Panzer Lehr. The 101st Airborne sallied out of Bastogne to attack the 26th VolksGrenadiers and expand their perimeter. In the north Hodges ordered the VII Corps to conduct an aggressive defence to block the enemy way forward from the Salm and Ourthe to Liège and Huy. Allied tactical aircraft appeared in increasing numbers over the whole theatre of operations, while heavy raids were made to the east on the Rhineland to disrupt the zone of communications of the German armies. These attacks from the air not only made movement in daylight lethally risky but also made it impossible to resupply the forward panzer units with fuel and ammunition.

On the December 24 Model realized that the game was lost. He and Manteuffel approached Hitler with new plans for a 'small solution'. They argued that although their troops had advanced 60 miles into Belgium they now had no chance of reaching Antwerp and only a slight chance of advancing to the Meuse because the strength of the Allied reaction had been grossly underestimated in the original plan, as had the logistic requirements for success. They advised that it would be better if they could concentrate on taking Bastogne, then 5th Panzer could move north between the Meuse and the Ourthe to Huy. 6th Panzer Army should advance between the Ourthe and the Salm to Liège. Then the two panzer armies could go on to attack Aachen whilst a force from the Roer advanced on Maastricht.

But Hitler rejected these plans. He insisted the attack must continue to push north-west taking Namur and Liège on the way, and that Bastogne be taken at all costs. Accordingly, the 5th Panzer Army launched a renewed series of assaults on Bastogne on the 24th and 26th, but all failed. In all, while under siege, Bastogne was attacked by elements of nine German divisions, but none of the attacks was sufficiently strong or co-ordinated to break the defence. Meanwhile the Allies steadily built up the pressure on the ground and in the air. The most forward of the German formations, 2nd Panzer Division, stalled a few miles from Dinant, was attacked from the north by the American 2nd Armoured Division, and destroyed on the 27th.

Next day von Runstedt advised Hitler that the offensive had failed and he should issue orders to form a line of defence held by infantry divisions east of Bastogne with a mobile reserve of panzers further back. The forward elements of the German army had run out of fuel and were isolated. They had to sabotage and abandon their vehicles and only a lucky few got back to their lines on foot. Many of the German soldiers who had advanced with high spirits and confidence a few weeks before were demoralized and anxious to surrender.

Still Hitler insisted the armies in the Ardennes must carry on the attack and promised they would be assisted by offensives mounted from the Saar and the Colmar pocket. He also at last realized that the 5th Panzer Army area was the more favourable for offensive operations and ordered 6th Panzer Army to send four panzer divisions south to reinforce new attacks on Bastogne and to the Meuse. But by then the US 3rd Army had six fresh divisions approaching Bastogne and these troops, with massive artillery and air support, were more than enough to defeat the German attacks on 3 and 4 January.

THE ALLIES ADVANCE

On 3 January Allied forces began to advance into the Ardennes from all directions. This advance was slow and costly because the mountain terrain and the bitter weather impeded all activity. The 1st Army moving towards Houffalize advanced at a pace of one mile per day. The British XXX Corps, attacking from the west, had to assault a series of entrenched positions on steep wooded ridges defended by desperate Germans who knew they could not retreat safely. But the Allied advance was inexorable and could not be stopped. Model was most concerned that he had seven panzer divisions west of a line from Bastogne to Liège and only one good line of retirement open. On 8 January Hitler gave permission for the panzer forces to withdraw to east of a line through Houffalize, but few tanks were able to get back as many were caught by Allied fighter-bombers in motion or wrecked by their own crews because their fuel had run out.

There was no time for the defeated German army to replace its lost men and equipment before, on 13 January, the Russians launched their offensive from the Vistula and the 6th Panzer Army was ordered to break off the action in the Ardennes and move east. The Allies continued to press on methodically as envisaged by Eisenhower. The 3rd and 1st Armies met at Houffalize on 17 January and St Vith was recaptured on the 23rd. When the Allied advance halted on 25 January the front was just west of where it had been on 15 December.

Hitler the gambler had staked all on a game in which the odds were stacked against him and his soldiers. His last adventure in the west was over and had ended with catastrophic failure and loss for the German forces. The Allies were encouraged by their success. When the time came to cross the Rhine they confronted a weakened enemy short of the means to defend this last great obstacle to their victory in Europe.

2
PRELUDE TO ACTION

Before the German attack began, many American troops were deployed in defensive positions in the Ardennes, recouping before the expected spring offensive. British troops of 2nd Army were deployed to the north, in the Netherlands. The senior commanders were disappointed by the position, as Omar Bradley remembered:

> The failure of our November offensive to crack the Siegfried Line [a chain of fortified posts running along the Western frontier of Germany] and push through to the Rhine had been a further jolt, leading Ike and SHAEF planners to conclude that we would probably be stalemated through the winter . . .

But Bradley was not willing to adopt a passive policy of resting and waiting for spring. He insisted on keeping up offensive pressure on the Germans. This entailed concentrating his forces in certain areas, such as the Roer, and leaving others with few troops in place. In early November Eisenhower and Bradley visited the Ardennes and, according to Bradley,

> Ike and I decided the sector could be held with four divisions. There was a calculated risk involved in manning the Ardennes front so thinly with so many green troops, but I thought the gamble was negligible. In the remote event that the Germans launched a spoiling attack in this sector, with our great mobility we could quickly see it off by diverting troops south and north from Hodges' and Patton's armies. Such an attack – another Mortain – would even be welcomed.

Eisenhower agreed with Bradley's view of the risk posed by this strategy:

In the Ardennes region we were running a definite risk, but we believed it to be a mistaken policy to suspend our attacks all along the front merely to make ourselves safe until all reinforcements arriving from the United States could bring us up to peak strength . . . we were in the best possible position to concentrate against the flanks of any attack in the Ardennes area that might attempted by the Germans . . . if the enemy should deliver a surprise attack in the Ardennes he would have great difficulty in supply if he tried to advance as far as the line of the Meuse.

Bradley agreed with the policy of maintaining the offensive:

My basic decision was to continue the offensive to the extreme limit of our ability, and it was this decision that was responsible for the startling successes of the first week of the German December attack . . . we tried to capture all those Germans before they could get inside the Siegfried.

British senior officers also wanted to keep up the pressure, and hoped that Hitler would intervene to insist on rash offensive action in the west. Montgomery's G-2 (Senior Intelligence Officer) GT Williams said of Hitler:

If he is ill I wish he'd recover and take command again . . . if Hitler were directing strategy on the Western Front, he might very well order another desperate and disastrous offensive like the one at Mortain. Such an offensive might enable us to destroy the German armies east of the Rhine . . . This would put an end to our stalemate and grinding war of attrition and enable us to cross into Germany . . . pursuing a mangled and fleeing army in fast-moving open warfare. However, believing von Runstedt to be fully in charge of the Western Front, we expected a textbook defense.

Montgomery felt it would be advantageous to use an offesive to force von Runstedt to commit his panzers early; at a conference at Maastricht on 7 December he remarked that:

A highly important factor in the winter operations will be to draw
into the battle and to defeat decisively, the enemy 6th Panzer
Army. This is his only strategic reserve on the Western Front,
and it contains the only divisions which could make any show
at all in a mobile campaign. These divisions must therefore be
so mauled during the winter months that they are out of action
when spring arrives.

By the middle of December the Allied intelligence organizations believed
that the German capacity for any kind of action had been much reduced.
On 12 December the weekly Intelligence Summary sent to Bradley included
this statement:

It is now certain that attrition is steadily sapping the strength
of the German forces on the Western Front and that the crust
of defences is thinner, more brittle and more vulnerable than
it appears in our G-2 maps or to the troops in the Line . . . with
continued Allied pressure in the South and in the North, the
breaking point may develop suddenly and without warning.

The view of Montgomery's G-2 was that, 'The enemy is in a bad way . . .
fighting a defensive campaign on all fronts . . . he cannot stage a major
offensive operation.' The G-2 of the British 1st Army concluded that with
reference to enemy intent to make a counter-attack 'Indications to date
point to this focal point as being between Roermond and Schleiden (north
of the Ardennes opposite Aachen).'

These estimates by the Allied staffs were supported by SIGINT, Signals
Intelligence and by ULTRA. As Bradley remarked, 'The fallacy that crept
into our thinking was that since ULTRA had not specifically forecast or
suggested a major strategic counter-attack, there was no possibility of one.'

In the meanwhile Bradley prepared for his own offensives, despite being
short of resources.

I had to commit every division I could lay my hands on, leaving
the Ardennes front thinly held and no reserves at army group
level. The weakest link in our front was the Ardennes sector . . .
we did not then consider it an unusually dangerous area. ULTRA

told us that it was only lightly manned by transient divisions or Volks-Grenadier divisions, composed of sailors and airmen.

However, Bradley did plan for the eventuality of a German attack on a limited scale via the Ardennes:

> If the Germans hit his sector, Middleton [General Troy H Middleton's VIII Corps] was to make a fighting withdrawal – all the way back to the Meuse river if necessary . . . since there were only a few roads through the area, we thought our tactical air forces could interdict them with relative ease . . . Middleton was to locate no gasoline or food dumps . . . within that line of withdrawal . . . he would slow the enemy . . . I would order reserve armoured divisions . . . and other units to close pincers at the base of the German salient and cut him off. Lacking the resources to continue our offensive and defend the Ardennes in depth, my defensive plan . . . was based on mobility rather than concentration . . . these plans . . . were based on the possibility of a limited German 'spoiling attack' of four to six divisions.

On the other side, German senior officers agreed with Bradley's analysis. Otto Skorzeny, veteran of many a high-risk adventure, commented on the overall plan, 'We realized we were being asked the impossible, but we had stressed the point to the Führer when the plan was first mooted and so our consciences were clear.'

Colonel-General 'Sepp' Dietrich, commander of 6th Panzer Army, told his American interrogators after the war:

> The whole attack was a big mistake. To use those two armies at that time of the year was the biggest mistake they made in the war.

Dietrich also complained that he had been given notice of the offensive much too late to prepare a suitable plan, and had even less contact with Hitler than Manteuffel.

> Manteuffel had better liaison with Hitler because he had been in command of the Grossdeutschland Panzer Div and knew many

of the men around the Führer's headquarters. I should have been given four weeks of planning instead of four days. I knew that the offensive would start, but not where. I was not in the area even once before the attack, and I couldn't look at the terrain. I didn't have time to prepare my thoughts and ideas in the way they really should have been prepared. Because of that, it is hard to give a detailed description. I am one of the oldest tank men in the Army, having been in tanks in 1916–17. If I had been asked, I would have been against that terrain with swampy territory and few roads. I would have gone by Aachen or Metz. The Ardennes was the worst terrain imaginable for a thousand tanks. Only four to five of them could fight at one time because there was no place to deploy. A big tank attack in this terrain is impossible. West of Aachen, one can see from five to ten kilometres in places and we could have gone to town. In the Ardennes, we could develop nothing.

He was also very critical of the lack of opportunity allowed for training his army for the offensive.

In regard to Gen Strong's [the British Intellegence Officer] question whether a tactical exercise by 6th Panzer Army in preparation for the Ardennes Offensive had taken place at HQ, C-in-C West, my answer must be 'no' as far as the divisions under my command are concerned. Also, there had been no large-scale preparations within 6th Panzer Army for the Ardennes Offensive during the three months of October to December 1944. Time was needed too badly for the training in attack and defense of units up to battalion strength and for the assembly of material. During this time, 6th Panzer Army was not under OB West, but was under FHQ. On 12 December 1944, at the conference in Bad Nauheim, the planned Ardennes Offensive was ordered by Hitler, but no exact date was given. I personally knew that a winter offensive was being planned by the Operations Division, but I did not know when and where.

Dietrich attributed all these difficulties primarily to Hitler's refusal to accept advice from his senior commanders. He described the arbitrary way in which decisions were made and imposed by the Nazi High Command:

At 15.00 on 2 December 1944, a conference of general officers took place at FHQ in Bad Nauheim. All the commanding generals of 5th Panzer and 6th Panzer Armies, as well as von Rundstedt, Model, Keitel, Jodl, and Hitler were present. Hitler declared at this conference that he had decided on a winter offensive because the Army's continuous setbacks could be tolerated no longer. The Army must gain a victory. He said that all preparations had been made and that thousands of tanks were at their disposal. Hitler continued at great length and referred to former campaigns. 'The German people can no longer endure the heavy bombing attacks,' he said, and 'The German people are entitled to action from me.' No one else made a speech. We were not asked. At the end of the conference, the generals were introduced to Hitler and each had an opportunity to talk to him for a few minutes. Hitler asked me, 'Is your Army ready?' I answered, 'Not for an offensive.' To this, Hitler replied, 'You are never satisfied.' With that my minute was up. The answers of the commanding generals were similar – 'not fully prepared for commitment.' After the conference, the generals who had been present met for a birthday celebration at von Rundstedt's house. No one dared speak about the Offensive. The death penalty hovered over the secret, and it would have been to no avail to discuss it anyway. By midnight all generals were on the way back to their units.

On the morning of 13 December 1944, I was ordered to Model's Headquarters for an orientation. On the same afternoon, I had a conference with my two corps commanders in order to make preparations for the planned offensive. The I SS Panzer Corps was designated as the attack Corps, and II SS Panzer Corps was to be held as 6th Panzer Army reserve. During the nights of 13, 14 and 15 December 1944, the divisions moved out to take up their positions. They covered an average of 100 kilometres per night. Even on 15 December 1944, Model and I were of the opinion that the attack was premature, and we requested an extension of at least two days. FHQ refused. This winter offensive, in my opinion, was the worst prepared German offensive of this War.

Manteuffel also held the opinion that the plans for the offensive were not realistic. After the war he complained that, with hindsight,

> The operation lacked the necessary personnel and material for the speedy exploitation of a successful breakthrough. There were not enough forces from which units could be brought up to eliminate pockets of resistance. The offensive failed. The reason for this failure was in my opinion the following: the number of forces launching the attack on 15 December was not in proportion to the objective [Antwerp], which had been placed too far ahead.

Like Dietrich, Manteuffel blamed Hitler and the staff of the Führer HQ for the errors of judgement that led to imperative orders for an offensive that was doomed. He commented that Hitler's style of leadership had effectively deprived the German staffs of their normal functions and capabilities:

> Efficiency, based on the ability to make decisions independently, which had brought the German Army very great successes in Poland, France and the East in 1941, had almost completely disappeared. Even the most experienced of our higher leaders had been forced to comply strictly with the wording of the order issued from Hitler's headquarters, and even in matters of minor tactical significance the hand of this headquarters interfered often – in fact as far down as the divisions.
>
> The German leading staff, which in earlier days had been so cheerful in accepting responsibility, had been crippled ever since Stalingrad and became more and more merely a mechanical commanding body – subject to the smallest details of the so-called 'Führer's orders' which originated from a headquarters far from the fighting front. This brought about the death of the German art of flexible command.

Hitler's distrust of most of his senior army officers grew stronger after the attempt to assassinate him on 20 July 1944. He relied more and more on the staff of his personal headquarters. Manteuffel felt that Hitler's closest military advisers lacked the experience of recent command in the field to make them competent:

My assignment to the operational situation of the Western
Front in the beginning of September 1944 – at the taking over
of the 5 Panzer Army by the German Armed Forces Operational
Command (I had just come from the Eastern Front and was not
acquainted with the situation on the Western Front as it was after
the Invasion started) – revealed to me, with frightening clarity,
that Hitler's military advisers were totally ignorant of the facts
at the front line.

Manteuffel explained to the British military historian, Basil Liddell-
Hart, Hitler's ability to dominate his professional staff and his supreme
confidence in his own powers of command:

Hitler had a magnetic, and hypnotic personality. This had a
very marked effect on people who went to see him with the
intention of putting forward their views on any matter. They
would begin to argue their point, but would gradually find
themselves succumbing to his personality, and in the end would
often agree to the opposite of what they intended. For my part,
having come to know Hitler well in the last stages of the war, I
had learnt how to keep him to the point, and maintain my own
argument. I did not feel afraid of Hitler, as so many did. He
often called me to his headquarters for consultation, after that
Christmas-tide I had spent at his headquarters by invitation,
following the successful stroke at Zhitomir that had attracted
his attention.

   Hitler had read a lot of military literature, and was also fond
of listening to military lectures. In this way, coupled with his
personal experience of the last war as an ordinary soldier, he
had gained a very good knowledge of the lower level of warfare
– the properties of the different weapons; the effect of ground
and weather; the mentality and morale of troops. He was good
in gauging how the troops felt. I found that I was hardly ever in
disagreement with his view when discussing such matters. On the
other hand he had no idea of the higher strategical and tactical
combinations. He had a good grasp of how a single division moved
and fought, but he did not understand how armies operated.

In December 1944, Manteuffel could not persuade Hitler to alter his general strategic intention nor postpone the attack, but he did obtain permission to modify some of the tactical orders:

> When I saw Hitler's orders for the offensive I was astonished to find that these even laid down the method and timing of the attack. The artillery was to open fire at 07.30, and the infantry assault was to be launched at 11.00. Between these hours the Luftwaffe was to bomb headquarters and communications. The armoured divisions were not to strike until the breakthrough had been achieved by the infantry mass. The artillery was spread over the whole front of attack.
>
> This seemed to me foolish in several respects, so I immediately worked out a different method, and explained it to Model. Model agreed with it, but remarked sarcastically: 'You'd better argue it out with the Führer.' I replied: 'All right, I'll do that if you'll come with me.' So on 2 December, the two of us went to see Hitler.
>
> I began by saying: 'None of us knows what the weather will be on the day of the attack – are you sure the Luftwaffe can fulfil its part in face of the Allied air superiority?' I reminded Hitler of two occasions in the Vosges earlier where it had proved quite impossible for the armoured divisions to move in daylight. Then I went on: 'All our artillery will do at 07.30 is to wake the Americans – and they will then have three and a half hours to organize their counter-measures before our assault comes.' I pointed out also, that the mass of the German infantry was not so good as it had been, and was hardly capable of making such a deep penetration as was required, especially in such difficult country. For the American defences consisted of a chain of forward defence posts, with their main line of resistance well behind – and that would be harder to pierce.
>
> I proposed to Hitler a number of changes. The first was that the assault should be made at 05.30, under cover of darkness. Of course this would limit the targets for the artillery, but would enable it to concentrate on a number of key targets – such as batteries, ammunition dumps, and headquarters – that had been definitely located.

Even before this SS raiding party went into action on 17 December, seen here beside a burning US armoured personnel carrier, sporadic incidents occurred throughout the Ardennes. Most frequently they took place in the darkness of the early morning winter hours.

Secondly, I proposed to form one 'storm battalion' from each infantry division, composed of the most expert officers and men. (I picked the officers myself.) These 'storm battalions' were to advance in the dark at 05.30, without any covering artillery fire, and penetrate between the Americans' forward defence posts. They would avoid fighting if possible until they had penetrated deep.

Searchlights, provided by the flak units, were to light the way for the storm troops' advance by projecting their beams on the clouds, to reflect downwards. I had been much impressed by a demonstration of this kind which I had seen shortly beforehand, and felt that it would be the key to a quick penetration before daylight.

After setting forth my alternative proposals to Hitler, I argued that it was not possible to carry out the offensive in any other way if we were to have a reasonable chance of success. I emphasized: 'At 16.00 it will be dark. So you will only have five hours, after the assault at 11.00, in which to achieve the breakthrough. It is very doubtful if you can do it in the time. If you adopt my idea, you will gain a further five and a half hours for the purpose. Then when darkness comes I can launch the tanks. They will advance during the night, pass through our infantry, and by dawn the next day they will be able to launch their own attack on the main position, along a cleared approach.

These changes did give the 5th Panzer Army certain advantages in the early stages of the battle, but could not overcome the effects of the fundamental weaknesses in the strategy and lack of preparation. The commander of 6th Panzer Army had much less time than Manteuffel to prepare his formations for the attack, and to follow the detailed plans issued by OKW. The 7th Army, commanded by General Erich Brandenburger, was the most badly affected by these factors:

The sole advantages which the German forces enjoyed were the element of surprise, and the favourable conditions in the enemy sector. However, these things were only of help to us at the beginning. As far as our estimate of the enemy's reaction is concerned, it may be said that the Supreme Command erred when it imagined that the enemy would content himself with a defensive reaction, and that the difficulties inherent in a unified Allied command would cause a certain time lag to intervene before the Allies fought back. These false suppositions had a particularly unhappy effect on the position of 7th Army, which was at least three or four divisions too weak to accomplish its mission.

Seventh Army also suffered from a lack of armoured forces, particularly disadvantageous when going on the offensive. While the high commands of both sides considered strategy, their soldiers in the field were occupied with their own concerns. Most of the American troops were expecting to pass a quiet winter in comfortable quarters. The German soldiers were training and preparing for defence of their homeland against an Allied assault in the spring. Until a few hours before the battle started they had no idea that they themselves were about to seize the initiative.

Every man was ready to do his duty, yet much depended on the leadership qualities of the officers on both sides. The 11th Armoured Division includes in its *History* of December 1944 a most telling paragraph, which described in detail the qualities that would be needed in the days to come:

> To be a successful chief of staff of an armoured division in operations requires an array of qualities which are not often found together. The holder of this post should first of all be able to function for long periods with very little sleep. When the battle is in its most mobile stage he will probably be listening and speaking on the wireless almost continuously for 20 hours a day. He must be capable of producing clear and coherent orders, long or short, verbal or written, at any hour of the day or night. He must make no mistakes in these, and he must be watchful for the possible errors of his staff. He must retain at all times a complete grasp of the situation, for not merely will he have to answer numerous questions about the situation, but he will also make a great many tactical decisions for which the attention of his commander is either not essential or not immediately obtainable. This means that he must be constantly available. His commander will visit his brigades and confer with higher commanders, but he must never leave his post. Hence, too, he must play his major part in conducting the battle without seeing a square yard of the battlefield, guided only by reports which reach him, and the map before his eyes. The command vehicle is his prison, the headphones are his fetters.

Though they would not be involved until after the first German assault, the British troops in the region, including the 23rd Hussars, were forced to change their plans, including those for their Christmas celebrations at the last minute and move into action.

When the full implications of the German attack were established, all available men and arms were switched against it . . . at first everyone dismissed the possibility of our being involved with a brave smile and a certain air of conviction. It seemed hardly credible that the only armoured brigade on the whole of the British front which had been withdrawn for rest and refitting with the latest British tanks would be called upon. In any case, we had no tanks and the whole thing was a minor affair . . . Christmas plans must continue to mature, be the enemy ever so busy. But our illusions were rapidly to be swept aside. By the 19th the German attack was beginning to take on a threatening air. A clean breakthrough had been achieved in the Monschau Forest, the highest part of the Ardennes, and it was known that 6th Panzer Army was thrusting in a north-westerly direction towards Liège with the 5th Panzer Army in a wider wheel on its left. But that was about the sum total of the information. The enemy had struck right into the rear areas and apart from the wildest rumours nothing was known of his real progress . . . this was a gamble on which they [the Germans] staked all. If it succeeded, they thought, the war might yet be won, or the end might be indefinitely postponed. If it failed, nothing could stop defeat.

By 19 December, it became clear that the German counter-offensive was in danger of cutting off half the Americans and all the British forces from their supply bases, as well as being a direct threat to both Liège and Antwerp. Eisenhower now made a crucial decision:

He ordered Field-Marshal Montgomery to assume temporary operational command of the US troops north of the penetration, for, because of the split it was obviously impracticable for General Bradley to retain control of the 9th and half the 1st US Armies isolated as they were from 12 Army Group Headquarters, located far to the south. Concentrations for the forthcoming Rhineland battle were therefore stopped immediately, while preparations were made to regroup in such as manner as, firstly, to seal the German bulge and, secondly, to collect an adequate counter-attack force on the northern flank. Meanwhile instructions were issued for the 7th US Army to side-step northwards from Alsace to the limits of safety, thus releasing as much of the 3rd US Army as possible to counter-attack the southern flank of the penetration.

Meanwhile, in the words of Montgomery:

> The situation remained unpleasantly vague, and I undertook emergency measures to get reconnaissance troops down to the line of the Meuse and to assist in forming effective cover parties for the Meuse bridges between Liège and Givet. Detachments of SAS troops and Tank Regiment Centre personnel were sent to the river in the Namur-Givet sector while armoured cars of 2nd Army established patrol links between Liège and Namur.'

CONDITIONS FOR THE TROOPS

Before the action began, military life went on as 'normal' with emphasis on training exercises and the renewal and maintenance of equipment as well as rest and recuperation. Close to the enemy, men were subject to the usual hardships and nervous strain of life in the field, and also had to endure the bitter winter weather.

At rest and in action, men were especially prone to trench foot, a debilitating problem exacerbated by sleeping with one's boots on. Some men found their feet so swollen that, as a result, they could not get their shoes on at all. Men of the 28th Division were issued with rubber overshoes (galoshes) which, worn without shoes underneath, remedied the condition within a few days, but many more were left suffering.

Since an army with bad feet could not even march into battle effectively, this list of dos and don'ts on the care of the feet and legs, issued on 16 December in the *Stars and Stripes* – the newspaper published daily for all US forces – was a warning as essential to the fitness of the troops as their training and preparation:

> DON'T sleep with your shoes on, especially if they are wet, if you can possibly help it. This is very important.
> DON'T lace shoes or leggings so tightly as to interfere with the blood circulation in the least.
> DON'T ignore athlete's foot, ingrown toenails, flat feet or any

other foot disorder. They add to the danger of your developing trench foot.

DON'T depend on anyone else to keep you from getting trench foot. They are your feet; you take care of them or nobody does. You must think of yourself first – FEET FIRST!

DO get your shoes and socks off a couple of times a day and rub your feet quickly. Team up with a buddy and massage each other's feet.

DO exercise your feet whenever and however possible. Wiggle your toes inside your shoes. Raise your feet and push against the wall every now and then. Bounce up and down on your toes.

DO keep shoes as waterproof as you can with dubbin. Wear artics if you have them.

DO change to dry socks as often as you can, or at least wring out the ones you have on. Body heat will dry extra pairs inside your helmet, shirt or jacket.

The advice was well taken, as Alfonso Trujillo of 82nd Airborne Intelligence and many thousand others would discover:

During the Bulge that was a horrible time, cold, no air support because it was foggy and snowy, and it was just ugly and we didn't have winter equipment. I recall a lot of the guys had trench foot because their feet would get wet because we just had ordinary boots. Their feet would get wet and cold and their circulation would suffer. One of the things they told us was to get dry socks – I would take my socks off and put them in here to dry [by my stomach] and change them every eight hours or so. I'd have my socks drying at all times inside . . .

Although the weather was frosty, the other constant enemy to good soldiering, in the Ardennes as elsewhere, was mud. Even on icy ground tanks could quickly churn up tracks into a quagmire. *Stars and Stripes* had plenty of sound advice for the troops in December 1944 in a column written by Joe Weston, Warweek staff writer (Warweek was a section of features within the main newspaper). Included was a report of a competition among GIs to send in the best suggestions for dealing with this inanimate enemy.

Like the men of the 501st Parachute Infantry, armed with bazookas, Allied troops were highly trained and ready to attack, and could defend themselves when 'all hell broke loose'. When, as here near Bastogne, rain fell during the day, it would still freeze hard at night.

MUD

This enemy never fires a shot

**[Mud] slows down our armor
at critical battle moment**

A GI's bitter complaint that 'everybody in the whole damned army talks about mud, but nobody does anything about it' started the whole business.

The Old Sergeant [the *Stars and Stripes'* personal advice column] did a little private snooping, asked for help – and got a deskful of letters proving that GIs from generals to privates are doing something about mud besides sleeping in it.

The letters ranged from a dainty packaged sample of Dutch mud contributed by a Signal Corps humorist to the much more practical 'Beat the Mud' program of HQ Advance Section, Cm Z, commanded by Brigadier General Ewart G Plank. General Plank, like every other solider, knows that the best way to lick mud is to prevent as much of it as possible in the first place. So, under the supervision of Colonel CR Broshous, his chief of staff, he got a crackerjack anti-mud campaign underway, which included a trip to Paris as a prize for the best preventive measures.

Mud commandments

Twenty-five GIs, sending in an assortment of suggestions won the 'Big City' jaunt starting 7 December.

Pfc Raymond Michael submitted the typical winning ten mud commandments:

1 STAY ON HARD SURFACES IF POSSIBLE
2 STAY OFF SOFT SHOULDERS
3 DON'T TAKE SHORT CUTS
4 DON'T TRACK MUD ONTO HIGHWAYS
5 KEEP VEHICLES CLEAN AT ALL TIMES
6 DRAINAGE OF STAGNANT WATER
7 FILL IN SOFT SPOTS
8 MARK BAD, IMPOSSIBLE SPOTS
9 USE FOUR-WHEEL DRIVE
10 DON'T DIG YOURSELF DEEPER BY SPINNING

The contest, which ended recently, was publicized via bulletin boards, company poop sheets, announcements at formations, posters and by other means. GIs were given time and material to prepare sketches on ways and means to beat mud.

The article goes on to give more advice pertinent to the handling of vehicles, the chief generators of mud, including handy DIY tips to stop unwanted movements such as side-spinning. Given the many hundreds of tanks and wheeled vehicles deployed in the Ardennes, these were practical precautions that contributed significantly to the war effort.

More mud-beating tips

From General Plank to Pfc Anders Swanson isn't such a long jump where mud is concerned. Swanson, with a Chemical Base Depot, comes up with a couple of ideas which he claims to be using with good results.

Swanson diverts the power to the wheel of any vehicle – self-propelled, fast-moving armoured or supply truck – which is not doing any spinning or revolving. For example, Swanson uses a truck which has both front and rear wheels on the right-hand side spinning.

If the wheels on the left side are on solid ground, he says, put brakes on the spinning side. The differential will then turn or divert power over to the left-hand side and the truck pulls out.

Swanson claims that braking is a cinch by just piping the brake-shoe fluid up to the dashboard. On the dash he rigged up cut-off valves allowing the driver to stop the fluid going to the wheel he wants to revolve. Then he puts the brake on – and he's out.

To critics who claim the operation raises hell with the differential, Swanson says, 'It ain't true' – and is willing to bet on it.

Swanson's second idea has to do with a wheeling device that goes in between and above the bogey wheels of a 6 x 6. It succeeds in getting all the wheels in the back assembly going at one time. Swanson recommends this method for use where trucks all get stuck in a particularly bad place. He suggests that a man be detailed to said place with his device – or any variation of it – because it is usually too clumsy to be carried by each truck.

No rules for mud

The above stuff, and much to follow, is all off-the-cuff emergency business and probably won't be found in the TMs [training manuals]. But mud can't read directions so 'you pays your money and takes your choice.' T/4 Hudson Robinson of an AAA Aw Ba, says: 'Mud! That's easy.' He suggests mounting dual wheels in front. Robinson insists that dual wheels in front of the 6 x 6 can and will pull other trucks of the same size out of the mud. He claims that the 25 per cent more traction created by this idea is surefire. Could be?

A SeaBee echoes the same sentiment. Says he, 'We gained extra power and traction by installing dual wheels in front and licked General Mud at Omaha Beach.'

From a hospital bed, T/S Herman Topel writes that shredded rags, knotted and wrapped around wheels helped out in a hurry. Knotted strands of rope were also highly recommended by Topel – if you have rope.

Corporal Edward R Oglin, who claims the enviable distinction of having put together a still on one of the Normandy beaches, passes on some good, old-fashioned New England mud tips.

Oglin's number one tip is to use the highest gear possible and lowest motor speed that will keep the vehicle going in the mud. He also advises dual front wheels and lower tyre pressure when going through soft stuff.

Corporal Bill Rowe, of a Harbor Craft outfit, claims that makeshift paving is the best and quickest answer. He suggests that special units from our own troops, PW details and French civilians be used for the purpose. Rowe advises that the bomb and shell rubble all over France, Belgium, Holland and Germany be crushed by roller and used to surface roads and areas. No dirt – no mud like that.

Jack Earle, Signal Crops, speaks for more than a few GIs in advocating the use of brush, stone, straw, leaves, hay and any other natural materials available to keep the main highway clear of mud thrown there by mud-churning vehicles.

Ounce of prevention pays

FX Purcell, of a GS Engineer regiment, who doesn't bother to mention his rank, if any, goes down the line with the program General Plank and his men mentioned earlier. He also says an ounce of prevention can cure a hell of a lot of mud and he sends in ten mud commandments to prove his point. Here they are:

1   Trucks turn off highway onto a side road to look for parking space.
2   Choose the best available ground – high and well drained – to park on.

A group of SS troops tries to extricate a vehicle stuck fast in the mud. When churned up, the snowy, unmade roads and tracks of the Ardennes were plagued by the 'inanimate enemy' that not only slowed and stopped vehicles by the score but blocked progress at the front.

3   Drive intelligently. Just because your Jeep or dual-wheeled truck will run in the mud doesn't mean you have to look for mud to test 'em.

4   Carry those boxes of ten-in-one a few feet to the mess tent instead of trying to back into it.

5   Improvise an exit and entrance to your bivouac area or dump. A few logs and a bit of gravel will do it.

7   For semi-permanent installations have roads and hard standing built in advance.

8   Consult the engineers before locating a dump or other large installation.

9   Even in digging a foxhole or a latrine, think of drainage.

10   Remember – no matter today – it's going to rain tomorrow.

SUPPLIES AND EQUIPMENT

Getting adequate supplies of fuel in place was also important, as Engineer Peter J Bertucci details:

[I] helped to supply Patton with a lot of gasoline for his movement across France. Since he needed gasoline more than anything else. We landed on strips that were anything but airstrips, however they were suitable for the C-47s . . . the center strip in the cabin of a C-47 is aluminum. Then you have folding seats on each side. Well we folded the seats up and loaded as many five-gallon jerry cans with 100 octane gasoline in the plane from the cockpit or the cabin all the way back to the doorway, with the door off, of course. And we tied them so they wouldn't move and we flew, and wherever we could land we'd slide, we had the pilot, co-pilot, the crew chief, and myself would just stand there sliding these five-gallon jerry cans full of 100 octane gas along these aluminum strips. And I would be a bit surprised if we didn't see some sparks flying. Fortunately we didn't blow ourselves up. And if the trucks were there to get the gasoline for Patton, we'd put them on the trucks. If they weren't there we'd just lay them on the ground and take off, because we couldn't spend too much time. And . . . we did quite a bit of that, I would say probably several trips.

. . . If we could find a road that we could land on, we would land on that road. There was no airstrips set up at all. Anything we could land on . . . a C-47 could land on almost anything if the wheels wouldn't sink into the ground. It was a very terrific airplane . . . this was some time in December, and during the Ardennes breakthrough the group alerted to a glider mission to Bastogne. This was canCellesd when the garrison – the besieged garrison – was relieved. But we played an important role in bringing up reserves to stem German threats.

As they rested in the Ardennes, expecting no action until the New Year, fortunate troops enjoyed some comforts, with warmth from log fires and good food. One was Sergeant John P Kline, a member of a machine-gun squad in the 106th Division in the northern sector of the Ardennes:

12/11/44

We left the woods near St Vith for frontline positions. Our destination was a defense line in the Ardennes forest atop the Schnee Eifel (Snow Mountain). The positions were 12 miles east of St Vith and were in Germany. A name we would learn to remember, Schonberg, was nine miles east of St Vith and three miles west of our positions. We were facing the German troops from emplacements on the east slopes [reverse slopes] of the German Siegfried Line, known as 'The German West Wall'.

We took over positions held by the 2nd Infantry Division and exchanged much of our new equipment for their old. The exchange was to be made as quickly and quietly as possible. The 2nd Division was being transferred to Aachen to participate in an attack on the Roer Dam area. My machine-gun position was a log bunker with field of fire obstructed by dense forest. Conditions were quiet. Excellent chow was served twice a day.

M Company, 423rd Regiment, was assigned positions along the front line to support the rifle companies. An infantry heavy weapons company, like ours, is equipped with 81mm mortars and water-cooled 30-caliber machine guns. A rifle company is equipped with automatic weapons and mortars that are only 60mm mortars and air-cooled machine guns. Our duty was to support the various rifle companies of the 3rd Battalion, 423rd Regiment. They were I, K and L Companies. Such was our deployment along the tree-covered ridge atop the Schnee Eifel.

The Ardennes forest is, for the most part, heavily wooded. It is interlaced with many small logging trails, fire-fighting lanes and streams. We slept in rough, but warm dugouts and enjoyed solid gun bunkers. Built by the 2nd Division, they were built of logs, with a log and earth roof.

We completed our changeover with the 2nd Infantry Division as darkness came. We had no time to become acquainted with the territory around our new positions. Because of that, and since we were new and inexperienced troops, our first night was unforgettable. We were facing, for the first time, an enemy that we only knew from newsreels and training films. It was a sleepless and anxiety-filled night.

I can personally confirm that a snow-covered tree stump will actually move. That is, if you stare at it long enough – and if you are a young, nineteen-year-old machine-gun squad leader peering, into the darkness, towards the enemy through a slit in a machine-gun bunker. Every sound was amplified. Every bush could be an enemy crawling towards you. Your eyes grow bleary from staring into the darkness. You are happy when the relief crew shows up. The next day, you take a good long look at the stump that moved during the night. You take note of all unusual objects, and then things start to settle down.

There were two gun emplacements (bunkers) for my machine-gun squad. One was higher on the hill, and the other a couple of hundred yards down the slope. When we first moved in, our gun position was in the lower bunker. After the first night we were asked to move back up the slope, to the alternative bunker. For what reason, I don't know. We did appreciate the move, for the alternative bunker was much warmer and drier. As in the lower bunker, there were 'trip lines' running from the bunker down into the forest and through the barbed wire. The lines were attached to hand grenades and flares. Then, they were placed in their shipping containers and attached to tree trunks. If we detected movement in the area beyond the barbed wire we could pull a trip line. This would cause a grenade to explode, after it was pulled from its container. A flare could be ignited to light up the area in the same manner. Our field of fire was good, but very limited. The 2nd Division had cut down a lot of trees and cleaned out the brush. However, the forest still offered the enemy excellent cover.

The 2nd Division were a highly experienced formation that had fought against German parachute troops in the battle for St Lô in Normandy. There they had learned all the arts of field fortification in cluttered terrain.

I remember one day being convinced that I could see a vehicle, in the woods, several hundred yards down the hill. The contours of the hill and the thick forest were playing games with my imagination. When I looked at it from another vantage point, the illusion disappeared.

There was one rifleman to the left of my bunker. He was entrenched in a log-covered foxhole. According to members of the patrols, this rifleman was the last person between my machine-gun emplacement and the 422nd Regiment. The 422nd Regiment was reported to be several hundred yards north on the Eifel. The two regiments sent alternate patrols across the unoccupied space each half hour. They reported very little German activity. The first days passed without incident. The most excitement we had in my bunker area was when a nearby 50-caliber machine gun started blasting away. The gunner had become bored and decided to kill a deer.

We left the bunker area twice daily to eat our meals in a mess tent. It was back of us, to the west, on the opposite side of the hill. To get to it we had to walk along a trail, through a clearing, and down the other side. The Germans had the clearing zeroed in. As we crossed the clearing, we had to be prepared to hit the ground in case they decided to harass us. The 2nd Division's squad leader that I relieved, said two men had been killed crossing the clearing a few days ago. Our daily trips to the mess tent were something to look forward too [sic]. The food was good and the Mess Sergeant seemed to be friendlier since we have moved up to the front lines. I did enjoy those meals, there were generous portions and we could chat with the others and get brought up to date on the local news.

Some had better luck. James Christie, serving with the 28th Division on the Southern flank spent time in Diekirch as well as in the field.

November '44 – moved from Hürtgen Forest, swapped places with 8 Infantry Division, and arrived at Dijkerk 'just before Thanksgiving'.

The 1st Battalion was sent into a defensive position outside of Dijkerk. We were on the right flank of the Regiment and the Regiment of course was on the right flank of the Division, and our front was along the Aure river, the . . . uttermost right boundary of the Battalion . . . was the Suere river. B Company held a piece of [high] ground some hundreds of yards back from the river [Aure]. A Company was on the right, I'm not sure where C Company was.

We remained in those positions for about two weeks, during which time we did some pretty heavy patrolling and got in a lot of replacements. Dug foxholes, dug positions, booby-trapped the whole place . . .

About the 10th of December we were moved back into the town of Dijkerk itself and placed in reserve. The procedure at that time was to place a battalion in reserve for one week, in the line for two . . .

And for Staff Sergeant John R Passauer of the 2nd Armoured Division Tank Maintenance, duty was done despite the grumbles:

We was always last because we was maintenance . . . we got orders to move out at night . . . we drove almost a hundred miles that night to get to Belgium. We went to the point of the Bulge where the Germans were coming . . . it was raining and freezing going down there . . . the next morning our tanks were froze fast to the ground, we had to beat on them with sledges and bars and everything to get them broke loose from frozen ground. If the Germans had known that we would have been a sitting duck . . .

No one had had a bath in all this time so they took us to a big long building where they set up showers where you went in and took everything off and anything that you wanted you put in a little bag, your belt, your money, cigarettes, lighter, everything except your dogtags you kept around your neck and everything else you threw away. Most of it weren't much good anyway, worn out and everything else. We walked in there, there was about 30 guys at a time taking a shower and of course after you got out of the shower they gave you a new uniform, new underwear and everything, new shoes, which was great . . . we hadn't been clean for a long time . . . it was sure nice to get a shower for a change . . .

With targets registered for the artillery, and bridging sites and approach routes identified and assigned, orders had been issued and the troops were briefed. The German armies were poised to launch their attack, despite their lack of supplies:

> **After Arnhem,** said wireless operator Hans Behrens, member of a
> Wehrmacht Panzer unit, we regrouped on the western Rhine-side
> and . . . just before the Ardennes offensive, we stocked up with
> what we had, and then . . . in due course we were given the . . .
> advance command to proceed to certain places. We did not have
> sufficient of anything. We had sufficient petrol to get to a certain
> distance, perhaps 20–30 kilometres, and were told: 'There's an
> American ammunition-dump . . . or a fuel depot. Go and get there
> and then load up again.'
>   It was incredible . . . on a shoe-string, how far we did advance.
> I remember Christmas 1944 we were I think at our most
> westerly point, somewhere between Bastogne and St Hubert in
> the Ardennes. Of course, the Ardennes . . . the whole offensive
> was called 'Wacht am Rhein', but to us commonly called the
> Rundstedt or the Ardennes offensive . . .

Their American opponents were much less ready to defend themselves. The plans for the offensive included the use of special forces disguised as American military police to spread confusion and take every advantage of the relaxed mood of the US troops. In the autumn of 1944, as the German High Command was planning the offensive in the Ardennes, Hitler had placed particular emphasis on the use of psychological factors as a way to counter the material and numerical superiority of the Allies.

Operation GREIF was the most audacious element of the overall plan. Brigadeführer Otto Skorzeny, a veteran of many adventures such as the rescue of Mussolini from captivity on the Grand Sasso, was to command. In October he was ordered to assemble a brigade-size force of English-speaking troops, to be employed behind enemy lines dressed in American uniforms, using American tanks, trucks and Jeeps. Skorzeny described the intention of the plan in this way:

> My three battle-groups should go ahead of the attacking columns
> and try to concentrate in the vicinity of the bridges [across the
> Meuse]. A reconnaissance party, in American uniforms, must find

out and report the position at the bridges . . . there would be
a good chance that a surprise attack, openly carried out
would succeed, particularly if the enemy had not recovered
from his panic.

The captured bridges could then be used by the advancing armoured columns of the panzer armies on their way to Antwerp and Brussels, and the infiltrators would then carry out their secondary mission which was to use initiative and imagination, 'causing alarm, confusion and despondency in the enemy ranks.'

Skorzeny was very doubtful about the whole idea of the Ardennes offensive, the more so regarding his own part in it:

There was great difficulty in finding suitable men and equipment
to form 150 Brigade, the formation to perform GREIF. [Skorzeny
recollected that of his men,] Category One, comprising men
speaking perfectly and with some notion of American slang, was
ten strong and most of them were sailors . . .

The brigade had only 15 American trucks and their two Sherman tanks broke down very early during the operation. In place of Shermans the brigade had 'twelve German "Panthers" . . . we camouflaged their guns and turrets to make them look like Shermans . . . they could only deceive very young American troops, seeing them at night from very far away.'

Training was inhibited because of excessive security measures, which meant that Skorzeny's men were not allowed to know what they were going to do until just before the offensive started. Ignorance of their intended purpose led to the emergence of wild rumours. One lieutenant in the Brigade said to Skorzeny:

Sir, I believe I know the real objective . . . the brigade is to go
straight to Paris and capture Allied Headquarters . . . men who
could speak English perfectly dressed in enemy uniform should
appear to be escorts for a prisoner of war convoy . . .

This particular rumour had a dramatic effect on Allied behaviour during the battle. Skorzeny and his staff decided to treat the rumours with a double bluff, 'we decided to let the rumours increase and multiply, while apparently doing our best to suppress them. We calculated enemy Intelligence would simply not know what to make of the medley of lurid and conflicting information . . .'

In the event, this policy of Skorzeny's added to the impact of his operation. This impact was primarily psychological because adverse circumstances prevented 150 Brigade from carrying out most of its planned actions.

THE BRITISH IN BELGIUM

While the Germans were planning their attack, British forces – destined to be involved in the battle a few days after the first assault on the Allies – were, like the Americans, settling down to enjoy some relaxation, though in their case much further from the action to come. The Fife and Forfar Yeomanry was promising itself 'a Royal Yuletide' which it imagined it 'deserved and began planning for the occasion'.

In Ypres in Belgium, Lieutenant William Steel Brownlie of the Second Fife and Forfar Yeomanry, was revelling in the peaceful atmosphere, and having some fun into the bargain:

> What a delight to be in a place like this, far away from the war.
> Of course the town had been flattened in 'the other war', but
> was now rebuilt, mostly in the old style. Piles of cut stones
> lay round the Cloth Hall, still to be completed . . . I got a bare
> room over a café near the station, the owner saying that she had
> married a WWI Tommy, who had died, and that she had been
> shot in the shoulder by a German during the occupation, for
> revealing the fact.
>
> We thought of a visit to Antwerp, but a taxi fare cost 3,000
> francs, so [instead] we went to *Thé Dansant,* a café on the square,
> meeting two nice girls who took us home for a pleasant evening
> with their family. Next day, we were discussing how to get to
> Antwerp, when Sir John Gilmour overheard, and said why not
> just take a Jeep? We had not considered such illegality. We
> went . . . and we had a splendid evening in the Divisional Club.

The men of the 23rd Hussars were having an equally good time, still waiting for new Comet tanks to arrive. These were similar to their predecessors, the

Cromwells, but had thicker armour and were mounted with a new high-velocity 77mm gun. They would also replace the American Shermans, which had given excellent service mechanically and survived far greater mileage than anyone had anticipated.

> Although an ambitious six weeks' training programme existed on paper, taking little account of the festive season, the fact that the new Comet tanks had not arrived and that all excepting a few of the old Shermans had been dropped off at Brussels, encouraged lively plans for Christmas and a natural instinct to make the best of superabundant hospitality. The four squadrons all had a generous area of the town and troops were billeted in private houses. 'B' and Headquarters Squadron shared the famous reconstructed Cloth Hall for a mess room, while Regimental Headquarters lived in a chateau on the outskirts of town in sumptuous seclusion. On all sides people got 'stuck in', their feet well under the table and, some said, their boots under the bed! By the sixteenth there was general agreement that the prospects were extremely good.

Elsewhere in Belgium, men were making the best of much more Spartan circumstances, though the situation was especially tough for the tank men who had come from action in North Africa. As Robert Watt, RSM of the 3rd Royal Tank Regiment recorded:

> I had become accustomed to war in the desert, where only soldiers and their machines were exposed to the destruction of conflict, but here every living thing and habitat had become part of the struggle for superiority and survival. Entire villages that had once housed generations of families had been reduced to piles of rubble. Deserted, silent and with the smell of death hanging in the air, this was indeed the tragic depressing face of war.

As well as making efforts to survive day by day and find enough food, Robert Watt's unit was also carrying on with training of new men recruited to make up for heavy losses suffered in the months since D-Day.

As our armies advanced to the borders of Germany, we moved forward to a village near Hasselt in the north of Belgium and, although information was limited, we knew by the demand for replacement crews that tank losses were high. Redirected men from Armoured Corps courses had slowed to a trickle. Tank men were definitely getting scarce and to fill the gaps, many from rear echelon units such as lorry drivers and pen pushers had volunteered to man the tanks, probably keen for a slice of the action before the war ended.

It was here on the moors that we set up a shooting range. Derelict farm buildings became our quarters and within a couple of weeks the permanent staff had turned this shambles of wood and masonry into a home from home. Once again, the ingenuity of man worked miracles. Holes were knocked in walls to be filled with frames complete with glass and a door, a brick oven appeared in the yard, made from new bricks and a forty-gallon drum, and an old barn floored with the steel platforms from two burned out lorries. I never dared to ask where all these materials had come from, but I did recognise that within any group of men, a wide range of skills lay dormant until necessity demanded. For example, an insurance agent who had done nothing but push a pen for most of his life built the oven and the two men who knocked the holes in the walls had no knowledge of buildings. By a miracle it did not collapse.

Here in our humble abode, remote from the daily routine and discipline of the unit, we settled down to a very pleasant and peaceful existence. Outside interference was limited to the regular arrival of rations and trainees.

By a stroke of luck, the supply of food appeared from a most unexpected source:

There were two other incidents that effected [sic] our way of life. Mysterious packages of food started to appear on our doorstep during the night and although, on occasion, we had been disturbed in the early hours by a dog which we inherited with the farm, he appeared to be barking at nothing. We had set up booby traps of parachute flares around the area but only one was fired and the dog did that. However, a few whispered remarks by one of the locals solved the problem. Our range lay across an old traders' or smugglers' route which was currently in use and the smugglers had no desire to attract attention by being shot at by our guards. With the additional issue of meat, fruit, vegetables and even drink, I saw nothing.

The difficulties of training, as well as entertainment and the weather, were also the preoccupation of Steel Brownlie, whose diary for 'December 15th etc' records:

The regiment arrived, and with it much chaos and hard work were put into their quarters. It is not easy to convert a mobile tank force into a static one whose object is training. Next day an Orderly Room was set up, and we were back to 'real soldiering' – barrack life. Vague reports came through of some kind of German offensive in the Ardennes, but we were too busy to bother much.

I collected Comet tanks from Menin, and took Colonel Alec in a Jeep to Gravelines, where a firing range had been set up. Our 'overs' would fall in Dunkirk, still held by the Germans and contained by 9 RTR and Czech troops. It was a good range, but more bleak than most, and 45 miles way. I resolved to go there as seldom as possible, interpreting my duties as Gunnery Officer to be mainly supervisory . . . yet I had to go occasionally, once driving back in the dark and freezing rain, one eye peering through a shrapnel hole in the opaque windscreen of a Jeep. The first time, I map-read Colonel Alec into the ruins of Petit Port Phillipe, which I later heard was thickly mined, by mistake.

Two more Comets arrived. I found a site for a miniature range, Pinkie Desmond and I visited the Victoria Palace to arrange a Squadron Dance, which was a roaring success and went on far into the morning. It was at this or another like it that I gallantly walked home a girl called Made. There was deep slush, I was wearing thin shoes, she passed out so that I had to carry her over one shoulder, she kept dropping her umbrella. I propped her up at her front door, rang the bell, and fled.

Also billeted in Ypres, and unaware of the action they were soon to be involved in, were the 2nd Fife and Forfar Yeomanry:

> *14th December* – The Regt moved to Ypres, advanced parties having set off a few days previously. Tanks went by transporter, personnel in tanks travelling through the night and arriving mid-morning.
>
> Billets were found to be excellent, comfortable and informal quite unlike the accommodation provided by the army at home. The Belgian people appeared friendly and everyone looked forward to a pleasant change from the discomforts of winter campaigning in Europe.
>
> Cadres classes were started on the Comet, a few of which had arrived, and which provoked general interest and approval, if not complete satisfaction.

But this 'normal' life was soon to end, and with it all thoughts of a peaceful Christmas. Though not in fact directed at the Ardennes, there were occasional warning signs:

> An occasional violent explosion nearby, wrote RSM Watt, jolted us back to the reality that there was still a war on. I took a tank to an area where smoke was still rising and discovered a damned great hole with lots of metal debris lying around. It was the remains of a V-2 rocket, but why there in the middle of nowhere? From then on we watched the sky to the west and saw the smoke trails of the rockets being fired apparently directed at London and Antwerp. Ours were the duds that went straight up and down. It was quite a shock to realise the frontline was so near.

Also concentrated around Ypres, the 29th Armoured Brigade headquarters was, like the other British troops, slow to hear of the launch of the Ardennes offensive.

> Very little news regarding the German offensive in the Ardennes was available at brigade headquarters since the only sources of information at first were the divisional situation

reports – some two days out of date when they arrived from Holland – and the BBC. It is hardly surprising therefore that the true seriousness of the situation was unknown; on December 18 and 19, a certain amount of concern was caused by the BBC reports which showed that the offensive was definitely gathering momentum rather than being checked. I realised that this was something much bigger than anyone had visualised at first, and there was a marked eagerness everywhere to know the latest official news. The attitude amongst many was, not unnaturally, that whoever else might be called in to help, the 29th brigade was surely one brigade which could not be touched [because it, too, was being refitted with Comet tanks], unless to fight on its feet.

Within 24 hours, however, all that was destined to change . . .

On the morning of December 20th, at two o'clock, the duty officer was roused from his bed by the telephone, and collecting his wits as quickly as possible, he realised that he was talking to the Chief of Staff, 21st Army Group. A series of orders came through as fast as they could be noted down: '. . . the brigade will move as quickly as possible . . .'; 'the Brigadier will start at once for Army Group Headquarters in Brussels to receive his detailed orders . . .'; '. . . the brigade will receive its tanks, ammunition, food and petrol from Brussels on the way to its battle positions . . .' So came the orders, and so ended sleep that night for many an officer and man.

The Brigadier was roused, and decided that nothing but disaster could result if he attempted to reach Brussels during the night; for outside was thick fog and pitch darkness. All commanding officers were warned to have their regiments ready to move as soon as possible and to rendezvous at the headquarters of 23H at 07.00 to receive such details of orders as were available.

Emotions were running high, but, for the brigade to be effective, they needed a plan of action and cool heads.

When the Brigadier arrived in Brussels at 09.30, he was given his detailed orders, and assisted by a staff officer proceeded to work out his plan. From such information as could be obtained from the Americans the situation appeared serious indeed. Seldom before could so much blue chinagraph [pencil] have been applied to the main operations room map. Never before in the campaign had the Germans assembled such a force – 24 divisions, of which at least ten were known to be panzer divisions and including the sinister and elusive 6th SS Panzer Army. It seemed that many grave breaches had been forced in the American lines, and although from everywhere came reports that our allies were fighting well, it was clear that somewhere on those snow clad hills, as yet only purple patches on maps that were quite new to us, the German armour was loose and rolling steadily westwards. Air reconnaissance had been impossible during the day owing to the appalling weather conditions; how fast through this blanket of fog could the Panzers travel? All depended on the answer to this question.

It was plain that in many places there was nothing between German spearheads and Brussels except for scattered groups of American base troops, quite inadequate in strengths to do more than harass the advancing enemy. It was not only in the operations room that the atmosphere was tense, for outside that evening Brussels seemed different. The streets were cold and dark; civilians clustered in small groups on corners, talking earnestly, some eager for a new rumour, the majority hoping for a morsel of encouraging news to take home with them. In many a Belgium home in the capital that night, despair gripped at the hearts of families as they contemplated the possibility of another German occupation.

Robert Watt's reaction at hearing of the German offensive, undoubtedly shared by hundreds on both sides, was the return of fear in the face of conflict:

A further jolt to our complacency was delivered with news of a German counter-attack in the Ardennes, south of our location and we were ordered to be in a state of readiness to move at short notice. This information shattered my dream world of peace and security, being remote from enemy activity for so long I had shed the mantle of constant nervous tension, for that feeling of foreboding, and uncertainty had returned. I had no desire to become involved in active warfare again and the churning sickness of fear in my stomach told me so.

He and his comrades may have been cheered, however, by the reaction of the Belgian civilians to the advancing British tanks:

In many places it was almost like liberation day again, with flags, flowers and even hot coffee for those who were fortunate enough to stop by the roadside for a few moments. As the tanks and half-track neared the Meuse, things became quieter; most people were indoors, and one became conscious of curious faces peering through windows and looking cautiously out of doorways. By the time that the first few vehicles of a convoy had passed, one or two people would venture out for a closer look, and having satisfied themselves that it was after all 'les Anglais' would call out their friends and families. Perhaps it was that they too knew that the Germans were using Sherman tanks in their vanguards? More likely that to these simple and delightful people one tank is much the same as another.

Strategically, the Commander-in-Chief decided that it was vitally important for the British to man the River Meuse as a stop line in case the German columns should break clean away, and to do so whatever the elements could throw at them. To make this work successfully, co-operation and quick thinking were vital.

As it happened, the 29th Armoured Brigade was the only reserve available to the Army Group, and even if it had no tanks it had to be given some – quickly.

So, during the morning of December 20th, the brigade began to move out of Ypres, led by the Rifle Brigade, some of whose vehicles, which were still arriving from Holland were having to be turned around on the road. They drove steadily all day through the fog, and arrived in the area of Waterloo just south of Brussels a little before midnight. The armoured regiments followed, mostly travelling in lorries, a few 17-pounder Shermans and some Honeys being the only armour in the columns.

Meanwhile, at Army Group, the Brigadier had made his plans and was ready to issue his orders to commanding officers as soon as they arrived. The task given to the brigade was no light one; they were to deny to the enemy the crossings of the River Meuse along a front of 40 kilometres, from and including the town of Namur in the north, to the bridge at Givet to the south. To help, various other units were put under command, including the 61st Reconnaissance Regiment, the 4th Army Group Royal Artillery, three troops of Bofors guns from the air defence of Brussels, and a self-propelled battery of anti-tank guns. Three field security sections, several civil affairs detachments and elements of the Belgian Special Air Service completed the 'Brigade Group'.

The office of the Colonel GS (Ops) became a kind of brigade tactical headquarters, and rendezvous for dozens of officers, each anxious to help in his own particular sphere. Maps, signals communications, air support, petrol, food and traffic control provided but a few of the problems which had to be solved, and the co-operation of these officers from the various branches of the Army Group staff was more than appreciated.

From the evening of 20 December, the final stages of preparation for these British forces now ran to a tight timetable.

At 19.00 the commanding officer of 8 RB arrived and was ordered to move his battalion at first light next morning, and to position one motor company on each of the main bridges still in existence over the Meuse, at Namur, Dinant and Givet. As soon as possible in the morning, one squadron of each armoured regiment was to move, to be followed later by the remainder of the regiments as soon as they were equipped. 2FF Yeo were to be responsible for Namur and its bridges, 3 R Tks for Dinant, and 23 H for Givet.

As dawn broke on December 21st, the Rifle Brigade moved away in the direction of the river, and men of the armoured regiments began the task of taking over their tanks. Ammunition had to be stowed, petrol tanks filled, Browning machine guns and wireless sets fitted before they would be ready to move out and take up their positions with 8 RB.

At 09.30 the Brigadier held a conference for commanding officers to discuss the final details regarding the holding of the crossings, and the responsibilities for the demolition of the bridges. The magnitude of the latter responsibility was never greater, in view of the large numbers of American troops still fighting far to the east. Authority for demolition could, at first, only be given by the Commander-in-Chief himself, but the responsibility was later delegated to the brigade commander, and subsequently to the regimental commander at each bridge. Throughout, the policy was that the bridges would only be blown in the gravest emergency, and as a last possible resort to prevent the enemy crossing the river in force.

By 13.00 the motor companies of 8 RB were in position on their respective bridges, and by 16.30 they had been joined by one squadron of each armoured regiment, this, as a result of almost superhuman efforts on the part of the tank crews. As darkness was falling the remainder of the tanks were on their way to the bridges and at 20.00, less than 48 hours after the telephone call in Ypres, Army Group were informed that 29th Armoured Brigade were complete on the river line.

The German attack set off similar activity and produced similar experiences for the 2nd Fife and Forfar Yeomanry as William Steel Brownlie's diary resumes:

20 December
Next morning, routine as usual, Desmond away in Eindhoven with three trucks to collect goodies for Xmas, bombshell. We were to move to the Ardennes soonest. Forget the Comets, leave all the heavy kit behind, pick up our old Shermans in Brussels, get to the Meuse and help stop von Rundstedt. Advance party to leave at 13.30, self for A Sqn, Jimmy for B Sqn who were short of

officers, in scoutcars. Cup of coffee in Aalst, Brussels in turmoil, population very scared. We laid out areas for billets, there being no time for details, and I was sent as regimental guide to a point in the suburbs where our column of trucks was expected. They were late, it was cold and pouring with rain, V-1s were passing overhead, very depressing. There were three of us in the Humber, so I arranged that we took turns – two in a café, one in the car. The column arrived, and I led them through the city – strangely quiet and the streets empty – to our billet areas. In minutes everyone had found a bed, and 'got feet under a table'. A Sqn HQ was set up, there was an O-Group at RHQ, and I got to bed with my crew about 2am.

21 December
Up at 6, we went to the reinforcement unit, where the Shermans of our 29 Armoured Brigade had been dumped and emptied of all ammo, etc. There was no time to sort out whose tanks were whose, and the three regiments got vehicles with any old regimental, squadron or troop signs on them, which was confusing. I was lucky – my Sherman was in Ypres as a trainer and Jock McKinnon drove it to Brussels. By midday, with a miracle of organisation, the whole Brigade were armed, rationed and fuelled. We moved at 2pm, Pinkie leading in a scoutcar, me following in his tank. There were cheering crowds in Brussels, worried that the Germans would be back and maybe we would stop them. The roads from there to Namur were deserted except for a few road blocks manned by local volunteers. Not much to stop the Germans if they got across the Meuse.

I was sent ahead in a scoutcar to arrange a harbour in Belgrade, a suburb of Namur, and picked a street of brick-built houses, where the tanks parked. We were most welcome, and my own billet was with a delightful damsel (but naturally), who was serving me a four-course meal, when her large policeman husband came off late shift, and she produced a baby daughter from the back room. You can't win them all.

Next day, he was still waiting for action, but ever on the alert, and aware of the differences between his current situation and the one he had encountered in Normandy:

First light we went through the town and over the Meuse bridge, which was wired for demolition and defended by a scratch force collected from all kinds of units, looking nervous and checking everyone's papers. There were latrine-rumours about German parachutists disguised in captured American uniforms, but our main worry was that some bloody fool would blow the bridges with us on the far side. We motored on a few miles to Erpent, and deployed in defensive positions on high ground. All we knew was that the situation was 'fluid', so that an enemy thrust could come our way. This was welcome in a way, for we were camouflaged with a good field of fire, quite the opposite of the situation in Normandy. But nothing came. We sat in the cold. Late afternoon I was sent back to Namur, to arrange sleeping places for all ranks, as near to the bridge as possible. There was a row of expensive looking houses right on the river bank, so I knocked them all up and told the inhabitants to expect our troops in a short time.

Speed was of the essence in the preparations of the 23rd Hussars:

The telephone in RHQ Mess rang at three o'clock on the morning of the 20th. The Colonel was to meet the Brigadier at eight o'clock in the Orderly Room, and till eight o'clock that was all we were to know, though there was no doubt that something was in the air, and those who knew of the message realised that our plans for celebrating December 25th would now almost certainly not materialise. At eight o'clock the Colonel, accompanied by the Adjutant, met the Brigadier. The Adjutant was dressed ready to go on short leave to Paris, but at one minute past eight, all thoughts of visiting Paris had been abandoned. During the night the Brigadier had been summoned to report to 21st Army Group in Brussels as soon as possible and the Brigade was put at two hours notice to move. We knew little of what was going on except that we were likely to move to the area of Brussels. Squadron Leaders were hastily summoned and were told, to their consternation, that they must be ready to move by eleven o'clock. Tank crews were to collect the Shermans once more and the Echelon was to be packed up and ready for war. We had brought back with us seven 17-pounder Shermans and four Honeys. These were to move to Brussels on their tracks under Captain Blackman. The remainder of the regiment was to travel in lorries, except for a small rear party which was to be left behind to keep a loving, and not unwilling, eye on our interests in Ypres.

Had such an order been issued in the days in England, the man who gave it would have been freely described as mad. Now no one questioned it. It was a little shattering but it could be done, and the rush was so great that no one had any time to have any headaches about it. The time for the move was constantly changed. At two o'clock in the afternoon eventually the Regiment was forming up and the CO was beginning to move off when a despatch rider drove up with a note to say that the move was once again put back one hour. Perhaps that further hour's respite was just as well. At the head of the column things looked all right, but rumours were abroad that, in the town, kit was still being thrown into lorries, and men were rushing out of their billets to jump on board just as the vehicles were beginning to move off. At three o'clock the column did get going. Though the delay of an hour had meant perhaps that fewer things were left behind, it gave us an hour less daylight for travelling. It was damp, cold and misty, and not till eleven o'clock at night did we reach the rendezvous where we were to meet the Second-in-Command who, as usual in all such cases had gone ahead with a harbour party.

So ended the first stage of a move which was certainly the fastest the Regiment had ever been asked to do. That it went off so well and, on the whole, so smoothly only showed how accustomed everyone now was to doing what at first sight seemed impossible. Each man knew his job and did it. Each man knew what bit of equipment he was responsible for and took it with him. So far as is known only one large item of equipment was left behind – the water trailer. Its absence was not discovered till Brussels when a very worried lance-corporal approached his Squadron leader and made his awful confession. Throughout the long journey from Ypres to Brussels he had been worried. He knew there was something not quite right. And then, when he halted in Brussels, an idea flashed through his mind. Hoping for the best but fearing the worst, he climbed down from the driving cab of his three-tonner, walked round behind and found that the Thing was not there. He had forgotten to hitch on the trailer which must still be reposing, where it had been behind his lorry, in a side street in Ypres.

Once in Brussels, even though it was late, cold and pitch black, there was more work to do on the tanks they thought they had traded in for superior models, and more miles to travel before they could take up their allotted positions:

That night we harboured in the streets of Brussels near the Second Armoured Reinforcement Group where we were to collect once more the tanks we had handed in only a week before and had thought that we should never see again. Those who had time to sleep were made welcome in the houses, but most had work to do. A general idea of the plan was now known. The Brigade was to take up positions as quickly as possible covering the bridges over the Meuse at Liège, Namur and Givet . . . it was not until after midnight that we were told which tanks we were to take. When the list was received they were allotted to the squadrons, and in the darkness the job of taking them over was begun. It was not easy to find the right tanks when one could not see the numbers. When they had been found they had to be checked for battle worthiness. When we had handed them in we prided ourselves that they were in good condition as could be, considering the miles they had done. Since then 'the mice had got at them'. Some had no wireless sets, or sets that would not work. In others the machine guns were missing. It was a case of every man for himself. Whether out of the stores or from the tank next door, the various bits and pieces were collected. At nine o'clock that morning 'C' Squadron was on the move to Givet . . .

The journey was not without its incidents. The Military Police were charged with the duty of conducting the column through

Brussels and, apparently oblivious of the imperative need for us to reach Givet with all speed, or possibly with the object of reassuring the townsfolk who had hear rumours that all was not well in the Ardennes, they took us on a sightseeing tour of the city before setting us off on the road leading south to Charleroi. Thus it was that at one moment the tanks were seen proceeding down one side of the street in one direction while on the other side were the wheels going the other way. It had its funny side, but we knew we were urgently needed elsewhere though we had no accurate information of what the situation was, and in any case the more of daylight we wasted in Brussels, the longer would we have to travel in the dark. It was a long drive. Some tanks broke down, as was inevitable, but by eleven o'clock that night, December 21st, we were moving into Givet little more than 36 hours after the warning order had been given to prepare to move from Ypres. It was an achievement of which everyone felt rightly proud.

For some, including the British 11th Armoured Division, there was still more waiting until the action began:

By as late as evening on December 23rd, no firm information could be obtained as to who, if anyone was on the right of the brigade, beyond Givet. A liaison officer was despatched to contact whatever troops he could, and in the meantime 198th Anti-Tank Battery was disposed in positions covering the right flank. It had also been decided that the bridges could be best defended by putting out a defensive screen on the far bank of the river where there were excellent hull down positions with perfect fields of fire. The object of these screens was to delay the enemy's advance to the river line itself for as long as possible, while inflicting upon him maximum damage, and avoiding casualties themselves.

All the pieces of the jigsaw were now assembled, and some were already in place. It was time for action.

3
THE ALLIES UNDER FIRE

During the night of 15–16 December German artillery units moved forward into firing positions from which they supported the infantry assault on the morning of the 16th. Early that morning, for Captain Arnold Albrecht, Military Intelligence 99th Division, 3rd Army, as for hundreds of others . . .

> . . . all hell broke loose and we had a major battle just beginning. The outfit to our right, the 104th Cavalry I believe, was completely annihilated and so was one of the regiments of the 99th Division, my outfit . . . We were awakened by the noise and confusion of battle and also by the orders to move out as quickly as possible. One of my interrogators lost his life there, the only casualty we had during the war. He was an officer as I was and he also had a decidedly German accent. Later, when we had time to talk about his death we were never quite sure whether his voice betrayed him or if it was caused by enemy fire.

Even after the German shelling began, some of the American troops refused to take the situation seriously. Like Private James Christie of the 28th Division, they had grown complacently accustomed to the sounds of gunfire in the Hürtgen Forest:

> Well, during the night there was a considerable amount of shellfire. I don't know exactly when it started. Sometime after midnight. It didn't particularly disturb most of us because having been veterans of continuing shellfire in the Hürtgen and other places, we weren't surprised to get a few artillery sounds, so most everybody just rolled over and went back to sleep, but come daybreak and we still heard a rumble and there was obviously more shelling going on, and Dijkerk was getting hit. As a matter

To impede the advance of German vehicles across Belgium, Allied engineers laid mines in strategic roads, and on bridges and culverts, all of which had to be carefully mapped. When a tank hit a mine it would burst into flames or, in army parlance, 'brew up'.

of fact we heard that the Battalion Motor Pool had been hit rather severely. We also heard that several other installations . . . had been hit, and someone decided that perhaps the accuracy of the German artillery fire was a bit more than it should have been. The rumour around the 109th was that a detachment was sent to look for an artillery-spotter with a radio, and that one was found. Well anyway here we were on Saturday morning with shells falling in Dijkerk, and I was getting ready to get the company to fall out for this parade. We quickly got word to fall out . . . and a tank or two rolled up . . . the men were put on the tanks and off they went into some mission – we didn't know what it was but it had something to do with the 2nd Battalion . . . [which] was apparently taking a pasting somewhere up there on the Our river. Shortly thereafter the word came down to mount up another platoon and another tank – maybe two – was sent down and off they went on some wild mission . . . we were left with the 2nd Platoon of B Company, the Weapons Platoon and Company Headquarters, and that was it. We had possibly 35–40 men.

About 9.30 that morning, Saturday morning, a Jeep pulled up in front of the Hotel de l'Europe and a medical officer jumped out. He saw me smoking a cigarette and sitting on the porch . . . he said 'Hey, listen. Do you know what's going on around here?' I said 'Whadya mean?' He said 'Well, I hear artillery fire, I see people running in every direction. Something is happening, and I've got to know whether or not anything is so bad that I've got to evacuate this hospital that's down the road here. Should we pull out?'

In the brashness of youth and in my stupidity I said to him 'Listen, we've had a few artillery rounds here but that's nothing unusual, and we can handle anything the Germans throw at us, so stand fast.' Boy, was I ever brash.

So he said 'Thanks a lot. You're the first person I've spoken to today that's said anything positive.'

Corporal John Albert Swett's battle was over in a matter of days after the beginning of the action, and he was mired in confusion:

On December 16th all hell broke loose. The Germans started shelling our positions. We were cut off by the 17th and surrounded in smaller groups and had no food . . . ran out of ammunition, and we were all surrendered by our regimental commanders on the 19th.

It's always confusing in battle and those that are down in the ranks – you don't know where you are or what's going on. We didn't even have the sun, it was overcast all the time . . .

What happened was about 3.30 on the afternoon of the 19th a loudspeaker went around on a military vehicle, probably a German speaking, saying that we had been surrendered by our commanding officers and that we should come down off the hill and form up on the road . . .

I had quite a few side-arms I had a – without any ammunition – carbine and a .45 and what we called a grease-gun, a small automatic gun. But we were trained to take all our weapons apart if we were ever captured and throw the parts around so they couldn't be reassembled and so it took me some time to disassemble all these weapons and throw the parts around the forest and then go down the hill onto the road.

In the camp . . . we had practically no food. We had a small amount of soup a day and a small piece of bread which got to be smaller and smaller over the three and a half months . . .

[When interrogated . . .] most of us would give nothing but our name, rank and serial number which is what we were taught to do and they insisted that we give them all the information that they wanted and they just took a group of us out and stood us in the snow without any overcoats or anything . . . some people said that we stood out there three hours I think it was less than an hour really . . . they got tired of seeing us standing there at attention. The worst thing that happened was that there was a fella that had been shot in the hand or had shrapnel in his hand and he was bandaged up and he had his hand in his shirt to keep it warm and a German came along and pulled it out of his shirt and hit it with the butt of his gun.

Yet others, like Thomas Jefferson Blakey, responded in a totally cool, matter-of-fact way, despite the absence of senior staff and last minute changes of plan:

Around 8 o'clock he [the CO] got this call and took it and went back to his staff and after dinner he cleared the table and told his staff what was going on. That the Germans had broken through in Luxembourg and we were moving at daylight the next morning, but we already had ammunition and supplies so it wasn't a big deal for us to pack our little kits and get ready to get in the trucks,

Early in the offensive many GIs were taken prisoner. As well the humiliation, there were supreme discomforts to endure. As Staff Sergeant Richard A Hartman described: 'We walked probably 30 or 40 miles . . . we were cold, we were hungry and we were lousy.'

the bigger deal was getting the trucks in there by daylight. At daylight we moved out. We went to Bastogne and they decided, Ridgway was out of pocket, Taylor was in Washington, Breton was out of pocket, Gavin was the ranking man; he took over as Corps commander. He sent us to Bastogne. We got to Bastogne and because we were there so early, they decided to send us to St Vith which was 60 miles forward and had the 101st come in and take our place. That's how it happened. That's how the 101st got to Bastogne and the 82nd got up there.

By December 1944, John A Neno, of the 254th Combat Engineer Battalion was in the Bastogne area when he came under fire:

We were 10 or 12 miles from there on a hill that we very rapidly called Buzz Bomb Hill because we were dug in and the war was sort of quiet, we were helping the officers drink their liquor rations, looking for packages from back home and everything tremendous. 'We're winning the war fellows, we're on the home stretch.' First off we got hit and we called it Buzz Bomb Hill because these flying bombs a lot of them, these missiles heading for England flew right over the top of our hill . . . on December 17th we had constant artillery fire because there wasn't anything between us and the Germans really. The artillery fire was very very heavy, much more than normal and 2 o'clock in the morning on December 17th they went running through our camp, the foxholes and such getting us all up and telling us there was a breakthrough and we had to get our bazookas out and take out the German tanks et cetera.

Then we got everything ready to defend ourselves the best we could and about that time they came to me and said, 'OK, you take your weapons carrier, we want to save as much equipment as we can because we're likely to be run right over' . . . Dawn was just breaking when we drove out of that area we were in. And we looked up over the hill, less than a mile away and we saw the silhouette of the tanks up against the skyline. And the guys say, 'Whoopee, there come our tanks. We're safe now.' A couple of minutes later we could see swastikas and that changed things a little bit, but in effect I drove out with a weapons carrier and about half a dozen guys, never fired a shot, it's what we had been ordered to do, but around the German forces coming in. The battalion, the rest of the battalion dug in deeper and tried to hold the line.

When I drove out of there we ended up in an old railroad station out of the area the Germans were coming through. And so for the next – I think – several days there was such a bunch of confusion over MIAs, killed and captured. We, none of us really knew what had happened to our whole battalion until they started regrouping and coming together and we found out that there were a bunch of them [MIAs] captured, some of them did escape. We lost a lot of trucks . . . but we really did hold the line and make it tough for the Germans.

THE BATTLE MAKES NEWS

Early news of the German assault in the Ardennes reached US forces on the pages of *Stars and Stripes*, the forces daily newspaper, on 19 December:

NAZIS HURL RESERVES AGAINST
1st ARMY IN 'LAST DITCH' BID

Security silence was ordered at 4pm Monday concerning battle-line reports of operations along the length of First Army front, where the German commander, staking Germany's military fate on what may be one last great bid to prolong the war and break the Allies drive for the Rhine, has thrown in an estimated half of his tactical reserves into three thrusts into Belgium and Luxemburg.

Despatches filed prior to this imposing of rigid censorship said the Americans were hitting back hard at the enemy and that frontline officers did not try to minimise or under-estimate the seriousness of the situation, which was described as 'fluid' at some points as the Germans struck with numbers of infantry, tanks and armoured vehicles, backed up by the heretofore carefully hoarded Luftwaffe.

'Necessary measures' were under way to counter the enemy moves, it was reported. US radio correspondents, giving their reports earlier Monday, said the Germans had penetrated 'a number of miles' into American-held areas and that there had been at least a dozen such penetrations. New York Radio declared that heavy US reinforcements had been hurried into the sectors most seriously pressed.

Before ordering the news blackout – which a Reuter SHAEF dispatch said need not cause anxiety, pointing out that such censorship had been employed to fool the Germans in the Third Army's dash through France – it had been admitted that German tanks had made gains in Belgium south of Monschau, bending back the American line on a seven-mile sector. Five of nearly 100 enemy machines reported seen in this area were knocked out and, Monschau, which is in Germany close to the Belgian border, still was in US hands.

A Reuter correspondent who toured this First Army front Monday said he saw US troops digging in to meet expected panzer thrusts, and tank destroyers firing at enemy armor. Bad weather impeded Allied fighter-bomber support, though the fliers were up in numbers to meet the Luftwaffe challenge.

Despatches said that the German drive, which began early Saturday with probing stabs all along the Ninth and First Armies' positions before the thrusts into Belgium and Luxemburg, had been resumed Monday after what was described as a 12-hour lull, not otherwise explained.

Spearheading the German blow, it was said, was a panzer division which had seen action on half a dozen other battlefronts in the war. Quick action rounded up most of the Nazi paratroops dropped behind both the Ninth and First lines. Prisoners said they had been formed over a month ago into special teams for the operation. The paratroops' mission apparently was a diversion to screen the Germans' main effort.

Monday morning, it was announced that disclosures of where the German columns had smashed through or how they had advanced would not be allowed. On Sunday, however, it was revealed that the Nazis had fought into Honsfeld, Belgium, west of Monschau, and into Luxemburg below both Vianden and Echternach, both border towns. Monday's despatches indicated that thrusts elsewhere along the front had been sealed off.

German broadcasts claimed that Field Marshall Gert von Rundstedt's troops already had crossed most of Luxemburg and hinted at new surprises by saying: 'British soldiers who have been promised leave in January may have to do without it.' British troops hold positions above the Ninth Army in Germany and along the Maas in Holland.

UP despatches said the German drive had come as a surprise, quoting reports from troops that in one instance enemy tanks had rolled into a town just as the Yanks were finishing chow.

Meanwhile elements of four divisions of the Seventh Army inched into the first of the three-held layer of 20-mile deep Siegfried defences before the southern approaches to the Saar Palabinate. Others, still on French soil, overran two Maginot forts near Bilche.

The Third Army made some gains in both Dillingen and the Sarrequemines area. Air reconnaissance was said to have shown the heaviest enemy railway movement yet spotted behind the Third Army Front.

NAZIS TURNED MACHINE GUNS ON GI PWs

By Hal Boyle, Associated News Correspondent

An American frontline clearing station, Belgium Dec 18 – Muddy, shivering survivors, mad with rage, told today how German tankmen tried with machine guns to massacre 150 American prisoners standing in an open field.

'Those of us who played dead got away later,' said Cpl William B Summers, of Glenville, W Va. 'But we had to lie there and listen to German noncoms kill with pistols every one of our wounded men who groaned or tried to move.'

'Those dirty —,' Summers said. 'I never heard of anything like it in my life. Damn them. Give me a rifle and put me back in the infantry. I want to go back and kill every one of those —.'

Trapped at road fork

Summers, who escaped with a gashed hand, is a member of an artillery observation battalion which was trapped at a road fork by a powerful German armoured column which drove several miles into Belgium when the Nazi counter-offensive started yesterday.

The enemy's Tiger tanks quickly shot up more than two dozen American trucks and light armoured vehicles. The captured Yanks then were led into a field and as the German column moved past, less than 50 yards away, the Nazi gunners deliberately raked the defenceless group with machine-guns and machine-pistols.

The survivors expressed hope that perhaps a majority of the men had escaped by diving to the ground and lying still, but three hours later, after the mass slaughter was attempted, less than 20 had made their way back to their own lines.

The news that reached the troops – and the world – on the next day was equally dramatic:

NAZI BLOW SITS 'EM UP IN US ARMCHAIRS

By Carl Larsen, Stars and Stripes *US Bureau*

New York, Dec 20 – Germany's sudden shift to the offensive in Belgium and Luxemburg, mounting American casualties and the stepped-up draft brought the nation a grim reminder today that the war in Europe was far from over.

Newspapers used their boldest headline type on the German thrust, while editorial writers drew parallels between the Nazi drive and the Germans' final offensive under General Enrich Ludendorff in 1918.

Although there was no attempt to discuss the threat lightly, Washington officials were confident it would be checked. They speculated that the enemy push might call for the Allied commands' plans.

Army spokesmen in the Capital admitted the German counter-offensive struck the weakest point of the Western Front. The sector was weak they explained, because of the wide dispersion of the Allied divisions and because the terrain was not considered important. These sources said the German offensive could go a lot further without causing serious damage.

Doesn't Expect Full Diversion

The spokesman, described the counter-thrust as 'probably as large an operation as the Germans were capable of making at this time.' He said they expected Gen Eisenhower to divert only as many troops as were necessary to halt it. They thought he would continue to concentrate on pushing forward on other fronts.

'On the whole the chances are that Rundstedt has made the best possible choice in the use of his strategic reserve, considering it was limited in size and that he has no hope of ultimate victory, but is fighting only to gain time,' Major George Fielding Eliot, *New York Herald Tribune* military analyst, said.

'If he is badly beaten in this attempt he is hardly worse off than if he had waited for an Allied breakthrough and then tried to defeat it in open warfare on the Cologne plain. It looks very much like Rundstedt had concluded that the battle of attrition along the Roer was going against him, his front could not be held much longer and that his best hope lay in defensive action aided by surprise while he still had such means at hand,' Eliot wrote.

Max Werner, military commentator for *Field Publications*, saw in the 'revival of the German blitz method' an attempt to break the offensive ability of the Allied armies – by shock and losses. Additionally, the German high command 'may possibly want to foster uncertainty, fear and even panic in liberated countries.'

Other analysts claimed the counter-drive was aimed at bolstering sagging morale on the Reich's home front by providing a 'Christmas victory'.

Out to break continuity

Drew Middleton, *New York Times* correspondent at Supreme Allied Headquarters, said the tactical objective probably was to break the Western Front's continuity, cutting communications between the First and Third Armies and opening in the American line a bulge that probably would have to be smashed before large-scale movements elsewhere could be contemplated.

Dave Boone, whose homespun philosophy is nationally syndicated, commented: 'It takes something like that sudden re-entry of the Germans into Luxemburg and Belgium in a surprise attack against our boys to make the home front realise this war ain't a Hollywood script in which everything has got to go our way.'

News of the German assault came thick and fast:

GIs FIGHT NAZI TANKS TILL GROUND INTO EARTH

By Wes Gallagher, Associated Press Correspondent
South of Monschau, Belgium, Dec 20 (AP) — Doughboys slugging it out with Nazi tanks until they are ground down in their foxholes, rescue in Western thrillers fashion of nurses and wounded from a field hospital captured by the Germans, infantrymen trapped behind German lines picking their way back to their outfits — these were only a few of the tales in the First Army's bitter struggle to smash the West Front German counter-offensive.

It was not all a story of acts of bravery. There were American

German SS troops, playing their part in Hitler's last gamble, move on enemy positions on 16 December with all guns blazing. Finding himself under attack in a foxhole, engineer John A Neno did as he had been trained and 'dug in deeper and tried to hold the line.'

formations which cracked under the Nazi onslaught. It was a front of wild confusion as officers and men, trapped for several days behind German lines, smashed through into the First Army side with Titanic tales, only to be greeted with calm disapproval by tough doughboy veterans who now have succeeded in plugging the holes and stabilising the front of this sector. The German infantry now is suffering heavy losses, but American losses, too, have been heavy, as the crowded aid stations testify.

Had just helped wounded

Sgt Ronald Johnson, of Creekside, Pa, stood in a station. He had just helped two wounded GIs over the mountain from behind German lines.

'When this attack started, artillery hit our company command post, killing everyone but myself and another fellow,' he said wearily.

'The Germans came in and took us prisoner but some of our boys attacked and we escaped in the woods. We made our way back to our units, or what's left of them, and the boys dug in again when we were attacked by those big German tanks.

'Some of the boys stood right in there fighting until the tanks ran right over their foxholes and smashed them. I got away again with two wounded boys and, by keeping to the woods, was able to bring them over to the American lines. That's all, I guess.'

The American field hospital was overrun by Nazi tanks and parachutists and the parachutists started loading nurses and wounded on trucks to be taken to Germany when Lt Col Charles Horner of Doylestown, Pa, dashed into town in a Jeep followed by two half-tracks, started shooting from the hip and recaptured the base.

Doughboys took over the town just in time to shoot up two Jeep-loads of Germans who raced into town in captured American cars thinking their forces held it. Tanks appeared next and Yankees and tank destroyers slugged it out with the Nazis, who were on the receiving end for the first time in four days. The town now is firmly held.

SPOTTER PILOTS' STORY

At a café in Liège, Sergeant Bill Davidson, a staff correspondent of the magazine *Yank* met up with some of the artillery spotter pilots. They were still in shock from these first terrifying encounters but determined to fight back:

> 'It's funny,' said the little captain with the southern accent. 'We were all in the sack in those two nice little houses we had fixed up near the front line when [Staff Sergeant] Riffle came running in . . . he said "There are engineers digging in the front yard." I looked out and sure enough, the engineers were out there making foxholes. Then I got on the phone to the battalion S-2 and he says he has been trying to get me and that there are enemy tanks in the town on our right flank. Then he tells me there are enemy tanks in a town on our left flank . . . "There are also," he

says "paratroopers reported in the town where you are." "Shall I get ready to move, sir?" I ask the battalion S-2. "That," says the battalion S-2, "is an understatement." And he rings off.'

The move was not an easy one. The pilots and the ground crews ran out onto the cowpasture field and piled everything movable into the little spotter planes. Then, one by one, the planes started to take off. As they headed down the strip, a Tiger tank pulled into sight across the road. The German vehicle halted uncertainly like a big awkward animal, as if it didn't know what to make of the swarm of tiny aircraft. It swung its 88mm gun once. Then it opened fire with its machine guns. At the same time, mortar shells began to fall at the far end of the field. The planes were headed right into the fire. There was nothing else they could do. Most of them got off. They went back a few miles, where they were once again driven out by paratroopers. Now they were here, ready to start looking for their artillery battalions in the morning.

Another cub outfit didn't fare so well. 'The first thing we knew,' said a tall, thin-faced lieutenant, 'we heard someone yelling in German in the road just outside the house, and the Jerries were there.'

These pilots and GIs didn't have a chance to even get out of the house. The Germans headed for the front door. 'For God's sake, let's do something – let's get down into the cellar,' one of the T-3 crew chiefs yelled. Everyone piled down into the cellar. A German approached the front door and blew it open with a blast from his Schmeisser. The house filled with Germans. They pillaged, ransacked the Americans' personal belonging and collected souvenirs. They especially grabbed helmets, .45s, flight jackets. They took cases of C rations out of the kitchen. One Jerry found a US dollar bill in a pilot's wallet and called excitedly to the others. They examined the dollar bill and talked in German about the picture of George Washington.

Then a German decided to go down into the cellar to look for cognac. The door stuck. He kicked it open. He started down the steps. At this point, there was a crash outside, followed by three others in rapid succession. The German captain said something and the other German dashed back up the steps. The American artillery was firing on the field, destroying the cubs so they wouldn't fall into enemy hands. The Germans took off. The American cub outfit took off immediately afterward.

Heroism was present in large measure on that shocking day, as Bill Davidson quickly discovered:

A Captain Stevenson sat over in a corner of the café, talking soberly to a Belgian girl. One of the pilots pointed him out. That afternoon Stevenson was flying a general out of the danger zone. Suddenly the captain spotted a column of enemy tanks moving relentlessly down the road to Spa at about 15 miles an hour. No one was firing at the Panzers.

Stevenson opened up the little plane as fast as it could go and flew like mad to a Ninth Air Force Thunderbolt base he knew. At the fighter-bomber field, he gave the group operations officer the exact location of the advancing German column. Five minutes later, a squadron of Thunderbolts took off. They caught the Panzers on the open road and clobbered them with 500-pound bombs.

Now Captain Stevenson sat in a corner drinking beer and trying to reassure the frightened girl that the Germans were not going to come into Liège.

There were more tales to tell, including that of Sergeant John Watts, an ex-oil field worker from Shreveport, La. His job was to keep the cub engines in shape.

The afternoon of the German breakthrough, Watts' outfit, too was in danger of being overrun. The planes were being flown out but there weren't enough pilots to go around. Two cubs would have to be left behind. Watts went up to his CO, Capt Howard Cunningham of St Petersburgh, Fla, 'I'll fly one of the planes out, sir,' he said. The captain looked at Watts for a long time. 'I can't give you permission to do that, Watts,' the captain said. Watts looked at the captain. 'turn your back, sir, and you won't know anything about it,' he said. The captain started to walk away. 'I just remembered,' he said, 'I've got to make a telephone call.'

Watts took the plane off and landed it undamaged at the other field. He just missed a tree on the take-off and flew still and nervous like a fighter pilot. But he got there.

Ten minutes later the other sergeant, T-3 Marvin Pierick of Highland, Wis, pulled the same gag . . . Pierick was a farmer who had worked on the assembly line at the Boeing plant for a few years before the war. He had flown exactly 35 hours . . .

AT THE FRONTLINE: DISARRAY AND DISGUISE

As the front dissolved into chaos the German special forces tried to infiltrate, with limited success. Before 16 December Skorzeny had felt that 'Operation GREIF' could only succeed 'if it was begun the first night after the offensive started and made full use of the enemy's surprise and disarray'.

But at a council of war on the afternoon of 17 December he concluded that there was no question of the panic flight which alone would have given Operation GREIF a chance. Nevertheless some useful minor actions were accomplished. On 18 December nine teams were sent forward. One reached the bridge over the Meuse at Huy where it gave false directions to a tank regiment, which duly got lost. Others pulled up tactical direction signs, cut telephone cables, laid mines, felled trees across roads and installed spoof warning notices. In the village of Engelsdorf, where two American companies were organized for defence, having established roadblocks and machine-gun nests, they were deceived by Germans dressed as Americans into thinking that the enemy had passed by, and gave the order to withdraw.

This sort of bluff could only succeed in an atmosphere of great uncertainty and started a real spy mania in the American back areas. The apprehensions of the American forces were increased and confirmed by the capture of orders about GREIF carried into action and captured from a careless German officer.

American units in the forward areas were already sensitive about security. As James Christie of the 28th Division near Dijkerk recalled . . .

. . . someone decided that perhaps the accuracy of the German artillery fire was a bit more than it should have been . . . a detachment was sent to look for an artillery-spotter with a radio . . . there was a cobbler's shop . . . specialised in making shoulder-holsters . . . in this shop was a young female blonde . . . the blonde was caught in the very act of sending a transmission and she was taken off on the sidewalk and summarily shot . . . justice was swift in those days.

Skorzeny's men caused inconvenience in the Ardennes but had a much greater impact amongst the higher levels of command. By cutting communications wires the German infiltrators deprived the American command of vital information, which caused acute anxiety. Captain Harry C Butcher, a member of Eisenhower's staff, visited Verdun on the 18th to find that . . .

> . . . there was an atmosphere around the 12th Army Group Headquarters which reminded me of the Kasserine [A battle in Tunisia in which American troops, in their first encounter with the experienced Africa Korps were pushed back] . . . The teleprinter line from the 1st Army press camp at Spa had been cut. The Germans had dropped many paratroopers behind our lines, many in American uniforms, and other enemy troops were infiltrated in captured Jeeps.

Inevitably, rumour magnified the scale of the German special operation. In the area of the British 30th Corps, Major Julius Neave, Adjutant of the 13/18th Hussars, wrote in his diary on 24 December:

> An interesting feature has been the mass employment of American uniforms and equipment. How the Devil they cope under those conditions God knows. They've not done it except in ones and twos on our front but if they do it much more its going to be a highly tricky problem.

Further back the rumours had a greater effect. Horrocks remarked that

> Rumours multiplied, particularly as regards the activities of the German commandos . . . not more than fifty Jeep loads all told were actually employed but their numbers were multiplied at least twenty times. It was almost impossible to move about freely behind the American lines unless one had an intimate knowledge

When the Germans attacked, many Belgian civilians decided it was best to flee, though they first needed their credentials checked by American MPs. Many more not only stayed put but gave refuge to Allied soldiers, sharing with them what food and shelter they had available.

of America, because the US sentries were not satisfied with passes and passwords. Everyone was grilled about America. 'What is the second largest town in Texas?' I was once asked. I had no idea.

The need for security was impressed on all the British troops, including the 29th Armoured Brigade:

The need for great security mindedness had been impressed on all ranks, a well advised precaution as was shortly to be learned. Many stories were circulating about the arrest of fifth columnists in Brussels, Liège and even Paris. The party in the latter city was reputed to have been on a mission to assassinate General Eisenhower. The first encounter which 29th Brigade had with such excursionists was on the night of December 23rd, when a

Jeep manned by three 'Americans' failed to stop when challenged by a US Army check post at Dinant. By pre-arranged signal, the 8 RB post a few hundred yards further back pulled a necklace of Hawkins grenades across the road, blowing up the Jeep, and killing all its occupants. They were found to be wearing US Army caps and greatcoats over German uniform.

In fact the spy mania was worst in Paris where it had a paralysing effect on Eisenhower's headquarters. On 23 December Harry Butcher noted:

> Ike is a prisoner of our security police and is thoroughly but helplessly irritated by the restrictions on his moves. There are all sorts of guards, some with machine guns, around the house, and he has to travel to and from the office led and, at times, followed by an armed guard in a Jeep.

This was because 1st Army Intelligence had reported that Skorzeny and 60 of his commandos were indeed tasked to kill the Supreme Commander and 90 others were under orders to attack other senior officers. In this way, as if in a game of chess, a move that had not even been planned but which was anticipated, had a most powerful effect.

In the earliest stages of the battle the American senior commanders in the theatre were not alarmed by reports of the German activity. Bradley was with Eisenhower in Paris, where . . .

> . . . later that afternoon, word reached SHAEF that the Germans had launched counter-attacks early that morning at five separate points . . . in Middleton's VIII Corps sector . . . my initial reaction . . . was that von Runstedt had launched a limited spoiling attack through the Ardennes in an attempt to force Hodges and Patton to slow down or pull back. I was not overly concerned.

At this time Hodges' army north of the Ardennes was attacking towards the Roer dams and Patton was preparing to attack eastwards to the south of Middleton's corps area. Eisenhower was not worried either:

> I was immediately convinced that this was no bad attack; it was not logical for the enemy to attempt a mere minor offensive in

the Ardennes unless . . . it should be a feint . . . this possibility
we ruled out . . . we had always been convinced that before the
Germans acknowledged final defeat in the West they would
attempt one desperate counter-offensive.

The British senior commanders were more alarmed. As Montgomery
recorded: 'I took steps to ensure that the right flank and right rear of
21 Army Group would be secure'. In effect this meant issuing orders for
30 Corps to move. Horrocks, the corps commander, was enjoying an
evening in the palace of Laeken when a staff officer from Headquarters
2nd Army telephoned him to say:

> The Germans have smashed through the American front in the
> Ardennes and the situation is extremely confused. Field Marshal
> Montgomery wants your corps, which is our only reserve readily
> available to move down and occupy a lay-back position to protect
> Brussels. Can you return immediately?

Horrocks was startled by the call. He remembered that . . .

> I don't think I have ever been so surprised in my life. Here were
> the Germans whom we imagined almost at the end of their
> tether, and whose air force had been practically shot out of the
> skies, pulling off the biggest surprise of the war and launching
> a large-scale counter-attack. It was so uncanny that, sitting there
> with the fog all round me, I felt very, very uneasy.

During 17 December commanders on both sides began to feel perturbed.
For Eisenhower:

> The morning of December 17 it became clear that the German
> attack was in great strength. Two gaps were torn through our
> line, one on the front of the 106th Division, the other on the
> front of the 28th. Reports were confusing and exact information
> was meagre, but it was clear that the enemy was employing
> considerable armor and was progressing rapidly to the westward –
> in view of the terrible defeats we had inflicted upon him in the
> late summer and fall, and of the extraordinary efforts he had been

compelled to undertake in raising new forces, we had believed that he could not be ready for a major assault as early as he was.'

On the evening of the 17th Skorzeny attended a conference at which,

Colonel-General Sepp Dietrich was present. The northern tank group had made headway after violent fighting . . . captured Bullingen and had a hard battle for Engelsdorf . . . an attack on Stavelot was in progress and meeting with strong resistance . . . surprise had been complete, but the idea of a sweep to the Meuse in a single rush, and the enemy retiring further without fighting, had to be abandoned. There was no question of the panic flight which alone would have given 'Operation GREIF' a chance.

SHOCK AND AWE

The shock of the German attack was widespread and devastating:

. . . the thin American line simply disappeared. An American division newly landed took the first blow and was rolled up. Another armoured division was caught on its flank and thrown completely off balance. Headquarters after headquarters were encircled or overrun, and a stream of flying bombs intensified the savage onslaught. The roads filled with fleeing civilians, hampering friend and unconsciously aiding the foe. Then, to spread the confusion, ostensibly friendly tanks appeared, only to open fire when within range. The first German prisoners captured had all the confidence of 1940 and arrogantly predicted victory of the Reich in a matter of months.

When Stavelot fell, the Americans lost one of their key points of communication. Now no one – least of all SHAEF – had any clear idea of what was happening, but it was obvious that since the first vague message on the 16th stating that 'some penetrations of the American line have been made using tanks,' things had deteriorated alarmingly. With incredible speed the Germans appeared in one village after another. It would appear that through the 17th of December the battle was out of control. . . . it was only the desperate resistance of isolated American units, fighting often without orders or information from above, which saved the day for the Allies. In the midst of utter confusion and bloodshed, the Americans held on when by all normal standards hope should have been abandoned. It was this early resistance – this and nothing else – which saved Belgium and Holland from being overrun once more.

By 19 December the shock effect on the Allied commanders had dissipated. Eisenhower decided that rather than mount a simple defence against the offensive he would contain it in the north, blocking the way to Liège and holding the Meuse, and make a swift and vigorous counter-offensive from the south using Patton's Third Army.

By that day the battle had been lost by the Germans according to Sepp Dietrich; when asked the question 'When did you think the attack was lost?' his reply was 'On the third or fourth day.'

Dietrich's I SS Panzer Corps was held up in the narrow valleys of the Northern sector. At about the same time the 5th Panzer Army in the south ran into the resolute defenders of Bastogne who presented them with an operational problem they could not solve, according to von Manteuffel:

On the night of 19 Dec the XLVII Pz Corps along the line to the east of Noville – east of Bizory – west of Neffe, faced an enemy who put up tenacious resistance. Our problem was whether we should gather all forces to capture Bastogne on 20 Dec or go back to the original plan for the 26 VGD to capture this place while employing the Panzer Divisions for a further advance west, bypassing Bastogne. The Corps, therefore, consulted the Army regarding this question. The importance of Bastogne, if held by the enemy would hinder all movements to the west and cripple our entire supply. This fact was emphasized to all at the conference prior to the attack. If it could not be overrun or captured by a surprise raid it would tie down our forces. Our own forces were considered insufficient in numbers and combat strength for both tasks: to advance to the Meuse, and protect the long southern flank, including Bastogne. Besides, Bastogne offered the enemy a threat, to bring up forces to start an assault from this area which could seriously endanger the German attack. All incentive for capture of Bastogne existed even more so now that the Seventh Army did not contain the strength originally envisaged. However, on the other hand, the XLVII Pz Corps would have to give up temporarily its advance to the west in order to capture Bastogne.

As the Americans reacted to the offensive and the Germans became ever more desperate to stave off defeat, the fighting intensified, though there was the heart-breaking business of withdrawing from towns and villages they had liberated and of abandoning the civilians who had welcomed them so eagerly a few months earlier. As reporter Robert Barr witnessed:

> During the night the town had been bombed a little, strafed a little, and the siren had wakened us up to give warning of paratroop activity. In the morning there was a rumour that German tanks were just over the hill. Armed patrols went out on the roads. Trees were felled as road-blocks and Thunderbolts and Lightnings came low over the town and began zooming and searching in the woods just east of us. Then the order came that everyone hoped would never come. We had to move out quickly. Somehow the news spread round the little Belgian border town and the people came out to see the leave-taking . . . there was handshaking and many questions. How near were the Germans? . . . was it true that German tanks were just over the hill? There were awkward silences. The GIs couldn't answer that question . . . a girl asked me if she should leave the town. She had been in the Resistance movement. Were the Germans really near? she asked. It was an awkward question, but the Germans answered it for me by sending a shell over the hill and into the town. The convoy began to move out, past rows of solemn-faced civilians. One or two were crying; others ran over to the Jeeps to wish us luck, and to hope that we'd be back soon.

AT THE MEUSE

One of the first troops to arrive at the Meuse, early on the morning of 20 December, was that led by Lieutenant Franklin of the Second Household Cavalry Regiment. Rather than finding himself face to face with von Runstedt's Panzer élite, all was quiet and peaceful:

As dawn broke I came over the last ridge of hills and looked down on to the little village of Andenne, just over the rivers, and a few houses shattered at each end of the concrete and steel bridge. I breathed a sigh of relief and ordered breakfast. In the road, Trooper Lees dug a hole, poured petrol into it, and a match completed the cooking arrangements.

I had been asked for a report on the blown bridge and reminded them that it had been blown up for the last four years and over, but they still seemed inquisitive, so off I went to a little hut and told the foreman there that I was going to build a new bridge and wanted the full particulars of the old one. I little guessed for what I had asked. Plans were unrolled before my gaze and the width, depth and speed of current, soil at banks and everything about the river was noted down by me in metres, centimetres and millimetres. I think that he almost expected me, like the devil, to build another bridge overnight. I am not sure that I did not give such assurances!

Being the only British troops in the area had its disadvantages, however:

As to what was happening south and east of the Meuse, we know as yet very little, for Major Sir Peter Grant Lawson had not been allowed to send his patrols beyond the river bridges. There was good reason for this veto because we were still the only British troops in the area, and it was General Dempsey's intention that, should the enemy arrive on the Meuse and effect a crossing, our armoured cars were to shadow their armour unremittingly until an effective British counter-attack force could be assembled.

We had been warned that the Germans had dropped parachutists behind the lines and that they were employing a number of trained saboteurs, both as civilians and in Allied uniform. For this reason patrols were soon halting Americans and checking their identity papers. They reciprocated with enthusiasm, and as nobody had been told what to look for, there were some tense incidents requiring tact to complete formalities without bloodshed to either party.

Our Allies appeared to be unconversant with what was happening farther east in the battle zone, and until we were permitted to cross the river we had to fall back largely on information gathered from refugees. This was either unreliable and hours out of date or else downright alarmist, but it appeared fairly certain that the Germans had reached Marche – a surmise which proved correct to within a few miles.

They, too, were aware of the rumours and speculation spreading like wildfire, and made more poignant by the dense fog.

Meanwhile the hours sped by as an orgy of spy fever spread over the countryside and long convoys of . . . transport continued to swirl over the Liège bridges into the darkening gloom, blissfully unaware of the thunder of arms to the east. We wondered what the maximum speed of the Panther tank would be in the thick fog which still enveloped the countryside. Much appeared to depend on the answer to this question, for on the entire river line Dinant-Namur there was still no sizeable body of defensive armour should the enemy choose to drive due west. This latter move was in fact taking place – for the stiff American resistance on both flanks of the bulge was beginning to canalize the German drive away from Liège and Huy and on towards Dinant.

Colonel Abel Smith, who had got no farther than Brussels before being recalled, arrived back at three o'clock in the afternoon. By dusk the situation had taken on a slightly more reassuring aspect. 30 Corps was in the process of establishing a strong striking force behind the regimental reconnaissance screen and preparing to bar the roads to Brussels. The intention was to strike at the right flank of the German thrust should the enemy succeed in crossing the river. News later came through that the Guards Armoured Division would be moving into position to our north within the triangle Diest-St Trond-Tirlemont. But having first to disengage from the Ganglet sector near Sittard, its units would not be arriving until the morrow. Darkness came with still no signs of the enemy, but refugees pouring back in ever-growing numbers.

The history of the Second Household Cavalry Regiment, in an account written by Major the Hon FFG Hennessy, gives a true insight into the events of 20 December, including repeated emphasis on the 'fog of war'. At Second Army Headquarters, Hennessy had arrived just ahead of General Horrocks.

'This is splendid', said the General. 'If we keep our heads and don't do anything silly this may shorten the war by months.'

It was now 9am, and already, by some brilliant driving through the night, the Household Cavalry had reported Liège and Namur clear of the enemy. This was wonderful and invaluable news. It left, in the Corps commander's words, three courses open. One, to try to hold the Meuse, possibly arriving too late and too weak in the vital spot. Two, to hold on to the 1940 Dyle positions, thereby abandoning a vast amount of equipment and stores. Three, to stand back in the Tirlemong-St Trond area waiting until he [the enemy] crossed the river and then go in with a whoop and cut him to pieces. The latter course he decided was not only the most attractive but the soundest. Could the Guards Armoured Division be formed up with one battalion group in Tirlemont and the other in St Trond ready to strike at first light next morning?

The Grenadiers have their own traditional formula for meeting every contingency. It consists of the straightforward reply, 'Sir'. Just as the Chinese economize in words and obtain their meaning and expressions entirely by inflection of the voice, so the Grenadier can, by skilful employment of this single monosyllable, imply everything from immediate co-operation to abject insubordination. On this occasion my Grenadier training stood in good stead. I played a 'Sir' and went away to think it out.

I was out of wireless range with Divisional headquarters; the orders to move and concentrate on the Diest-Louvain area had already reached the troops and in fact some had already started; they would be arriving through what promised to be another foggy night – to change the destination of the whole division to new concentration areas under such conditions and without previous reconnaissance was a risky task, especially when one considers that at least five divisions were on the move at the same time. And the vital American supply route which passed through our area has also to be kept clear at all costs.

But it was a risk-taking season. And we had always been rather proud of our march discipline. Now was the time to put it to the supreme test.

'Sir,' I repeated in a quite different tone of voice. By now it was midday and the Household Cavalry had just reported back to Army, under whose direct command they were now working, that the whole river line was clear of the enemy as far as Givet.

The fog was now less thick, but their task had not been an easy one and they had carried it out with outstanding skill and alacrity. Furthermore, their commander had organized five scout car patrols with orders to make a wide sweep of the Ardennes itself. It must be realized that at this time no one at all at any headquarters, either British or American, knew how far the spearhead of the German advance had penetrated. It was, however, confidently reported from every quarter that they had passed through Marche, an important centre of communications only some twenty miles from Liège and Namur . . . Things were beginning to look much better.

But there were still uncertainties to be faced, tricky situations to overcome and convincing arguments to make to get troops into their desired positions. A sense of humour was a useful means of communication, too.

Back in the divisional sector there was much speculation during the day as to whether we should ever succeed in extracting ourselves from the line. The enemy were showing themselves very restive to our front. Should they attack, as was confidently expected, any chance of relief was out of the question.

In fact the attack never came in and, as dusk fell, the Division started pulling back over our Affreuse Old Meuse and on through a cold and misty night to a dispersal point which we had set up at Hasselt. Here, through one of the longest nights I can ever remember, harassed officers and MPs strove to convince doubting drivers that they were not fifth columnists endeavouring to turn the column straight into the enemy lines, but there had been a change of plan.

'Who are you?' 'First Grenadiers' – 'Straight on down the road to St Trond – halt with your head short of the main Louvain-

Namur road and get off into the fields as fast as you can at first light. Above all keep that main road clear – it's the American supply route and I reckon they are going to need it.'

'But Diest is my destination.'

'I know, but the hotels are terrible, and, my dear, the drains! Please try St Trond. They say that they make some wonderful brandy out of petrol there.'

'First Coldstream, are you? Turn right and carry on to Tirlemont. Yes, I did tell him St Trond, but you've changed brigades now. You'll find yourself under 32nd Guards Brigade tomorrow morning.'

'How's it going?' I said to Pat at about 3am.

'Well, it's going – only the grey light of dawn will reveal how,' he replied.

As dawn broke on 21 December, the Guards Armoured Division were indeed arriving safely. On the same day permission was at last given for them to cross the Meuse, but progress was not easy:

As our patrols had been given no American passwords they were frequently detailed and in one case even arrested, when a patrol was placed in custody for the night in spite of the most vehement protests from its commander that he was not Otto Skorzeny. Fortunately the Americans forgot the wireless set, and the Troop Leader was able to relay back a stream of information, including lists of US headquarters locations taken off the map in the detaining formation's own operations room!

From now on the Regiment maintained one squadron patrolling daily south of the Meuse along the westerly limits of the German breakthrough, while the remaining three squadrons manned the river line in anticipation of a role which, thanks to the tenacity of the Americans, never materialized.

4

IN THE THICK OF THE FIGHT

THE ARMOURED FORCES

In May 1940 the German Army Group A had advanced through the Ardennes in three days led by Panzer Group von Kleist consisting of seven panzer divisions and an independent regiment with a Luftwaffe flak corps attached. In December 1944 Hitler expected the 5th and 6th Panzer Armies to motor through the wooded hills to the River Meuse in one swift move, then dash on to take Brussels and Antwerp. He took no account of the difference in both weather and road conditions, nor of the great increase in the size of tanks that had occurred since 1940. He wanted tanks to lead the attack to take most advantage of their mobility and shock effect.

In the southern sector the 5th Panzer Army actually sent infantry shock troops ahead of the tanks to infiltrate and disrupt the forward defensive positions of the Americans. In the north the 6th Panzer Army followed their orders more literally, and their advance was led by the I SS Panzer Corps with the II SS Panzer Corps in the second echelon. There was not enough space on the narrow winding roads to allow an advance on a broader front. The way was led by the Battle Group commanded by Jochen Peiper, who had a reputation for brilliant fast manoeuvre actions on the Eastern Front. His orders told him to get on westwards to the Meuse as rapidly as he could. It was expected that the mere appearance of masses of German tanks would panic and paralyse the American troops in the Ardennes.

However, dense columns of tanks with infantry and engineers to the rear proved vulnerable to ambushes and blocking actions by small bodies of enemy troops at defiles and other choke-points. The mechanical difficulties of navigating the steep, icy roads added to the delays imposed on the armoured columns. They could not just push on and exploit in depth as had been hoped. Often they had to stop and wait while sappers and infantry came forward with artillery support to assault and clear American obstacles and defenders.

On the Allied side, tanks were involved in responding to the German offensive from the beginning. Armoured units led the way in lining the west bank of the Meuse with a defensive cordon to confront any panzers that managed to get that far. In the north the US 7th Armoured Division seized and held St Vith to hinder the 6th Panzer Army advance, gaining time which the Germans could not afford to lose. In the south tanks from Patton's Third Army in the Vosges rushed north to attack the left flank of the 5th Panzer Army and relieve the hard-pressed American garrison of Bastogne.

Infantry formations followed up the panzers as well as they could to secure the rear and flanks of the spearheads and to help them when they were held up, and were accompanied by their artillery and engineers. However, most of the soldiers going into action had no idea of these strategic developments. They had no reliable sources of information and lacked the time and the energy necessary to think about such things. Their horizons were close and confined, and their vital interests were immediate, as their personal accounts of the experience of the battle reveal.

The 1st SS Panzer Corps was led by the 1st SS Panzer Division with Colonel Jochen Peiper's battle group out in front. But their advance was delayed or blocked at choke-points along the roads. At Stoumont the lead unit of the 1st SS Panzer Division eventually forced a way through, as described by Lieutenant David Knox of the American 30th Division, a veteran formation that had fought against some of the best German armoured troops in Normandy.

> Just before daylight I checked the men in position and changed some of them. Then four tanks arrived in our defense area which made us feel much better. At about 08.30 tanks or half-tracks began to cover over the rise to our front. The tankers with us wasted no time with them. Two were knocked out and no more were trying to come over. We realized, however, that there were probably plenty behind. We knew this because they kept throwing direct fire rounds into buildings. At the same time we could hear a hell of a fight going on to our right, in the area defended by Companies I and K. About this time Lt Parramore called me on the sound-powered phone and told me that these two companies were getting pushed back. That wasn't good because our flank would soon be vulnerable. I immediately checked with battalion. They told me that there had been some

trouble but that everything would be OK. I could hear the other company commanders on the radio occasionally. Discussion was held on use of Powell's stuff, which meant artillery. The answer seemed to be that it would be available if we could hold out an hour. The mortars were set up and could fire. Lt Conway, the mortar observer arrived at our CP about this time. It was now about 09.00. Lt Parramore called me again and told me that Companies I and K were being pushed back again or still and that I had better find out what was expected of us. That was a mighty good idea and one that had been occupying my mind no little bit. I called on the radio, 'Hullo Thorn3, Hullo Thorn3, we are concerned about the situation on the right. Can you tell me what is going on?' Here is Colonel Fitzgerald's answer that I will always remember: 'I too am concerned – the situation is grave. You will continue to hold.' So I told Lt Parramore we would have to hold. I didn't like it any better than Parramore did but he had just a little more realistic picture of the whole thing because he could see men practically running to the rear. I kept close to the radio. The Germans had by this time set up a machine gun or a tank just behind the rise to our front 250 yards and were firing down the street just outside our CP. About that time I heard Lt Kane, the company commander of Company K call up very excitedly. I knew he was being hit by plenty of tanks from his flank and rear. Our orders were to hold. It wasn't good. About this time the tanks with us started to pull out. Now it was bad – very bad. I wasted no time in getting hold of the radio. I said, 'What do you mean hold and you take the tanks away. What do you mean?' The answer: 'Continue to cover the withdrawal of the battalion.' Lots of things went through my mind in a hurry. It sounded like an order to sacrifice Company L to save what they could of the other units. I asked, 'Give me clarification. It is useless without the aid of tanks. How long do you expect us to hold?' Then I got the answer I wanted, 'I will have to leave that to your judgement,' Colonel Fitzgerald said. My mind was made up. We had better get out in a hurry . . . it didn't take us long.

The advance was also strongly resisted at Stavelot, as recollected by Second Lieutenant F Pfeifer of the 1st SS Panzer Division. He was forced to

Well protected from the bitter cold, a US mortar crew on high ground near St Vith fires on enemy positions. Such support was vital to the progress of the armoured divisions, but shells bursting in the trees had a devastating effect, causing severe injuries from fragments of wood.

attack before he was ready, under pressure to get on quickly to the west:

> Shortly before Stavelot I gave orders to dismount from the
> vehicles because the artillery fire became too heavy and I preferred
> to go through the town in the infantry manner . . . civilians
> had evacuated the area south of the river and it was also free of

enemy troops. We arrived during the afternoon and I suspected a trap; my suspicion was confirmed because we found two dead comrades and an abandoned Tiger immediately in front of the bridge from which some bricks were still falling. When I returned from my reconnaissance of the bridge Colonel Sandig appeared suddenly on a motor-cycle. He said things were going too slowly. I told him I needed fire support from the heavy weapons of the 4th Company; however it had been delayed and I had to risk the attack with my 1st and 3rd platoons whilst my 2nd and 4th provided fire support. When half of us had reached the north side of the bridge we were shot to pieces. With two squads we stormed across the little square on the north side into the first houses.

Pfeifer went on, but was unable to clear and secure Stavelot, which changed hands several times. In the area of 5th Panzer Army, early success made some of the panzer troops exultant, however, the panzer troops were supremely confident in the superior quality of their tanks. Typical of their attitude was this comment by Hans Behrens, a tank wireless operator who attributed the failure of the offensive to shortages of vital commodities, particularly fuel for the tanks.

Another main turning-point for me – perhaps *the* main turning-point for me – about the folly and the terrible pain that war instils is when . . . Bastogne was taken several times to and fro and one time we were coming down a cobble-stoned S-bend, and on the left-hand side was a Sherman tank with its gun-turret open. For some reason we stopped. I got out of our vehicle, climbed on top of the Sherman tank and looked down inside, and what I saw there was a young man, absolutely charred black, and one clean hole into the side of the turret. Some of our armour-piercing ammunition was devastating. It just . . . almost burned a hole through it and exploded inside and I saw this young man and I said to myself then, and I've never forgotten it, 'This could have been me'. He had a mum and dad somewhere.

The Sherman tank had a sinister reputation for catching fire easily. In response to the question 'Were your tanks better reinforced than the Americans'?' he replied:

Throughout the battle many German tanks, like this one destroyed near Bastogne, suffered a similar fate. In the absence of tracks in the snow, a 'grinding, rumbling noise' and the ominous sound of a rotating turret were often the first signs of an approaching enemy tank.

The main tanks were, definitely, yes, the Tiger and the Panther. They were superb vehicles for that sort of terrain, and indeed armour . . . it's well known now . . . since the war I've read up on the information . . . and the various tank sizes, the Cromwell and Churchill and Sherman, they weren't really adequate.

After the Bastogne incident, we progressed further west, and I believe St Hubert was the most westerly point my division reached; there was one . . . north of us, who went a few kilometres further west but these were the extreme lengths, and we . . . had great losses. It was very, very cold. Food was getting extremely difficult, and so was fuel. I remember not having washed properly for three weeks. We must have stunk, I would imagine. How we got back again to where I was finally caught in February '45 . . . I don't know.

The infantry were especially alarmed by encounters with tanks, as the experience of the 84th Division proves. On the other flank of the battle they were ambushed and routed by a lurking tank, and hampered by having to contend with snow up to their knees.

> Moving farther into the woods, Campbell took over the point. A frame hut was spotted on the right flank. The patrol halted, and the lieutenant crept to the door, .45 drawn and ready. He burst in. The hut was empty. The men went another fifty yards. A farmhouse became visible, and the patrol halted. Leaving seven men behind with Scott, Campbell picked George Bond and Walter Roman to cross the clearing with him and check the place out: George, the slender six-foot ASTP boy just back from the hospital; Walter, the serious little fellow from the Bronx, whose issue overcoat ended well below the tops of his combat boots.
>
> The three men studied the farmhouse. No tracks in the snow-covered clearing, no smoke from the chimney, no movement around the house or the neighboring trees. They headed out, Campbell in the lead. Their combined firepower: two M-1s, one pistol, and half a dozen grenades.

Bowditch remembers his first inkling that the enemy was waiting.

> Three pine trees alongside the house started to move and we heard a grinding, rumbling noise. Olson at first didn't comprehend what was happening. 'I was leaning against a tree, scraping frost off the trunk, when I heard the engine start on the tank. It didn't register – it just didn't register.

Willy Herrell was equally surprised:

> We were about forty yards back in the woods when Campbell, Bond, and Roman headed out. That was one of the worst experiences of my life. I've had a lot of nightmares from it. That German tank seemed to come from nowhere . . . the sound of the rotating turret stopped the three in the snow-covered meadow. It didn't require Campbell's 'Go back!' to turn them. Each step was an effort. The tank held its fire. The three made it halfway to the

woods before the tank fired. This was one time Campbell wasn't afraid. He figured it was too late for that. As he zigzagged toward the woods, he said to himself, 'What a stupid way to die.'

When the German gunner fired the first high-explosive round, Bond was hit and went down. The other two men moved toward him. His wounds were massive; Bond was dead. The next round, seconds later, dismissed any thought of carrying Bond back. Roman and Campbell were both hit. A shell fragment ripped a hole in Walter's throat. He was bleeding heavily and unable to speak. Campbell took hits in his neck, arm, shoulder, and back. Both arms were immobilized.

Olson watched as the shells exploded.

Bond was down, and Campbell and Roman stopped to check. Campbell's suspender straps on his cartridge belt had been torn loose by shrapnel. Then back in the woods we took a tree burst. We didn't know where that tank was coming from or if it was coming after us, and we weren't going to stick around and find out. We got the hell out of there.

In the confusion of the shelling, the two groups lost contact. Scott tried to get the rest of the patrol under cover. When the firing stopped, Scott led his little group down the hill, but couldn't find the company. He headed for the battalion and gave a report on the tank encounter to be passed along to artillery.

Shells bursting in trees had a particularly devastating effect. The explosions produced many secondary missiles consisting of fragments of wood torn from trees. These caused particularly nasty wounds, especially likely to cause infection and gangrene, and with the fragments invisible to X-rays. The German infantry were equally afraid of American tanks, particularly the effects of the main armament at close range.

The Americans also had effective means to fight tanks, including the 57mm anti-tank gun, which could stop tanks but was vulnerable to German infantry and artillery. American machine-guns and mortars could maim and destroy German infantry; and the US artillery, if available, could engage German guns with counter-battery fire. Each side tried to disrupt the all-arms coordination of the other to gain the advantage.

The Americans also had the tank destroyer known as the 'wolverine' armed with a 90mm gun that was very effective. Together with the British Firefly, a Sherman fitted with a 17-pounder gun, the TD was the only Allied A/T system that could engage and destroy the German Tiger tank at a good range. The Chaffee was a light tank designed for reconnaissance and scouting.

The tanks employed by the British were American Shermans and Honeys. Captain JA Kempton, 2 i/c 'C' Squadron of the 3rd Royal Tank Regiment, takes up the story, with the weather, once again, playing a significant role:

> ... within 48 hours of being under training at Poperinge, we picked up our tanks, put them in order, filled up and were in battle positions. The country was excellent tank country, open and rolling and the frozen ground made the going fair over all the area.

The Allies made considerable and effective use of anti-tank guns such this 57mm version. Also extremely effective was the 'wolverine' tank destroyer, armed with a 90mm gun. These weapons could be used with great accuracy in all but the poorest visibility.

That night 'C' Squadron Commander and the Squadron Sergeant Major decided to try and contact the Americans at Marche again to get some more information from them. This they did after a very exciting ride in a Jeep. The journey back being even more exciting, as according to the Squadron Sergeant Major, they passed four German armoured vehicles. They reported to the Colonel that an American Infantry Division was now in Marche and the General said that he would hold on there and the US 2nd Armoured Division was due to move in on our left flank to the north-east.

The next day, the 23rd, dawned foggier than ever and brought an even bigger drop of rumours. Regimental HQ had established itself in the fine Château at Sorrines. An Air Liaison Officer turned up, as did a Liaison Officer from the 2nd American Armoured Division. The main snag was that American troops in half-tracks were difficult to differentiate from Panzer Grenadiers in similar vehicles, especially in the fog.

Luckily the move out at first light into battle positions was accomplished without incident. The Americans confirmed that the Germans were in Celless.

First blood was to 'C' Squadron who brewed up a Mark IV about 9 o'clock. Full marks for the 17-pounder gunner as the Commander was relieving nature. Then the report came in that the road between 'C' Squadron at Achene and 'A' Squadron at Sorinnes had been cut by infantry. This made 'C' Squadron's position very insecure and they were withdrawn to the north west. The next contact with the enemy was at Boisselles when 'A' Squadron knocked out a half-track and another vehicle.

Visibility was poor early on, and it soon became evident that the advanced elements of the 2nd Panzer Division were trying to push through to Dinant in the mist. However, the mist cleared a little and two Panthers moving up to Sorinnes from the South East were knocked out by another troop of 'A' Squadron.

About this time the Brigadier visited the Regiment and later General Bols, commanding the 6th Airborne Division, and we learned that by Boxing Day a Brigade would arrive from England and would be on the ground in our position.

We also learned that at last we had some Gunner support.

Admittedly it was only two mediums, but medium stonks are very useful especially against tanks. About this time one troop of 'A' Squadron was pulled back and 'A' Squadron took up a closer position at Sorinnes. Two carriers of the 8 RBs in Foy Notre Dame (between Sorinnes and Boisselles) were extracted from an awkward position. It was certain that the Germans were in Boisselles and Foy Notre Dame in some strength and probably in or had passed through Achene.

The Colonel then decided that as the Germans might very likely have a go at the bridge that night, we should have to take up defensive positions in a semi circle to defend the bridge and as the rumour of parachutists was very prevalent (some had been dropped further south) 'A' Squadron were withdrawn behind the river in an anti-parachutist role.

The position was 'B' Squadron on high ground south east of Gemmerchene with a detached troop well to the south in contact with an American Troop of two anti-tank guns, and 'C' Squadron to the north side of the Dinant-Ciney Road with Regimental HQ at Gemmerchene. That evening the Regiment fell back on Dinant in tighter positions, 'B' Squadron forward looking south, south-east and east. 'C' Squadron, echeloned back a little, looking east and north-east.

The order at this stage was to defend the bridge at all costs . . .

As often in battle, orders were quickly made, and just as quickly changed again. After several changes of plan, however . . .

At 9.30 that evening fresh orders came through from Brigade, Squadron Leaders were called for and later that evening, Christmas Eve, we learned that the Regiment was to advance on the morrow. It was believed that the Germans were running short of petrol. Our objectives were to be Sorinnes, Foy Notre Dame and Boisselles. The advance was to be made two squadrons up. 'B' Squadron on the north route from Dinant to Sorrines, 'C' Squadron on the south route from Dinant to Boisselles, 'A' Squadron in reserve, who were to follow 'B' Squadron.

That night was quiet but full of anticipation and Christmas morning dawned bright and clear. Each had a platoon of the

Rifle Brigade attached to them and 'C' Squadron a section of Recce Troop.

The advance began at first light and 'B' Squadron occupied Sorinnes without much difficulty. 'C' Squadron got into Boisselles after a dash down a forward slope under fire from a German tank, all ran the gauntlet successfully except one tank of Recce Troop which was hit low down, the crew escaping safely. Lieutenant Robin Lemon personally evacuated wounded members of the Honey, took over another tank and remained on observation. The bag in Boissells included an armoured car, half-track, a truck and a Jeep. The position was unpleasant as the village was overlooked by a wooden hill to the north-east, in which were four tanks, one identified as a Panther.

A 17-pounder was manoeuvred into position and eventually got a few shots in, whereupon the Panther pulled back. The next incident was a Squadron of US Lightning Fighter Bombers, half of whom bombed the German tanks, the other half ground strafing 'C' Squadron. This attack was repeated an hour later, fortunately the bombs again falling on the Germans, although the machine-gunning on 'C' Squadron continued. Very luckily the only casualty was one Infanteer from the 8 RBs, but it was not serious.

By this time 'B' Squadron had contacted the Americans again and had got into Foy Notre Dame. This village was ablaze and yielded up a very fair bag of German PoWs, vehicles and half-tracks. 'B' Squadron and the infantry of the US 2nd Armoured Recce Squadron doing a first class Allied combined Operation.

Unfortunately a premature report came in that Foy Notre Dame was clear and Major Dunlop MC, 'C' Squadron leader, called a conference at HQ, now established at Sorinnes, decided to go the short way via Foy Notre Dame. He was most unlucky to be hit in the mouth by a German sniper, while travelling in a scout car through the village.

By nightfall the position was the Americans had occupied the Farm Mayenne (Panther Farm), Foy Notre Dame was a smouldering ruin in which half of 'B' Squadron and the Americans leaguered for the night after going round the village and getting Germans out of cellars like ferrets after rats.

HELP – AND HINDRANCE – FROM THE AIR

By the autumn of 1944, the Germans had only 4,500 aircraft on all fronts and only 1,000 serviceable machines in the West, compared with the Allied number of 10,000 in the West alone. The aims of the Allies – when the weather finally cleared – were first to gain air superiority, then to isolate the battlefield by clipping off the enemy's communication lines and destroying bridges and roads, and to provide support to the ground forces by attacking enemy troops, tanks and strong points.

Late on Christmas Eve, 1944, the fog, which had lasted for five days, finally lifted – the best gift the Allies could have been granted:

> Christmas Eve [was] a great day for the Allied air forces; for hour after hour the air was filled with the ceaseless roar of thousands of engines and with fuselages gleaming in the brilliant sunshine, planes of every size and description – hundreds of them – were seen flying west to spread havoc and chaos amongst the communication lines of von Runstedt's armies, hitherto spared by the weather alone, from the furious onslaughts of Allied air power.
>
> [The next day . . .] The air forces were out again in great force, hammering at the bewildered enemy far to the east, smashing at his road junctions and defiles. One particularly successful attack was carried out during the morning by Rocket Typhoons controlled by the RAF officers at brigade headquarters. A column of German tanks and half-tracks were spotted by an Air 'OP' and were caught by the Typhoons in a sunken road just south of Celless, very great damage being done in an almost incredibly short space of time.

Edward Norton, who was working as an interpreter/interrogator for the British Army, was relieved to see the offensive being held up:

> When the skies broke and the air force could move again, the Germans were stopped. The air[craft] stopped the tank offensive, and what made a tremendous difference was the fact that they were using cannon – not with bombs. But the fighters had cannon – 50mm machine guns, not ordinary 20mm but 50mm – and the cover on the tank, the top, was thin metal, so as they

hit them, the bullet would penetrate, and it would spin round
and knock them out . . . that did most of the damage . . . by
penetrating the cover, and spinning round.

Captain John F Amsden of the Seaforth Highlanders witnessed the German
assault from the air:

It was snowing heavily and it was very cold. To add to our
amusement, the Germans started firing their V-1 flying bombs
and many of these were targeted on Liège with the hope, I
suppose, of putting out its bridges over the River Meuse. But
V-1s were very inaccurate and the bridges survived. The ridge on
which the house was situated was almost in the way of the V-1s
and they came over us at almost roof-top level – certainly not
more than 50 feet up and when, occasionally, their engines cut
out too soon, they landed on the ridge with a terrific explosion,
but fortunately they hurt no one. There is no doubt they were
intended as a terror weapon against civilians – they were too
inaccurate for anything else; unfortunately, they were also too
fast for the Allied fighter planes to catch them until the first
Meteor jet planes came into service and got rid of them – often
by flying closely alongside and tipping their wings with their
own until they went back the way they had come or down into
the sea or open country. Not very pleasant there for us, but it
did make us feel closer to our families at home who were also on
the receiving end. The V-1s weren't the only things to miss the
bridges. They used to tell the story in Liège that when the Yanks
were advancing on Liège after the breakout from the invasion
beaches, the US Air Force made repeated bombing attacks on
German lines of supply, but there were few civilian casualties
because they all hid under the bridges.

With renewed fighting came the inevitable losses and hardships, and the
weather continued to play its part in the action. However, the British
troops behind the Meuse were still better off than many of the Americans:

At last their bombers and fighters could take to the air again
and, sweeping in from aerodromes all over France, Belgium and

England (they even came over enemy-held territory from Italy), five-thousand aircraft pounded and strafed the German bulge.

The battle ground began to resemble what we had seen in Normandy . . . the carnage in vehicles was appalling. In addition, nearly every one of von Rundstedt's supply roads was now under crossfire from the stranded American garrisons that refused to give in, and the effect was to wither up the German supplies until only a thin trickle of petrol and ammunition was reaching their spearhead to the west.

All through Christmas Day and into Boxing Day the German spearhead, led by the battered 2nd SS Panzer Division, pushed and struggled to gain the Meuse, ignoring the ominous signs of their comrades digging in on both flanks. On the hard ice-bound roads, tanks locked in deadly combat waltzed and skidded from village to village. Even the petrol in the carburettors solidified when engines were stopped, and men froze to death in their foxholes during the night. We thought of the hardships being endured by the American infantry on the exposed ridges of the Ardennes and blessed our good fortune and relative comfort behind the Meuse.

The improving weather also meant that the enemy could launch air assaults on the armoured troops. Captain Cooper of the Second Household Cavalry Regiment managed to drink a Christmas toast, nonetheless:

Christmas Day – Flying bombs arriving overhead very often. A hard white frost and up by six o'clock – breakfast with Regiment at Poucet, then left for 29th Armoured Brigade to relieve Jim Seely as LO. Intensely cold even in tank suit and sheepskin coat. Thousands of planes going over all day in clear blue sky. Their Tactical HQ on Onhaye over the river; German tanks are filtering through, but the Americans seem to have the situation in hand (more or less). Met General Horrocks at Onhaye and picked up Corporal-of-Horse Jenkins and driver. They were cut off at Rochefort and fought their way out . . . got billets in a downstairs parlour of a café, with my wireless going with a lead through the window as usual. Christmas dinner with Towler consisting of tea, captured German pork and biscuits – perfectly bloody! Met

Brigadier Roscoe Harvey and one or two others I know – freezing hard all the time. The German tanks got almost into Dinant. Supper with Brigadier Harvey in next-door house. Locals came in and we all drank champagne. Wireless touch with the Regiment good – they are over forty miles away.

December 26th – Still freezing hard. Breakfast cooked by Towler on the Belgian kitchen stove – bully, beans and biscuits. Got a lot of information back. The SS and Panzer Grenadier Regiments opposite us have advanced a little during the night – quite a few of their prisoners coming in. Got some Typhoon rocket targets for the air! Twenty German tanks and soft vehicles hit . . . 'C' Squadron's patrols as usual down to the fighting round Marche, etc. German planes attacked during the night, machine gunning the road. They flew in very low and also dropped a few bombs. The civilians are still very frightened about the German advance and hundreds of refugees are still coming back. We lost two sappers killed on the road this morning.

The Third Royal Tank Regiment also benefited from the arrival of air support from the RAF:

Observation was obtained by Recce Troop and 'C' Squadron of Celles and the area to the south-east. As a result of those observations of the road from Celles, south-east, on which a great deal of German movement could be seen, air support was called for by the Regimental HQ. Within 20 minutes a Squadron of Typhoons did devastating work on the Celles road, four Panther tanks, various Mark VIs and half-tracks were brewed up together with other sundry vehicles. An extremely fine piece of work by the RAF as red smoke, the usual Allied method of indicating target for aircraft [at that time] was fired by the Germans on an American pocket staunchly holding out to the east of Celles. Fortunately the Typhoons took no notice of the red smoke, and set about the German reinforcement column with devastating results.

The next morning 'B' Squadron advanced from the leaguer area and brewed up two Panther tanks believed abandoned as a result of the air attack. Later 'A' Squadron moved into Celles and reported vehicles destroyed and abandoned in the woods east of Foy Notre Dame as two Mark IVs, four half-tracks, three 88mm anti-tank guns, a 105mm gun and various transport.

Later that day the American General, commanding the US 2nd Armoured Division, visited the Colonel at Regimental HQ and, though it would be invidious to say, congratulations were made on both sides. It is certain that every single trooper in the 3rd Royal Tank Regiment who saw the American Medium Tank attack from Achene towards Celless (across our left flank) did and will have nothing but praise and admiration for the magnificently executed attack on Boxing Day morning by our Allies.

Come the New Year, the men of the 48th Fighter Group were still recovering from the celebrations when they were taken by surprise:

At approximately 08.45 hours when some of the Group had taken their hangovers to work and most had just kept them in bed, an amazing thing happened. An unfamiliar drone of engines was heard – the first was immediately recognized as an Me109. The plane was accompanied by five more of Göering's Groundhogs and they were busily preparing to clobber St Trond/Brustem Airfield. Upon the alarm that enemy planes were attacking the field, offices and boudoirs were evacuated for more substantial dug-outs . . . by this time the Mes had made their pass and were preparing to take another one from the opposite direction. For a while they were all over hell and gone and half of Belgium. They strafed the runways, they strafed the planes, they strafed everything that got in front of them. Later a pilot who was captured said that all he did was press the trigger every time the field swung in front of him. The ack-ack boys on the field made a good showing for themselves. They accounted for five enemy planes destroyed and one probable that was smoking from the field when it left. Highlight for some of the personnel of the 493rd Squadron was when ack-ack hit a FW-190 near the edge of the field. It caught fire and the pilot pulled up and bailed out. Half of the 493rd Squadron rushed out into an open field and formed a welcoming committee for the hapless pilot. He was not lacking in military escort when he was brought to the squadron area. There were at least nine carbines and three sub-machine guns stuck in his back. His plane crashed and burned . . . on the 492nd side of the field, ack-ack scored a direct hit on an Me109; he crashed near one of the runways. The pilot earned a wooden cross rather than an iron one . . . damage to our aircraft was negligible in spite of the amount of Nazi ammunition expended. We had two of our planes totally destroyed with 14 slightly damaged. Most of these were back in flying condition within the next few days.

For the airmen themselves, on both sides, the experience was both exhilarating and dangerous, as this letter from a German pilot testifies:

Dear Parents, especially Dear Dad,
I almost forgot your birthday. We are very busy here. They almost got me on my last operational flight. You must realize that we are now the first unit in the West to meet the enemy. As you know 800 fighters accompany the bombers as escort. Our unit is praised again and again. All heavy fighters ask for us as losses are high. Two of my best friends did not return last Sunday, and never will. In our Staffel with ten pilots you feel that sort of thing. But now I am finding just how useful experience is. Aachen is our sector for ground strafing missions. That is a terrific sight. When one sees the front for the first time. You hear nothing, but below you see clouds of smoke and guns flash. The flak fires like mad. In this madhouse you force yourself to be calm, seek your target and shoot. I have four operational flights now, among them two against enemy bombers over Reich territory . . .
Yours ever,
Kurt

On the morning of the 23rd, wrote Lieutenant Howard W Park of the Ninth Air Force, 513 Squadron, the first lifting of the weather, we took off two abreast under a 200 foot ceiling. Flying at a fixed rate of climb for one minute, then a 180 turn, continue until we broke into the clear which was up at 12–15,000 feet. We would

Once the weather cleared and flying became possible, Allied bombers were able to attack targets throughout the Bulge. Here, bombs dropped from B36 Marauders rip into a bridge across the River Our, trapping thousands of retreating enemy troops in the battle zone.

contact ground controller (Capt James Parker), and given as much altitude as possible in the clear, up to a couple of thousand feet weather permitting, we began a high-speed dive towards designated targets – tanks, troops and guns – then jinxing violently away from the target . . . I had flown continuously since early May '44 and had never before experienced such intense light flak. Intelligence informed us that about 700 four-barrel, coaxial mount 20mm flak guns were about Bastogne . . . the flak tracers were like garden hoses with projectiles arcing lazily through the air towards me. I remember so vividly my slipping and skidding as streams of flak fire reached for me, sometimes within three feet of my wing surfaces. Despite skill, a lot of luck was needed to escape unscathed. The flak took a toll. It seemed as if the 513th was always first out and it seemed we lost one of four in lead flight every time. Actually, we lost five of the 513th in three days, and seven in a week during which the group lost a total of 10 pilots. Most of those who didn't return were recently transferred to us from the States and had no feel for the flak as those of us who dealt with it regularly.

By 27 December the number of missions had significantly increased, and with it the danger of being hit by enemy flak:

Our group of three squadrons flew continuous cover over the city and environs in missions of eight – two four-ship flights – approximately four missions per day for each squadron. This occupied about ten daylight hours of target time per day. The missions were on a rotating basis, like a conveyor belt, with rotation of the entire roster of pilots (32) per day for each squadron. This is about 96 sorties per day; the record shows we flew 105 sorties per day. Each individual flight consumed about four hours of time with briefing, field preparation for takeoff, mission flight time of two and a half hours, conferring with the crew chief on return, and debriefing . . . the whole five days – the critical days – seem almost a blur in my memory . . . it was the first time in the war where I felt I didn't have enough control over my own destiny! So much depended on luck in evading the flak. Usually, during the infrequent air-to-air and 'normal' flak, I felt as if I could survive on the basis of my abilities, but not so the winter war over Bastogne. It seemed as if it came down to the luck of the draw . . . we went out on the mission determined to help our ground forces, especially as we had developed a relationship with the men of the 101st who were bivouacked with us at Mourmelon. [We were] on the alert each day from the 18th to the 22nd, champing at the bit to go as unfavourable reports of the German advance kept coming in. Then, as we began, we had a sort of rude awakening because none of us could believe the intensity of the flak. The enemy, without an effective air force, could only utilize the predicted weather and an ungodly number of flak guns to protect his ground movements. On each of those missions, I think back, and believe that I just took a fatalistic turn of mind, figuring I'd do my damnest to evade the flak, but knew the odds were pretty tough in carrying out the requests from the ground. Capt Parker suggested our targets and we never shirked regardless of flak or feelings. I do not believe I was consciously scared, just fatalistic.

THE ARTILLERY

In the American and British armies the partnership between the field artillery and the infantry was vital to survival. In addition, the Allies had very powerful medium and heavy artillery that showed great flexibility in delivering overwhelming firepower against the enemy. On their side the Germans enjoyed the advantages of some technical innovations in artillery equipment and tactics. The famous '88', which could engage aircraft or tanks with devastating effect at long range, was of great advantage in defence.

The Nebelwerther, a multiple-rocket launcher, was an area weapon which had strong psychological effects as well as physical ones on those whom it engaged. But in general the German artillery was not as powerful or useful as that of the Allies. Although the Germans did field self-propelled assault and anti-tank guns, many of their batteries were horse-drawn which made them slow and vulnerable. The German infantry were more inclined to rely on their own organic heavy weapons, their mortars and infantry guns of 105mm and 150mm calibre, than on the conventional artillery. The Allies also made best use of their great advantages in logistics: their gunners usually had far more ammunition than the Germans. It was an Allied principle never to send a man where a shell would do.

The German artillery was heavily involved in supporting the offensive. Work in the observation post of a battery was particularly hazardous. The forward observers had to go right up to the front lines of leading infantry, or emplace themselves on conspicuous high ground from which they could see targets ahead. They were a prime target for snipers, and could be left isolated by unexpected changes of forward positions.

The effects of shelling, both physical and psychological, added to the misery of field conditions and were described graphically by Lieutenant Otts and Staff Sergeant Egger serving in the 26th Division. The German 88 was feared as a powerful weapon, and because it was particularly accurate at long range, due to the superior power of the optical glass used in the sights:

EGGER: Fockler went to the aid station yesterday morning with frozen feet, and Stribling had been missing since January 5. He had fallen behind that night as we were walking to the rear.

We were told this morning to be ready to move on line in the afternoon. As we were moving from the woods to the road on which the companies of the battalion were strung out in a long column, an 88 shell made a direct hit on a lieutenant standing in the road. George Company filed past the lieutenant, who had been an artillery observer, and the column halted for a few minutes when I was right next to the remains. I scanned the scene quickly and looked away. All that was left were a mound of bloody flesh and intestines, a blotch of crimson snow and two feet encased in overshoes. Maybe it was a better death than some had to endure, as it was quick, perhaps painless, and unexpected.

The column took off at a fast pace and the usual one-third of the men fell behind. We took over some old positions in a dense stand of hardwoods about a quarter of a mile from Mon Schumann crossroads. I made some improvements in my foxhole before the bedrolls were brought.

OTTS: I overheard him telling some of the men of all the wonderful times he had in Paris while we were enduring periodic shelling in our frozen foxholes. It really burned me up, and none of the men would have anything to do with him. I don't think it is any disgrace for a man to crack up under the mental strain, but to desert your company and fellow soldiers in combat is the worst thing a man can do.

EGGER: The frequency of the shelling increased today, especially near meal time. The Jeeps carrying our meals would dash up, leave the containers of hot food and coffee, two containers of hot water – one soapy, one clear to wash and rinse our mess kits in – load the containers from the previous meal, and speed four miles back to the kitchen. A few men at a time would run down to the road, fill their mess kits, and run back to the foxholes, eat the meal before it froze, and then dash back and wash the mess kits. It was not a very relaxing way to enjoy our food. This went on twice daily. If we wanted lunch we heated a ration.

The kitchen was taking more risks to provide us hot meals than they had in November. In the bitter cold weather, hot meals were important for the morale and nutrition of the troops.

Without the minimal comforts of hot drinks and food troops could become mutinous or lapse into a miserable apathy. Life in dry foxholes could be improved by putting in straw to provide insulation and digging deep to get out of the wind. Deeper holes were safer against shells and mortar bombs too. Egger's account continues:

> Junior Letterman, who had been with the platoon since November 9, was hit in the hand and a few minutes later Harold Schroaf, also from the 2nd Squad, was wounded. Both were able to walk to the aid station at Mon Schumann. Alex Stoddard's leg was broken by shrapnel and I helped carry him up the road until we met a Jeep. He was suffering from the pain but did his best to hide it. Only Letterman later came back to G Company.

Periodic shelling had a very powerful effect on the military spirit of its victims. It played on their nerves, like a toothache. This effect was intensified by the trickle of casualties it caused, as Otts notes:

> 1st Sergeant Germain received a battlefield commission and became our platoon leader.
>
> Bob Lees of the 1st Squad went back with frostbite today. He came back to the company in June.
>
> . . . About every half-hour during the day and at intervals during the night the Jerries would throw a barrage of from 200 to 250 rounds of artillery, mortars, and nebelwerfers into our area. The sound of exploding shells was deafening and the ground shook all around. We could hear the rocket bombs coming from miles away and they made a terrible racket when they crashed in the road and woods around us. The bombs did not throw much shrapnel, but the concussion was terrific – enough to kill a man if he were too close.
>
> The snow all around was black from the exploding shells and the ground was littered with tree limbs. We were suffering several casualties a day, and the percentage of combat fatigue was running high. A couple of men shot their fingers off – anything to get out of that hell.
>
> [Egger continues] The Germans increased the shelling again today. We had heard they were running short of ammunition, but

you couldn't tell it from the amount of metal they were dumping on us. The interval between barrages was so short we hardly had time to get out of the foxholes to relieve ourselves. There was nothing to do but roll up in a blanket and keep warm.

The trees increased the hazards of the shelling as the rounds that struck the branches would explode in the air (tree bursts) and shower shrapnel downward and out, while a shell hitting the ground propelled fragments up and out. The pieces of shrapnel were jagged and made a whistling sound as they whirled through the air.

We could not move much because of the constant shelling, so I slept except when I had sentry duty. Moores, Sturgis and Packer had the only foxhole with a log cover. If axes and saws had been available we could have provided the same protection for the other foxholes. The Germans were so close we could hear the mortars pop as they hit the firing mechanism in the mortar tubes. Then in a few seconds we could hear the shells whispering as they dropped from the sky to land near our positions.

For some of the artillery, the only option left was to surrender. Staff Sergeant Richard A Hartman of the 590 Field Artillery Battallion, 106th Division, was . . .

. . . completely cut off and our whole battalion just surrendered practically all at one time. We were mired in there. It was bitterly cold, and snow, and we tried to create a road down through a valley and across a stream and in the middle of the night we just got bogged down. The next morning they began lobbing in the 88 shells and eventually one of the officers put up a white flag.

They had also lost radio contact . . . we'd had radio contact for the first two days and after that I think we'd completely lost it. It was very dramatic. I can remember having a feeling that we'd let down the whole country. Good Lord, we'd been sent over there to fight and we weren't doing much fighting. They marched us, they rounded us up and marched us back . . . and lined us up in the city streets, at least the group I was with. They lined us up there and searched us and some private came along and tried to take my watch. I yelled for a German officer and he came and I told him my father had given me the watch and he wouldn't let this kid take it. So at least I had that. And that night they put us out in a courtyard right off the main square in Bleiauth [sic] and we spent the night there. It was bitterly cold, and we spent that first night sitting on the ice in this little courtyard . . . my recollection is I had an overcoat, most of 'em didn't for one reason or another, I guess they left them in the trucks when they were captured . . .

We were cold, we were hungry and we were lousy. Within a matter of weeks everybody had lice and you never got rid of them till the end, till we finally got back and were deloused after we were liberated. That was the most miserable part . . .

We walked probably 30 or 40 miles back into the interior of Germany. Coming towards us in hordes were these big German Tiger tanks and just thousands of troops. It was their last hurrah and we walked past them. We were going one way they were going the other . . . they put us on boxcars, about 65 men to a boxcar. We all could not even sit on the floor at the same time, some had to stand and others sat. They moved this train [and] . . . we were there the 24th, 25th, 26th and 27th of December on a siding.

Having been taken prisoner, there was little cheer for these men, and still danger aplenty:

By that time the weather had cleared a little bit and the British Mosquito bombers were up and the night of the 24th December, Christmas Eve, the railyards at Limberg [sic] were their target. We were locked into these cars and then somebody said, 'Look at the flares' and the red flares were coming down, the lead bomber drops the flares and everybody else is supposed to put the bombs on the target. Somewhere after maybe ten or fifteen minutes, somebody, I never found out who, it must have been a German, opened the doors of the boxcars and the guys just ran out. This friend of mine . . . he and I ran one way and kept running till a bomb dropped in front of us and we went back another way eventually ended up in a cave, it was a quarry outside the train station, or rather the train yards. We got back in this cave, this was where all the German guards were so when the bombing stopped we were politely led back to the car. They knew where safety was. Unfortunately, there were 7, so I've been told, 7 people from the train were killed and there was a PoW camp very close, you could see it from where the train was and the bomb killed 65 prisoners there. We stayed there 3 or 4 more nights while they repaired the tracks, and then they moved us through Frankfurt. That was one of the most humiliating experiences as we went slowly through the train station at Frankfurt there were just hordes of Germans down shouting, spitting, waving their fists at us. Very understandable, our bombers had just literally destroyed their town and we were as close as they could get to the enemy. It gave me a terrible feeling to see that . . . it was a British PoW camp [between Leipzig and Dresden] they took us in there and we were there for about a week I think, I know we were there on New Year's Eve and New Year's Day, and then we were put back on another boxcar train and moved further east to a camp on the Oder river between Berlin and Posen, Poland. Again that was a terrible experience on the boxcar because when we got on, there were already machine-gun bullet holes through the sides of the boxcar and it was a 24-hour trip and periodically the air raid sirens would go. You know, you just thought we're going to get strafed again, they're hitting everything that moves. Fortunately they never did and we got to the destination on the Oder River. That was an American camp. I was a Staff Sergeant and that was a camp for American non-commissioned officers. We stayed there for just about a month I think. Bitterly cold, never been so cold in my life . . .

THE ENGINEERS

Sappers on both sides performed many invaluable support tasks for the other arms. They constructed bridges across rivers, often under fire, and operated ferries in assault river crossings. They both created and demolished defensive positions using whatever materials they could bring or find. Minefields and booby-traps were prepared and cleared by the engineers, often by hand, and the improvement and opening of routes and tracks were their routine tasks.

As engineers, explains combat engineer David L Williams of the 104th Timberwolf Division of the US Army in his record of the battle, we had to put in antitank mines, place explosives on bridges and culverts, and put cratering charges in the strategic roads. All the explosives and all the mines had to be carefully mapped. We were busy.

A cratering charge requires five holes about two inches in diameter for a two-lane road. The holes on each edge and in the center are about four-feet deep and hold 40 pounds of nitromon. The two holes in the center of each lane are about six-feet deep and hold 80 pounds of nitromon. Nitromon, as an explosive, has a push rather than a blast, as TNT would have.

Digging these holes was tough. We started these holes with three-pound TNT shaped charges. The shaped charge stood on 10 inch legs and had a hollow cone in the lower half. This configuration directs much of the blast straight down. It would make a two-inch wide hole four feet into the pavement. We would finish the holes with jack-hammers and a power auger . . .

It is a little bit of a thrill hanging head down in the hole putting electric blasting caps in 40 or 80 pounds of explosive. But it was done and the wire leads run to a safe spot.

Putting in antitank mines in open fields was relatively easy. The snow had to be scraped off the ground and then the mines were dug in according to a pre-designed grid. They were then mapped and marked and sometimes a barbed wire fence was put around it.

It was more difficult to mine a paved road with antitank mines. We had to use jack-hammers and crow bars to place the mines. But, in some places, we still wanted to be able to use the road. Once the holes were dug, we filled them with cut sections of logs and stacked the boxed mines near-by to be installed when and if needed. It supplied us with endless work, making sure the logs had not frozen in place.

Williams also provides a good picture of the other difficulties the weather posed for the engineers operating in the Hürtgen Forest:

The snow was so deep that we couldn't get off the road, and sometimes we didn't know where the road was. The first five or six demolition sites we checked showed intact circuits. At the next one, it did not check out. The break was easy to spot. It had recently been run over by a tracked vehicle – half-track, tank – ours or theirs passed through our heads. We had to fish around under the snow to find the broken wires. Bump said to stay low when we tied these wires back together because sometimes there is enough of a current surge to set off the blasting caps. I didn't know if he knew what he was talking about, but I believed him, I tied them back together and nothing blew up . . .

The circuit checked out so we headed off to the next one. We were winding deeper into the forest when we came to a small town. Normally, a town would have division signs and here would be a dozen or so trucks and Jeeps. There was nothing. We turned the engine off and there was silence except for the wind. A shutter was blowing back and forth, banging once in a while. We looked into those blank windows and thought the entire German Army could be hiding there.

We went through the town and off into the forest again. The snow got deeper until finally we realized we could go no farther. Bump marked our map as impassable at that point. By digging a little snow from under the Jeep and physically bouncing the front tires up and down we got the Jeep moving. Thanks to the four-wheel drive we were able to turn the Jeep around and head back. We had been in the forest for over five hours and we had not seen a living soul!

There were lighter moments for the engineers, too, when they were 'lodging' in a cellar in Langerwehe:

The house immediately next to the cellar had been badly blasted apart. In climbing over the rubble one day one of the guys found a top hat. We each had our picture taken wearing that top hat, standing in front of that blown apart building.

Another thing we found was a metal, portable, full-length bath tub. We soon propped it up on bricks and filled it with water. There was lots of brick and coal around so we built a small fire under it and warmed the water. I was the first one into the tub

. . . and it was great. Doc Biddick took my picture soaking in the suds with the steam rising and snow all around. It was a great bath.

THE MALMEDY MASSACRE

During attacks the sappers went forward with the tanks and infantry and were fated to be involved in the notorious events that took place at Malmedy. This appalling incident was reported in *Stars and Stripes:*

MURDER ON THE WEST FRONT

An item from Time *magazine, Dec 25th, 1944.*

Murder

Despite their other crimes, the Germans had generally observed the rules of war in their treatment of captured US and British fighting men. But last week even that record was blotched by the cold-blooded murder of scores of US soldiers.

It was in Belgium, in a sector where the Allies had stood for nearly three months. On Sunday a column of 15 to 20 Nazi Tiger tanks, spearheading the new German drive, cut off a US 1st Army unit which had only light weapons to defend itself. The Americans were quickly overcome: 143 were herded into a field with a few others the Germans had captured earlier. The Germans took away the prisoners' watches and any other possessions they fancied.

A German officer gave an order to a tankman, who opened fire on the Americans with a pistol. Another German in an armoured car methodically sprayed the helpless captives with a Schmeisser sub-machine gun. Some fell to the ground dead or wounded. A few fell, shamming death. After the sub-machine gun was silent, German noncoms walked among the Americans, systematically shooting all who moved or moaned.

For an hour the survivors hugged the ground, not daring to look around. Gradually the German tanks rumbled off, and when a furtive glance showed only one left, every American who could run or stagger made for the woods nearby. Fewer than a score reached Allied positions.

One survivor of the massacre was Harvey E Thiede:

[I] Marched to the Massacre of Malmedy, survived the Massacre, don't know how I survived, I guess the good Lord wanted me to live and come home; I survived the Massacre of Malmedy and two of my buddies got killed there instantly with machine guns. Germans were drinking warm beer – warm black beer, drank a lot of that – and they would jump on a tank and would shoot a machine gun into the GIs and whoever they messed, they were dead. My driver and gunner got killed instantly.

In the northern sector, Sapper Herbert Woodrow served in the American 30th Division. He had a tense encounter with German infiltrators:

Arriving at Malmedy, Company C located a vacated paper factory. The large building had a basement that easily held our entire

At Malmedy, bodies of Belgian men, women and children await identification before burial. The town was bombed by the Americans during the battle and almost destroyed. It was also the location of the infamous incident in which Allied prisoners were shot in cold blood.

company; it quickly became our command post. Cots that were in the basement and had previously been used by paper factory employees became our beds.

Trying to get into and through our lines, the Germans were dressing in American uniforms. Company C had received word that Germans dressed this way were going to try to infiltrate the lines. First squad was sent up a road past all other American squads. This was the road that the Germans would travel and we were on duty. The snow on the road was very deep. There were no tracks in the snow, which indicated the road had not been used for a couple of days. Another squad was placed on duty about a mile behind us on the same road. In case Germans approached, we were to let them through and notify the other squad of American soldiers that they were on the way.

In the middle of the night, I was on squad duty and heard an approaching Jeep. After I reported to the squad leader, he awakened the other soldiers. I stood in the middle of the road and stopped the American Jeep. The soldiers in the Jeep were all very clean with clean uniforms. The officer in charge was the only one speaking. If they had been Americans, they all would have been talking about food and women. I knew they were Germans! Asking them to relate the password, I said, 'true'. The officer replied, 'blue'. We had been instructed to ask other questions such as, 'Who won the World Series?' The officer answered every question correctly. All of the soldiers in the Jeep were much too friendly. I stepped aside and allowed them to proceed. As quickly as they drove away, the squad leader notified the other squad that a Jeep load of Germans was converging. When the Germans arrived at the location of the other squad, they were ambushed.

For the engineers, there was a brief pause in the usual round of work in order to eat a traditional Christmas dinner in Malmedy.

Christmas, 1944, arrived at Malmedy. Company C celebrated at the Company Command Post at the paper factory, where we resided in the basement. We feasted upon a Christmas dinner that included turkey, dressing, and all the trimmings. Since we continued with all of our regular work on Christmas day, I do not recall any other distinguishable events.

Some Company C soldiers were guarding a bridge. We remaining soldiers were given the assignment of laying a large minefield. We proceeded to the side of an enormous hill outside the city. Our mission was to slow or stop Germans approaching from across the hill. We placed 4,500 antitank mines on the hill. While we were laying the mines, American planes approached and bombed Malmedy. Many American troops and Malmedy citizens were there. The city was under American control. It was completely destroyed. As the bombs fell, we viewed from about a mile away explosions, fires, smoke, and dust. Realizing that German soldiers could break through the American lines and enter the city, Company C soldiers were preparing the bridges for demolition.

Laying mines and carrying out demolitions were also routine tasks for engineers intent on delaying enemy movements. Attacks by friendly aircraft were a frequent form of tragedy. The sappers also had to accompany armoured forces into action. The consequences were not always so unfortunate.

Early the next morning an American tank approached. The soldiers in the tank had just arrived at the Battle of the Bulge and had never been in combat. They wanted a squad to go with them into the Ardennes Forest to assist them in getting a 'feel for combat'. My squad was sent with them before breakfast, being told that we would be gone about one hour. We traveled trails in the forest. Meeting a German tank on a trail, we backed up and the tank crew called for artillery fire. They gave our position instead of the German position. Artillery began falling all around us. We ran to get away from it. Hurriedly, the American tank left and we did not know its fate. We removed ourselves from the artillery fire and were lost. All lanes and trails appeared to be alike. Trying to find our way back, we were unable to stop very long for rest because of the severe cold. We would have frozen. While we were walking, we approached an area in the forest where we could see Germans. Darkness was falling and we knew we would freeze after dark. We discussed surrendering but decided that we would rather freeze to death than surrender to the enemy. Walking for several hours after that in very deep snow and subzero temperatures, we became tired and sat down to rest. While we were resting, a soldier reached into the snow and hit a wire. He pulled it up to see what it was and discovered it to be a telephone wire. The Americans had placed it there. Supposing that the wire would lead us to American lines, soldiers pulled it to the top of the snow as we traveled. Following the direction of the wire, we arrived at the hill where our company was bivouacked.

This was a lucky discovery, since the telephone cable was a lifeline back to the company, in particular to hot food and relative safety.

Since the entire company was on the hill, our company kitchen was also there. The kitchen was on the back of a truck, where the cooking took place. When the kitchen crew had completed serving a meal, they cleaned the pots and pans and began preparing for the next meal. But on this night, the company commander requested that the food be kept warm and ready for our squad. We returned after midnight. We had traveled since seven o'clock that morning . . . [about seventeen hours] of walking with little rest. Talk about good food! I can still taste the hot coffee!

Engineers also had to prepare the way for infantry to go forward across streams into attack.

There was a place at the top of the hill at Malmedy called Five Points. My platoon stayed overnight there. We were in the basement of a bombed house that had only four walls standing. The basement had bins full of potatoes. I slept on top of a potato bin. We were there because the Americans were going to attack the next morning. We engineers had to build a duckbridge across a very deep stream. We carried the sections of the bridge to the stream and attached them as we moved across the stream.
  As the infantry crossed over the bridge, engineers journeyed

back toward the basement. German artillery fire was dangerously heavy. We ran into a barn. Many cows were in the barn and were tied to keep them housed inside. We could hear shrapnel hitting the sides of the barn. I pushed my way between some yellow cows for protection. The cows were scared, prancing, and bumping each other and me. I would try to push them away. I finally decided that if I were going to get killed, it wouldn't be by a group of cows. I'd take my chances with shrapnel. Forcing my way from between the cows, I made a mad dash to the house basement. During our stay in the Ardennes Forest area, we constantly worked. As we arrived we were working on defensive measures, such as laying mines, scouting, guarding, buildings cleared and cleaned, and cleaning the streets of Malmedy.

Later, as the Germans retreated, we were on the offensive and preparing to leave. We cleared mines that the exiting Germans left behind, took up our mines, and cleaned up the roads and streets. Always, we assisted the infantry.

5
ARDENNES CHRISTMAS

Wherever they were, and whatever they were doing, there were few in the Ardennes who did not celebrate or remember Christmas in some way, even if it was only with thoughts of their distant families and of better times past and to come.

Army chaplains conducted services as and when they could, and the season brought with it deeper thoughts about the nature of the war. Reverend (Captain) John H Humphries, a Methodist minister, recorded in his war diary on 24 December:

> Somebody wrote of war, 'Waste of muscle, waste of brain.' It is so terribly true and yet *is it* waste to give muscle, brain and heart for things one holds most dear? Unless such lads were prepared to 'waste' their lives there would be few things left to hold dear . . .
>
> Held a Carol 'sing-song' instead of the usual evening service. Teddy Cain and I made a programme for it and all promised well. Until 6 o'clock . . . my most important figure for the evening – an organist with a soul – absent . . . there was nothing else for it and I had to play by ear . . . we lifted the roof with our hearty, if tuneless singing. For two hours we sang . . .
>
> Still confined to billets and on guard against enemy airborne troops, the boys could not make whoopee in local cafes but they did their best to make Xmas Eve lively within the limits imposed on them . . .
>
> My mind was constantly turning homewards . . .
> *December 25 Xmas Day* – The outstanding feature for me was the Xmas service in the hut at 11.00 hours. I had hoped to take an earlier service for 689 and 231 at their billets and arrived for the purpose at 09.15 only to find breakfast just beginning. Poor

beggars! There was a 'flap' during the night and they had all been 'standing to'. What a way to spend late Xmas Eve and early Xmas morning. The food was more essential than a service and I said so to the RSM who was a little embarrassed when I arrived.

The 11.00 service was well attended: the singing went well.

Peace on earth and mercy mild.

When possible during the 'festive' season, many made the best of what little food they had, and others managed to rustle up – or be treated to – veritable banquets in incongruous surroundings.

For many troops on the ground, and civilians, too, the best Christmas present of all was the fact that the skies had cleared on the previous night. The record of Captain Clyde of the Household Cavalry summed up both the mood of the Allies and the generosity of the owners of the château in which he was quartered:

Squadron Headquarters spent Christmas Day in a château south of the river. I will always remember the bright clear sky which was creased from dawn to dusk with the vapour trails of the endless flow of American bombers. The château had an excellent cellar and a most accommodating host. Strangely enough, by midday, traffic on the forward net was fitful; by three o'clock all touch was lost, but the air miraculously cleared in time for the 'return home' order.

Countess Rene Greindel, wife of the Governor of Luxembourg Province, Belgium, who lived with her 12 children in a manor house occupied by troops a few miles from Bastogne, watched as . . .

Shortly after 3pm we could watch a real fairytale sight, which, for three days was to be repeated several times a day: the first parachutes! From the South East, we saw at least 150 Dakotas flying at about 600-feet high, and which dropped over a plain, situated between our home and Bastogne, a swarm of yellow, red, blue, green and white parachutes. The plain was indicated to the pilots by a pink cloud. The scene cannot be described: the dazzling snow under the bright sunshine, and in perfectly blue sky the extraordinary dropping of lovely shades! The colours indicated the nature of the supplies.

Given the good weather, the 23rd Hussars decided it was a good day for 'tank hunting':

> Christmas Day broke brilliantly fine and bitterly cold. The full force of the German thrust appeared to be spending itself and there [was] ground for believing that the Germans were running out of petrol and supplies, which it was reported were being dropped from the air, and that some tank formations had become stranded. In view of this, the news that we were to move forward to go 'tank hunting' was received with great applause. 'Brewing Tigers' instead of roasting turkeys was to be a novel pastime for Christmas Day, though . . . no enemy was seen.

Despite the disappointment, they managed a Christmas celebration in what turned out to a memorable day. They returned to camp . . .

> . . . for a Christmas dinner of iced bully and frozen cheese sandwiches. In the evening, proper billets were found in Beauraing, for is became obvious at once that there was no question of camping out in a field or 'bedding down' in a barn, or, perchance, 'kipping' inside outranks. We would all have frozen to death, and as no one had the least desire to experiment in that form of decease, it was thought best to make certain of comfort and warmth at night, the enemy being in a like plight. During the day no fires could be lit and Regimental Headquarters found that the splendour of its post was more than outdone by its coldness and that the sun never reached it all day and never would. However, it stuck there for the following days while the three squadrons 'basked' in the valley below, keeping itself warm by tobogganing on map boards or improvised sledges, or by attempts by its members to push one another down the hill.

For the men of the 2nd Fife and Forfar Yeomanry . . . a typical Christmas dinner was a cheese sandwich and a cup of tea. But some of the tank crews were luckier. From the refugees who kept streaming back from the battle zone they received welcome gifts of coffee, fruit and cake. Christmas night arrived with no sign of peace on earth and not the faintest hint of goodwill towards men. Indeed, from their exposed positions on the high ground [they] were able to see from behind enemy lines the launching of V-2 rockets aimed at Brussels, Antwerp and other areas of Belgium.

Major Bowes Daly of the 2nd Household Cavalry had both a celebration and a shock:

Christmas Day was spent at a village called Marche-les-Dames on the river between Namur and Huy. On Christmas Day itself my whole Troop was most royally entertained by the local inhabitants. A large meal was provided, and also largish quantities of Pernod, which was certainly a new one on most of my chaps, were consumed. By the middle of the afternoon their visibility was about five yards, so you can imagine my horror when some expert came over and told us that parachutists were reputed to have dropped on an extremely high hill overlooking the village. How we got to the top I have not much idea, except that I can remember pulling a Bren gun up most of the way. We took one look at the top, said we couldn't see a thing, and returned absolutely furious at what had proved to be a false alarm.

For some, the Christmas celebrations continued well into Boxing Day:

Those of us not on duty soon found excuses to borrow a vehicle and pay calls on neighbours along the river bank. On the road from Tirlemont to Diest, Major Williams's Headquarter Squadron was billeted in the village of Bunsbeek, as were most of the Squadron echelons. The houses were most adequate and the people, as usual extremely hospitable. Lieutenants Oliver (when he was not in Brussels) and Hughes were unearthed, living quietly and comfortably with the village priest and his old housekeeper. The priest was a dear old man with sound and philosophical

Small comforts, like a warming fire, helped make Christmas in the Ardennes bearable if not merry. Some troops managed more lavish celebrations, but for many the day 'went hardly noticed,' bringing no let up in the battle nor the treatment of the wounded and dying.

ideas on the *marché noir* [black market], which he insisted should in many of its 'beneficial' activities merely be labelled 'Le Marché parallel'. He possessed some excellent brandy, and his Household Cavalry guests drank, between Christmas services, to the successful outcome of the Battle of the Bulge. I seem to recall that one session was interrupted by a ring on the doorbell and a parishioner came in with a 'marché parallel' (boiling fowl) which the old priest promptly secreted under his cassock with a gentle smile.

In their turn the echelons repaid calls, bringing adequate allocations of cigarettes, gin and whisky and other NAAFI supplies collected by Captain Firth and his staff. RQMS Goody and the storeman, Corporal Wincombe, could always be relied upon to get that something extra from the supply point, and this time they had exCellesd themselves.

There was champagne, and the men soon found out how to obtain sacks of freshly baked American white bread. We bought bottles of sickly sweet beer which tasted like bad Guinness and treacle, and discovered some 'Burgundy' in Huy, purchased at an outrageous price and fortified with chips of sandalwood and colouring matter. We exchanged bully beef for eggs and cigarettes for cheese, and a Belgian barber in Andenne offered free haircuts and shampoos to the men. One Household Cavalryman, a road-mender in civilian life, came back in some confusion, reeking of scent and having had his eyebrows plucked. With a nice feeling for foreign habits he explained: 'I didn't dare stop the barber because I felt that this might be a Belgian custom at Christmas time.'

WOMEN AT THE FRONT

Among the women at the front was Rosemary Langheldt, who worked for the American Red Cross on a Clubmobile dispensing coffee and doughnuts to GIs. She was 'Captain of the Clubmobiles' in Southampton, and copies of the letters she sent back home feature next to her own, more detailed, journal accounts of her nursing activities, including her surprisingly lavish Christmas in 1944:

Saturday, December 30, 1944
Dearest Family,
Christmas is over and it's been a little hectic. We've been stationed here so long we had a cheery one in many ways as we know lots of people to wish a Merry Christmas. We're working day and night – our Christmas celebration was sandwiched in between loadings and hospital ships and emergencies.

We managed to get to mess for a turkey dinner on Christmas Day, but our celebrating consisted mainly of amusing the GIs going through the Port all day and most of the night. I made Ski skip part of the night shift as she is still weak from her hospital stay, but our Clubmobile was bright with holly and greens and mistletoe and the GIs seemed so to appreciate our being on hand. Think the job Eloise and Kari did on their Clubmobile was the biggest hit with the guys. They decorated their truck with a little evergreen tree, then punched holes in the tops of C ration cans and threaded string through to hang them on the tree as ornaments. They wore adhesive tape on several fingers each when they finally got the holes punched and, as Eloise remarked, if anyone reached into the tree they might bleed to death. The final touch was tying mistletoe above the serving window so it hung over the GIs as they were served. The guys kept complaining it was hung in the wrong place as it was over them instead of over the girls.

It was, and still is, bitterly cold – hoarfrost weather, the English call it. Christmas Day was beautiful and freezing, all the rooftops and streets white with frost, but the GIs didn't notice the fine holiday weather. They were too busy feeling sorry for themselves being so far from home. When they talk to us and realize we're just as far from home it seems to cheer them up a little. One huge bunch of troops had the docks rocking with their 'Jingle Bells' rendition before we finished serving them.

The European situation is certainly grim and we're seeing some of the most heartbreaking sights. The results of the German drive have affected us so directly, the stark horror of war impresses itself upon our minds more strongly each day. I wish I could say more as there's so much I'd like to write but it will have to wait until a later date . . .

December 30, 1944 – Just sealed my letter home and am feeling frustrated because I can tell the family only light and trivial details of a Christmas week so shadowed it broke our hearts. Hope they read between the lines and know there are more important things going on than those I am permitted to write about.

The day before Christmas Eve we started work at 04.00 to feed several shiploads of troops. Just as we finally finished, the boys were suddenly offloaded, and I was informed the ships were to reload that night with infantry replacements. A high-security operation and a real rush job because of the German drive in the Bulge. I already had made crew assignments for Christmas week and knew several of us hoped to grab a few free hours to be with

friends after finishing work. But when I asked for volunteers
(sure to be six extra hours – at least – in the middle of the night
on a bone-chilling cold, damp, and foggy docks), all I got was the
usual 'Okay, coach, which piers and how many?' It's no wonder I
love my crew.

The division being rushed over was the 66th. On December
23rd, they were yanked out of camp so fast – without any notice –
they still wore 66th snarling Black Panther Division patches
on their uniforms. Usually all division insignia is removed if
it's a high security operation. The cooks had to leave stuffed
turkeys and Christmas dinner preparations behind. They'd all
had Christmas parties planned and suddenly they were eating
K rations and headed for a channel crossing. Always especially
tough in winter.

They dragged into the dock area exhausted and it was easy to
see they were not in a happy frame of mind. They began arriving
early evening and our crews were there to serve units before the
Port started loading the two troopships waiting at Pier 38: the
British-controlled ship *Leopoldville*, a huge Belgian passenger liner,
and the SS *Cheshire*. It was so cold in the dock sheds some of the
guys lit little bonfires to try and keep warm during the long wait.
There seemed to be more than normal confusion in the loadings
and we'd see an occasional 'lost' platoon wandering through the
piers trying to locate their company. The men seemed so young.
Many carried Christmas-wrapped boxes or goodies that wouldn't
fit into their packs and told us they were determined to celebrate
Christmas wherever they happened to be.

I used the *Joker*, the wonderful Canadian truck Tom gave us,
to check supplies and shuttle more coffee and doughnuts where
needed. By the time I drove into Pier 38 the troops crowded
into that huge cavernous shell were in full-voiced rendition of
'White Christmas', the reverberating sound of thousands of
voices seeming to swell the shed in a mighty plea. I broke out all
over in goosebumps. Eloise and Kari were in charge of our main
Clubmobile and I noticed their eyes misted over too.

For hours we served the men, and sang and talked and laughed
with them. We did, as usual, a lot of listening and admiring

pictures in wallets. We lingered past midnight to stand by the gangplank and wish the last units well and cheer them off as they finally boarded. It was so dark you couldn't see much, but every now and then a GI leaned over to kiss one of us on the cheek or give an awkward one-handed pat on the shoulder.

Most of us sleepwalked our ways through the loading schedule for Christmas Eve as it was just as busy – and just as long. The docks and Hards were full of embarking troops being poured cross-Channel. Late on Christmas Eve, Eloise and Kari reported, they rushed over to serve a hospital ship that arrived unexpectedly. They spotted it coming in to dock ablaze with lights, white sides gleaming, a huge Red Cross symbol clearly visible on each side because hospital ships speed straight across Channel brightly signalling their presence to friend and foe alike. Eloise kept thinking how familiar some of the walking wounded looked as they came down the gangplank and, being Eloise, bubbled out to one hollow-eyed boy in a dishevelled uniform, 'Gosh, you look familiar, friend!' And the boy said, 'You're right. You just served us last night – on the *Leopoldville*.' And that's how they heard that the *Leopoldville* had been sunk just before entering Cherbourg Harbor. Eloise was so shocked that the GI was gone before she could ask him anything else.

When Kari and Eloise finished work it was pretty close to midnight and they decided to go to church. They'd never discussed religious preferences but just felt the urge to go, so they attended midnight mass at a nearby Catholic church. It was lit mostly by candles and packed with GIs, British and American sailors, Royal Marines, and Royal Engineers in all sorts of garb. Kari and Eloise stood against the back wall and could see the only attempt at dressing up was that all the men had their hats off, the candlelight flickering on their freshly combed hair . . .

Christmas Day was beautiful but freezing cold hoarfrost weather – and devastating, as rumors flew around the Port about the *Leopoldville*. While I was checking our work schedules early Christmas morning at the Maritime Chambers, the Port loading headquarters, Colonel Jim told me the details. The ship was in sight of the harbor when it was torpedoed and they feared at least

800 lives or more had been lost. Since I've been stationed here other ships have hit mines crossing the channel and been lost, but the *Leopoldville* was large transport with over 2,200 troops aboard. The thought of it going down was horrible.

When Barbara drove into the dock area for her very early Christmas morning assignment she spotted a British 'dockie' holding a soggy life jacket from the *Leopoldville*. He told her it had just been brought in by one of the channel patrol boats. She sat down on the dock and began sobbing. Told me she couldn't help it as she remembered all the guys she had talked with and all those pictures of wives and girlfriends she'd admired and all the singing during that long night.

So Christmas Day was especially difficult. We served thousands of troops being rushed over to try and stop the German drive. It was obvious they all knew where they were headed. On the Hards, looking up into the clear sky, we could see literally hundreds of contrails from a flight of bombers rendezvousing overhead. The bomber flights had been grounded by fog for days, unable to help out with the German breakthrough. But since Christmas morning dawned clear and bright, they could again fly. When the big flight started to head off toward the channel, first a few GIs, then instantly everyone on the Hards, looked up, waved their arms, and shook their fists skyward as they joined in a shouting mass chant, 'Go, Go, Goooo!'

In her letter home, to her family in Winchester, Massachusetts, Lieutenant Mary Louise Carpenter, ANC, a graduate of Vassar and the Massachsetts General Hospital School of Nursing in 1941 and working in the 13th Field Hospital, also described her Christmas with feminine detail:

December 29 – We arrived in time to get somewhat settled before supper, Brownie and I in a small room on the second floor of the isolation ward of a large Catholic hospital . . . the next morning some machine-gun fire was going on, about four blocks away, and one of our officers said he didn't know what the firing was about but that it was small arms, and it would be wise if we packed our musette bags [lightly] to make a quick get-away . . .

At breakfast the next morning there was an unexpressed feeling of triumph that we hadn't been moved and that a crisis had been weathered . . . we expected to spend Christmas peacefully in our isolation wards, and soon after breakfast the smell of roasting turkey pervaded the building. Very soon after came orders, pack up and move. By 01.30 we nurses were again packed into ambulances with only our small luggage this time (our bedrolls, etc, were all in another vehicle) for a ride through wintry, war-pocked countryside, and through one large city of death where the houses are all empty shells.

We arrived at our destination in time to settle in a flimsy looking but not uncomfortable barracks before going to our turkey dinner at our mess hall. In the evening we opened little presents we had placed for each other under a small tree we had brought and decorated with ornaments taken no doubt from ruined German houses – lovely, original things like white-stemmed, sparkly, red-topped mushrooms and a pretty, gold-robed doll angel. Then the officers came in and we drank gin and grapefruit juice and ate Schrafft's nuts, and fruitcake until it really was Christmas. Christmas Day itself was sparkling clear. Such was the war at the time of the German breakthrough as I saw it.

For the staff of the 107th Evacuation Hospital:

Christmas came and went, hardly noticed by the men absorbed in the great drama of the Bulge. The only things that might be associated with Christmas were the Jeep shows being put on in each ward, a fine turkey dinner and a brief session of Christmas carols. It was also the occasion of the transfer of the 107th back to the Third Army, with which it finished the war.

Christmas presents? There was one which thrilled everyone as nothing else could have done. Clear skies for our air force! Those clumsy C-47s flying supplies to the besieged men at Bastogne, those fleets of mighty bombers roaring over the Sedan skies to settle accounts for Malmedy; to us they seemed like avenging angels on an overdue mission of retribution.

THE UPS AND DOWNS

For some, Christmas brought a temporary lull. For certain engineers, including David L Williams, Combat Engineer in the 104th Timberwolf Division, US Army . . .

> . . . activity eased off . . . we were more relaxed. One night I got the chance to go back to Weisweiler to a movie. We knew nothing about what we would see until we got there. It was called 'Laura' and starred Gene Tierney and Clifton Webb. We hadn't seen any shows for so long we thought it was great. It may also have been the complete surprise that made it seem so good . . . the great feeling more so than the picture.
>
> One of our infantry companies moved into a warehouse on the Roer river and discovered it was filled with cognac . . . just before Christmas, somebody decided to give one bottle of cognac to each squad. My squad Sergeant, 'Bump' Clark, and I had the detail of delivering the cognac to the other platoons. We were cordially received and had to have a drink with nearly everyone we saw. Bump and I were not worth much the rest of the night. I couldn't stand the heat of our cellar so I went to sleep in the snow outside. A big burly Mexican guy named Rodriguez from our squad was on guard duty that night. He picked me up and carried me back to the cellar two or three times. I woke up the next morning in the cellar with a horrible headache . . .

William Steel Brownlie's Christmas was also recorded sombrely, as he struggled to write home. This is his diary entry:

> *25 December* – No more parties, and we were sent much further forward, to a crossroads with three or four houses: Lez [sic] Fontaine. No wind, the weather bright and sparkling, miserably cold. I tried to write letters home, but my fingers were too stiff. No mail, no rations on the tanks, so the cooks' wagons came up with supper in 'containers': stone cold. I slept with Desmond in a small bed in a dirty cottage. Merry Christmas indeed.
>
> Meanwhile our 23 Hussars was down to Givet, and 3 RTR at Dinant, guarding the Meuse against the von Runstedt break-out,

Battle of the Bulge, whatever you like to call it. His leading troops, 2nd Panzer Division, got to within a few miles of Dinant, ran out of fuel, and were attacked by 3RTR. We envied this opportunity to have a go at old enemies: at least I did.

After another awful morning sitting in the cold, we moved through beautiful countryside to Dinant, finally descending the long, winding road into the town, a cliff on one side and a chasm on the other. The surface was solid ice, the tanks kept slithering towards a three-foot wall, all that was between them and the 200-foot drop. With great caution and good driving, we all made it. Through Dinant, a most inviting place but no chance of a halt, we went west through Falmignoul and Falmagne, and into billets.

This was a small village, Walloon-speaking so communication in French was just possible, and most hospitable. Squadron HQ was in half of a small house. The old woman saw our rum ration being delivered, and insisted that we drink it mixed with hot milk, which she boiled in a pot. She supplied the same mixture while we were there, to the whole Squadron, who queued up at the door each evening. Only one troop at a time had to be out on guard duty. News of the battle was that the RAF had been able to get at the German supply columns, with better weather. I had a parcel from home and one from Ida Bowie of Dreghorn. Monty's Xmas present was promise of much UK leave, and we drew up lists. For fun we organised intelligence tests for all ranks in the village school. Colonel Alec sent Desmond Chute to get better billets (I for one was sleeping on the floor) in Mesnil St Blaise, but Brigade HQ got there first.

The importance of Christmas to the troops was not lost on the reporters of the *Stars and Stripes* and other newspapers:

HOW C-47s SUPPLY GIs CUT OFF IN BELGIUM
By Richard Wilbur, Stars and Stripes *Staff Writer. With the 434th troop carrier group over Drop Zone in Belgium.*
Christmas bundles from scores of C-47 troop carrier planes have just plunged down by green, yellow and red parachutes and landed near a snow-covered field, marked by colored smudges

On 25 December the skies were clear, making flying possible after days of enveloping fog. For the 101st Airborne encircled in Bastogne by enemy forces, the dropping of food, small arms, ammunition and medical supplies from C-47 transport planes was especially welcome.

from smoke spots, to re-supply an American unit surrounded by German forces below in the Bastogne area. GIs are streaking across the snow, and from this plane 500 feet above ground, we can see them beginning to collect the bundles – tons of ammunitions, K-rations and medical supplies – the kind of Christmas present the German-encircled GIs really wanted.

This is the second consecutive day that the unarmed troop carriers have roared across from England, sped deep into France, and, with fighter support above, made the final run through flak concentrations in Belgium to drop parabundles for the ground men, cut off from the American lines by von Rundstedt's breakthrough for more than a week. The C-47 I travelled in, piloted by Maj Thomas Ricketts Jr of Richmond, Va, was flying so smoothly that is was possible to typewrite in the long cabin from where door loads, each filled with 200lbs of 30-cal ammunition, were ready to be dropped.

A gale of winter wind blew into the ship as Cpl Kenneth Cade, of Kansas City, crew chief, opened the cargo door near the drop zone so that the door bundles could be shoved out, at the same time that six parapacks, each loaded with 300 pounds of 75mm ammunition, slung under the ship, could be released.

The aerial supply missions for soldiers trapped in Belgium – first combat job given Troop Carrier Command since the airborne landing in Holland – were planned as soon as the Germans broke through the First Army sector, but bad weather grounded the C-47s until yesterday.

Lt Col Joel L Crouch of Riverside, Cal, opened the aerial supply operation, without fighter escort, by landing paratroopers to direct other troop carrier planes to the drop zone.

SOLDIER'S MAIL . . . IT DOES GET THROUGH
By Igor Cassini, Warweek *Staff Writer*

A couple of weeks ago it was St Nick's turn to grumble about an aching back, because the old guy had quite a load to tote around the foxhole circuit this Christmas.

Half a dozen of his pet reindeers are laid up with round heels, having delivered millions of packages and letters from Eschweiler to Belfort. The white-whiskered guy and the APO worked overtime to beat the Dec 25th deadline.

High-tailing the mail from Akron to Aachen and points east and west is a devil of a responsibility and a rugged detail for the sweating mail clerk who is doing the best he can. His mail is part of the load, too. So, if a package turns up with a little mould on it or a broken string or a faded address, don't ream your company mail orderly and the APO too violently. Most of the stuff gets through in good shape – and in fast time.

More important
At this time of year the whole mail problem becomes more important than usual to the solider – and to the APO. More

packages are sent to and from home. More letters are written. The need for news of home is more urgent around the holidays.

Thirty million parcels were sent from the US to soldiers.

Some British troops were still travelling to the battle zone on Christmas Day, like Private Ernest Rooke-Matthews of 9 Para Regiment:

On Christmas Day we reached Dover and were soon on our way across the Channel to Calais . . . our Christmas dinner was tinned sausages and baked beans.

Lieutenant DH Clark, RAMC, also spend Christmas in transit in far from comfortable conditions. His journey had begun a couple of days earlier:

On 23rd December we were put into lorries and driven all through the night, then embarked at Folkestone on a ferry to cross the Channel. We set off – and then stopped. The ship put down anchors and we remained for 24 hours. There was little food, except biscuits and tea. It was Christmas Day – and we thought bitterly of all the turkeys and beer we had left behind. It was a brilliant winter's day and we were in 'The Downs' – the traditional anchorage – from which we could easily see the sunlit English coast. The boat, of course, was full of rumours. It was known that the Germans had mounted some sort of surprise attack, and that the parachutists were to stop them. We were told that they had also mined the Channel and that was why we could not cross. Certainly there were many small Navy boats scurrying about on the sea, and many planes overhead. Finally the anchor was raised and we zigzagged across the Channel. We disembarked in the dark in a shattered port and climbed into lorries which drove all through the night. As morning broke we crossed the Meuse – a wide dull grey river running between snow-covered banks – and were then sent off in different directions.

Militarily, reported Cyril Ray, Christmas brought no unqualified rejoicing to either side. The Germans had undoubtedly gained tactical surprise, and days of misty weather had been worth many squadrons of fighters to von Rundstedt. The American First Army had taken a lot of punishment, the advance to the Rhine had been halted, and a threatening salient was established. On the other hand, the line of the Meuse was intact, Allied resistance in the north was growing, and the magnificent stand of the US 101st Airborne in Bastogne limited von Rundstedt to a narrow front which he was unable to expand as long as the airborne men held on.

All through Christmas, McAuliffe and his men were holding out in Bastogne in the siege destined to become famous. On 25 December, as had happened since the 23rd, supply dropping was happening on a huge scale:

> Only one drop, consisting of food, went astray. One man told me that they went into cellars and air-raid shelters as supply planes came over. If you were out in the street, in the middle of the town, a bag might easily hit you on the head . . .
>
> [Christmas day was] Splendid . . . Splendid – that was the day we got twenty-eight German tanks.

On 25 December, as on other days of the battle, there were injuries and deaths in combat. Despite the season, atrocities were still committed as the German troops perservered in their onslaught.

It was a week into the offensive and German troops had arrived in Bande a few days before Christmas. On Christmas Eve the male residents of Bande and the neighbouring village of Grune were taken away by SS troops for questioning. The younger men were separated from those aged over 30 and interrogated first. One of these men escaped and made his way back to the nearest American troops with the news that the Germans were systematically shooting their captives. Private Ernest J Rooke-Matthews, along with the rest of 9 Para Regiment, was taken to see the carnage by the locals, with whom they could barely communicate as neither shared a common language.

> We were taken to a building where we saw the victims – rows of young men lying on straw on the floor. The bodies were frozen stiff – it was a gruesome sight. Every man had been shot in the back of the neck behind the ear. It looked as if the murderer was

probably standing just alongside the victim when firing the fatal shots. I was deeply shocked, as were my comrades. Most of us had seen other victims of war – we had seen crushed bodies, men who had suffered severe injuries, but this was callous, calculated [killing] of young men – civilians.

After the battle was over and won, many of the troops were eventually able to have 'real' Christmas celebrations, and when they did it included the traditional role reversals between officers and men:

As 29th Armoured Brigade had been in the Ardennes on 25 December, the Brigadier decreed that the third weekend in January was Christmas. So Friday 20th [January] was Christmas Eve, a regimental holiday, Geoff and I ending up at a dance in the Flamshuis. Next day it was visits from one Mess to another, then the officers and sergeants converged on the men's cookhouse to serve them their festive meal, a well-established Army tradition. We were surprised to be met by the whole regiment of other ranks, armed with snowballs. There was quite a battle. In the dining-hall, which was so small that normally there had to be two sittings, all were crammed in, and we had to walk on the tables to get the piled plates to those furthest away. It was not elegant, but it was a successful regimental occasion.

6
INFANTRY AND AIRBORNE

As always in battle the infantry – and the paratroops dropped or brought by road to the battlefield – bore the brunt of the action in the Ardennes, and suffered the most in terms of privations, risks and casualties. They fought in open ground, around isolated farms, in the woods, in villages and in towns. Other arms could destroy enemy forces and drive them back but only the infantry could clear, secure, control, defend and hold ground. And it was only the infantry who could penetrate certain kinds of terrain. The densely wooded steep ridges of the Ardennes were really infantry country where determined and well-trained foot soldiers decided the result of every clash of arms. Richard Hottelet of CBS expressed this high regard in an account filed on 22 December, 1944:

> I can tell you how much it means to have seen this strength
> of ours poured down into threatened areas. There have been
> several misty, cold mornings this past week when I have come
> back along an empty road from sectors of the front that I
> knew were held only by patrols and cavalry screens, and I've
> wondered what would happen if the Germans attacked there.
> And then, following a couple of Jeeps, would come a looming
> convoy of trucks and tank-destroyers and half-tracks and tanks,
> and I'd lean out of my Jeep and squint to get a look at the unit
> identification. Sometimes it was an outfit I knew well; sometimes
> it was a strange bunch, from pretty far away, but I always felt
> better on the way home because I had seen our strength.
>   And it's the same with the infantry. You know the Army is big
> and powerful, but you're out by yourself in the dark or under a
> miserable grey sky and you want to see some tangible proof. Well,
> you'll see it here now. Again this morning I saw another bunch
> thundering down to the front and everyone – soldiers, civilians,
> and war correspondents – looked at it and smiled.

But all this couldn't have happened if it hadn't been for the work and courage of the average GI. All day and all night they've driven scores of miles over roads jammed thick with convoys moving, moving, moving. Vehicles in ditches were pulled out, lost vehicles and convoys were put right, and in between MPs fished out Germans in Jeeps who were riding behind our lines to get information and do damage. With units pouring in from everywhere it's been hard to see how they could all be managed, but they were.

Because they had to hold the ground they were most often required to live in the open, no matter what the weather, so they suffered the worst hardships most frequently. Because they fought each other at close quarters and also had to deal with tanks and endure artillery fire in places, they also suffered the highest rates of casualties. The infantry were also hugely strengthened and sustained by bonds of comradeship in the face of the extreme tests and rigours of life in the field and combat.

Like other infantrymen, the US 84th Infantry Division made the best they could of the harsh conditions in the Ardennes, and realized the life-saving importance of digging themselves into foxholes, keeping warm and staying on the move. Resourcefulness was an asset, too:

In this cold and snow, the problem of taking cover was supreme. It took a good two hours to get through the frozen crust of earth. Riflemen reported that it took them as long as five hours to dig down as far as three feet. Not only was digging a foxhole a job in which a whole day's energies could be consumed but it was practically impossible to dig a good one at least five feet down. When the freeze came, rest went. In that terrible cold, there was only one thing worse than not sleeping – and that was sleeping. The quickest way to freeze is to lie still. Men went to sleep in overcoats and woke up encased in icy boards. It was practically impossible to bring up rations and supplies in anything but half-tracks. Water froze in canteens. Frostbite was as dangerous as all the Germans and their guns put together. In one respect, the snow was on our side. Some of our units used snow suits effectively. One unit, the 335th's 1st Battalion, made their own snow suits out of long white winter underwear.

It was the lot of the infantry to live out in the open, keeping warm as best they could in foxholes, where even a night's sleep brought the threat of deadly hypothermia. Snow cover made camouflage ineffective in open spaces, adding to their vulnerability.

Company Commander Robert E Foster, US 94th Division, like many infantrymen, witnessed many cases of frostbite:

> ... they issued what they called snow packs to replace our combat boots but I think, I know the people in the rear got theirs

a lot sooner than some of our troops did and some of our troops never did get them. And we had a lot of cases of frostbite . . . if you got it too serious, you lost that man. He had to go back. He couldn't walk.

That was not the only problem, because the Germans regularly used shoe-mines . . .

. . . Lieutenant Clutch, he stepped on a shoe-mine. His whole platoon, there were probably as many as eight or nine casualties. Where they had shoe-mines sitting in the snow, they'd break your ankle, shatter your ankle.

I was wounded, when we crossed the Saar river, and well, the afternoon before we'd crossed the river, Captain Brightman was killed by a stray round from across the river. Right through his chest, right through his heart. There was no chance that it could have been an aimed rifle that it came from, it was too far. So they were scattering, firing machine guns and so forth, and they hit him, and killed him right off. I became the Company Commander at that point. And that night, after a tremendous artillery barrage across the river on our part, we crossed the river on rubber pontoon boats and climbed the cliffs on the other side, and that's where we really saw the bunkers that the Germans had built on the Siegfried line. And we stayed there till the morning, or during the next day we sort of collected ourselves and then we had the attack order to move out again, and we were on a ridge about four miles beyond when suddenly we could hear German voices all the time. They had apparently realized that we were in the woods and the artillery started to come in on us. We had some casualties there, and I picked up a shrapnel wound in my left thigh. And I was bleeding, and Lieutenant Mackey then took over. He was the only other officer in the Company. And with the help of one of the GIs, I managed to drag myself back to the river where they'd set up an aid station and they carried me across, and then I was flown to a hospital in Belgium.

Other divisions also had to deal with the consequences of mines, including the 69th Infantry (known as the fighting Sixty Ninth) in which corporal Louis C Sarube of the 271st Regiment was serving in a regimental HQ wire section.

We reached the Siegfried line and set up in a German pillbox that had some concrete walls 15-feet deep. We immediately set up a switch board and started to run lines to different stations. The snow was so deep our wire lines sank. They said it was one of the coldest and snowiest winters on record in Europe.

One day we lost a wire line and me and another crew man went out to fix it. The sun was out that day and started to melt the snow. That's when we saw dead German bodies laying around. Our wire line was laid about ten feet from a dead German soldier whom we never saw in the deep snow. The poor bastard had stepped on a mine because the lower part of his body was gone. My buddy said to look at the big gold ring he was wearing and suggested we chop off his finger and take it. Not me, I said, I don't want any part of a dead man. He also left it alone. Seeing dead Germans didn't bother me. But seeing dead American GIs did. We got the line fixed and returned to our pillbox. One day our sergeant wire chief broke his arm in three places so I became wire chief. We had two wire lines laid to the 28th division on our left flank. One early morning about 2am, the switchboard operator on duty woke me up saying that one of the wire lines to the 28th division went dead. What should we do? What a decision to make. I said, 'Look, don't report it any further. I can't send anyone out on a night like this because the Nazi's had that area zeroed in with artillery.' We called that area 'Purple Heart Corner'. Also the German night patrol, if they found our wire lines, would cut them and tie a hand grenade at one end so when we would pull it, it would go off. I said as long as one line is good, let's pray to God it stays like that. As soon as dawn broke, the other men and I went out and fixed it. The only ones who knew about the situation were the switch board operator and me. And we were not going to mention it.

Captain William D Bowell, of the US 507th, flew into France, near Chartres. It was not a comfortable experience, as he explained later:

They put us in cattle trucks right off the airplanes – in cattle trucks – and took us to the front. In fact, as I remember, we went ahead of Patton . . . Patton's tanks. And, well, to begin with . . . Midnight Charlie, we called him Midnight Charlie, a German airplane, came over strafing the convoy. And I was on the bottom of the goddamn cattle truck and I, by the time he was ready for a second pass, I was just getting off. So, everybody else was spread out all over the fields. And I got underneath the truck engine. And I was wondering where the hell is the goddamn machine that was in, in the cab. He should have been up there shooting the damn airplane. And hell, he was out in the field with the rest of the guys. And I was the only one under the damn engine. Well, the rest of the trip I rode on the outside on the top of the cattle truck. As a kid, for fun we used to hook cattle trucks, you know, and ride them. I rode one truck for a hundred and seventy-five miles when I ran away from home at the age of 13 on the back of a cattle truck. So, I was experienced. And so we got up where we were getting into battle and the 88 fire was furious. I mean, it was furious. I remember one time I was diving for a foxhole and I saw the flash out of the corner of my eye. So, I get in the foxhole and things lightened up. And I got out of the foxhole and my god, here was a five-gallon gas tank that had been not four foot from me that had exploded because it got hit with shrapnel. And that was the flash that I saw as I was diving in.

The 'trucks' he blew up were in fact horse-drawn carts.

Horse-drawn carts, if you can imagine. And the Germans used a lot of horse-drawn carts. And . . . other than the pineapple grenade that we had, we had Gammon grenades which you could run up to a tank and slap it on and explode. The Gammon grenade was actually plastic. You'd form a ball and stick your finger in and put a cap in it. And . . . that was very effective. I can't quite remember. We had some way of directing the force of the explosion by putting something over the Gammon grenade which directed the force into the tank or whatever we were blowing up. But . . . literally, you have to visualize it, these, these horse-drawn vehicles, you know, were something else. And even, even the payroll wagon was horse-drawn so that it made it pretty damn easy to, to attack them and, and they couldn't, they couldn't run.

. . . We did find, when we were making our progress . . . a tree with a couple machine guns, 50-caliber machine guns in it, which we needed desperately. So we got those down and, and used those. I can remember crawling on my belly as we're moving forward and reaching out and putting my hand on a piece of striated metal, a chunk about that big, striated, and I thought, my god. And then I realized, it was a piece of the shell from the, the artillery from the ocean that come all the way inland and blown up. And it was a piece of the shell.

Stretcher-bearer Private Lester Atwell was another infantryman to experience the worst of shell-fire:

There came towards us, as if splitting the night sky, an enormous gathering shriek and a jolting, deafening crash. I had taken a few steps on hearing the scream begin; as usual I was looking for a comfortable place to fall. But the scream had come like a thousand furious whistles, so fast and loud, I fell over any place, landing on my side, burying my head in my arm. The explosion pounded me and the earth all about. I had time afterward to say, 'My God! Russ, are you—?' when another long, flying scream started through the sky, coming straight down at us. I banged my head into the snow as the explosion roared out with a blinding light and with what seemed like a great hissing of the snow. For a moment I waited, holding my breath, hearing the shrapnel flying angrily about, striking the building and the saplings around it.

Another shell had started for us and I found myself trying to shrink through the snow, to press my body by main force down into the earth. The roaring explosion deafened me. Shrapnel was flicking and pinging against the trees and the building, dropping into the snow. There was a long moment of silence.

His story continues a few days later:

New Year's Day, Rondu . . . moving forward – I heard Don Stoddard saying to the man next to him, 'This is called the Forest of the

Ardennes.' The cold evening air, the snow, the trees – everything turned blue, as if about us deepening veils of that color were sifting down. Somewhere in the distance shells were falling. The road turned and we emerged into a small, flat, open stretch of country. A roaring explosion went off. There was a confused outcry from the men.

'Hey! What's happening here? Look at that! Way out there!' In the indigo twilight, something burned red-gold like a cannon ball. 'That's an ammunition dump!'

'The hell it is! That's one of our ammo trucks – it hit a mine!'

A barrage of tracer bullets streaked over our heads, and there came the whistling, loud crash of a German shell landing very near us in the field. While the enemy shells continued to come in, the two big trucks began to execute a full turn on the narrow icy road, going into reverse, coming forward, going into reverse, coming forward. At last, at snail's pace, the trucks headed back out of the clearing. Some of the men had dropped to the floor; others, standing, pounded on the side rails, shouting for the driver to get up speed . . . there was no plan. No one knew what to do. My stomach suddenly went into knots. In the same place as before, the trucks halted and waited stupidly.

'What the f— is this?' the men were shouting. 'They're zeroing in on us! Let's get the hell down!' A few started to climb over the side, but another barrage of tracer bullets drove them back.

From below us on the road an officer's voice cried, 'Don't get down! Stay where you are!' Large shells whizzed and smashed about us, sending up explosions of snow and great spinning clods of earth. 'My God! Don't you think we'd better jump down?' I asked Phil Schaeffer.

Someone hopped into the lead-off Jeep and it suddenly spurted ahead, bumped off the road into the field, cutting a wide curve in the smooth snow. With one arm raised, the driver made circles over his head, looking drunk or highly nonchalant. After an astonished moment, I realized it was a signal for us to follow, for we started up and lurched crookedly down off the road into the field with half the excited men yelling, 'Get us the hell out of here! Get goin'!' While the other half shouted frantically, 'No!

No! For Cristsake, they're taking us right into it!' The truck, carefully following the curving lines made by the Jeep's tires headed for a narrow line of bushes and saplings that bordered the intersecting road. If we can only make those trees, I found myself saying. If we can only get out of sight! Behind us the barrage had intensified. We smashed through the bushes and bumped crazily down onto the other road.

For me, following upon any such unexpected crisis, there always came a space of mental blankness. Around me the men were still chattering excitedly, holding a post-mortem, 'We ran into our own road block! The whole road must have been mined!' Darkness came fast, but we continued down the side road with no plan, it seemed, except to set as much space between us and the German artillery as possible. Gradually everyone settled down.

One of the 'perks' of battle – for all the troops but especially the infantry who were often first on the spot – was loot. Private Atwell and his buddies had many a good find, though as he describes, it often had to be jettisoned afterwards:

Almost everyone had loot of some sort. Even Phil had an onyx inkwell he had picked up in a previous town. Its pen-holder was formed by the brass antlers of two stags' heads. 'What am I doing taking something like this?' he asked after having it a few days. 'Am I a thief?' It was his only piece of loot and he abandoned it, disturbed by the thought that he could not return it.

Usually, leaving a town, the infantrymen were loaded down with bottles of wine, books they could not read, clocks, statuettes, pictures. They carried them along, and then as the hike grew lengthy, they'd begin to drop them. For miles in the snow on the sides of the road, you'd see a trail of books, ornaments, carving sets and little clocks. Generally, the officers were just as avid and as guilty as the men. Advance housing parties made hay while waiting for the battalion to arrive; then the line-company boys poured through the houses, working excitedly in teams, ripping out drawers and scattering the contents on the floor, smashing locked chests with the butts of their rifles, overturning tables and bookcases. By law, men were allowed to take as souvenirs only captured German Army equipment, but frequently, with a superior officer's connivance and signature, chests of silverware were sent home, silver dishes, banquet cloths, mother of pearl opera glasses, cameras, jewelry, ancient dress sabers – everything from paintings to thimbles – and this while we were still in Allied territory.

Silly Willy . . . showed me a six- or eight-piece tortoise-shell desk set he had just picked up. 'A thing of beauty,' he said reverently, taken with the phrase, but not quite sure what a desk set was: the long letter-opener and the rocking blotter were mysteries to him. He showed me also two gilt-edged missals with red velvet backs and ivory covers carved with chalices and roses. They looked as though they had never been used, and the script inside was in Latin and German. What Silly was going to do with them, he didn't know, but he and his assistant had 'bags full of stuff' out in the ambulance, the cab of which was plastered with reclining pin-up girls, all legs and brassieres; the wife of neither was anywhere in evidence.

UNDER ATTACK

The Allied infantry bore the brunt of the Germans' unexpected offensive. In mid-December Hugh Kingery of the 106th was among men assigned to take over the 2nd Infantry Division's positions in the Siegfried line . . .

. . . Just, place for place, billet by billet, which they had been using. And they were assigned to another sector, because they were gonna make a move on the Germans in a sector to the south of us.

. . . [The] Germans had backed up and they were licking their wounds. And we were running out of supplies and waiting on more to catch up to us, you know. And so, they said, you know well you guys, try to walk around and try to get conditioned. It's early you know. Flex your muscles a little. And clean your gun, whatever you had to do to get ready for attack or whatever you get ordered to do.

We pulled up on the line on the 12th and sure enough you could hear all the guns and screaming mimis, and shells coming over us on the 16th. And those were the Germans coming after us . . . a complete surprise, a total complete surprise. A lot of folks claimed that they knew they were coming, but our head command didn't know. We weren't ready for them. And we were guarding a twenty-six mile tract, one division. And they brought about ten divisions through us . . .

I went with Creel up to the front, where the infantry was. And they'd been shelled very long. I don't know about any injuries or deaths or whatever, but they demolished a lot of stuff. A lot of debris around.

I wasn't enjoying the Howitzers at all . . . anyway we got orders to pack up, we're gonna move so we got our gear, geared up and in our trucks and all and equipment all together and we were gone and I didn't know where we were going and they did know where we were going because they kept running into new directions . . . and I thought what in the world is going on here. We found that the Germans were behind us so they were in a hurry to get west. They weren't too worried about us, yet. But then they knew they only had about a half a division come out. They could take those off of recruits or something. But, we didn't know that see, and so, come daylight one morning we were bottled up in a dead end street . . . that was blocked by German troops somehow that went ahead of us. And this warning came up we had pulled our Howitzers up off the road for several units, side by side, just a beautiful tract you know. And wait for them, our equipment up, off the side of the road. And sure enough here come these Howitzers, so but, you know coming over, and they were 88s. Boy they rained death and destruction on that draw there. But we were downhill from them, uphill from them and didn't catch anything. But Creel said, let's get out of here boys. I think I know another way out. So about 20 of us took off in another direction . . . he had a compass and he had a map and he knew some of the area. We didn't know where we could go.

We were on foot now. That's the way it was. So we were lightly dressed, field jackets and no mess kits or anything. I had a spoon in my pocket, a spoon hanging in the frame out there in the side room out there and . . . we went over hill and dale trying to skirt the wooded section but we were in a field and all the time getting

raked by machine gun fire and it was tracer bullets. They were
.50-calibers I guess. And . . . the tracer things. You know . . . what
they're shrieking at. And they weren't, they weren't trying to kill
us altogether, just got a little burst. And I think they'll probably
run out of ammunition too . . . so we dropped our guns and had
about a hundred yard walk up to this tank . . . so they frisked us
and took the stuff off us. They were a polite bunch of soldiers
really. Tough-looking guys but they were following orders and
they wound us up and decided they were done with us, they
couldn't make sense of what we were saying and we couldn't
make sense of what they were saying. But they aimed us, one red
crew took us off on our trail, off to the side of where we were.
And steered us on to a small road and we were alone for a while
until they ran into another column from another road and then
another column and pretty soon we were about six wide and a
mile long, heading east into Germany.

At 'Dead Man's Ridge' near the Meuse, men like Ed Jeziorsky of the 44th
Infantry Division were also under attack from artillery fire:

On December 17th . . . when we first heard that the Germans
[were] counterattacking . . . we were immediately alerted and
it was not the next day, it was within hours that we were at the
airfields, but the airfields were socked in and we could not
get across on December 24th, Christmas Eve Day, we were on
the runway and it began, fog began lifting and they served us
Christmas dinner on the runways. We got aboard the ships and
we flew on over and then we were immediately began being
trucked on up into the battle area. We were put on the Meuse
river . . . and the orders were that, we stay here, they do not pass
us. They stop here.
   I crossed the line of departure at eight o'clock that morning
and my only change was I asked Merritt to leave my light
machine-gun behind. I didn't, I [left it] in the deep snow with
the tripod it would have been ineffective anyway. We left it with
another squad and took that squad's BAR, Browning Automatic
Rifle, and I had one BAR on my left flank, I had one on the
right flank, and we had fire, fire movement there. I'm not an

overly religious person . . . We came under artillery fire, we were probably, oh, a thousand yards into our attack and Jerry artillery fire started coming in aerial burst. And then I keep yelling for the men to spread out, spread out, spread out further, spread out further, I just lost one man. A boy by the name of Wooten who had his foot severed by a piece of shrapnel . . .

But any, any rate, we kept moving, I kept the guys moving, and we were doing real well. And then more artillery joins in and it's American artillery. In that deep snow we couldn't have gone that quickly, yet we had. So you know, our own artillery was helping them out, but ah, we were in aerial bursts and they cracked very closely to me . . . I felt the breeze, and ah, I stopped. And how long I stopped I don't know. Maybe a second or two, or three or four. But the guys were moving and with the move and a voice says, 'Don't move'. It might have been my conscience, yeah it probably was. How long I stood there I don't know. Again, I started taking another step a voice says, 'Don't move!' Louder this time. Just then, *whisht*, right in front of me, comes up vapor. A piece of shrapnel had been spinning in front of a suspended end, hot steel hit the stuff and the steam came up. I'd have walked right into it. Like I say, I don't know, it might have been St Mike sitting on my shoulder or whatever. But that, that, that's you'll understand, I'm telling you true. As I can, it actually happened. But any rate, we took, we took the objective.

The British were also fighting alongside the Americans at the Meuse, as a result of Montgomery's rapid reaction to von Rundstedt's threat:

It was British armour and infantry which captured the two villages south of Rochefort on Wednesday, and yesterday another British force joined in the attack on the Americans' right. East of Marche they pushed the Germans back nearly a mile, with a series of thrusts into the hills along a five- to six-mile front.

British troops have actually been fighting in the Rochefort sector since Christmas Day, but they were holding defensive positions in the Meuse valley behind the American 1st Army several days before that.

When the Germans broke through in the first weekend of the

their offensive, Field-Marshal Montgomery at once brought British divisions south in case the Americans needed them and, as the German threat developed, the roads leading back into Belgium were packed with British convoys day and night. It was remarkable how quickly and efficiently we moved thousands of troops with all their guns, tanks, ammunition and engineering supplies. The Belgians lined the roads and cheered the Tommies, as the convoys moved towards the front.

The troops forgot about their Christmas plans, and in rain and sleet they dug defensive positions in the valley of the Meuse. The men who had helped to liberate Belgium were determined that they would not let the Germans come back. But, as it turned out, the main German assault toward Liège was held by American troops alone, and until Christmas Day the British forces had only the role of long-stop. By then the Germans had captured Rochefort, and had sent a series of armoured columns probing towards the Dinant sector of the Meuse, but at Ciney and Celles the British and Americans caught them. The Germans were stopped, and most of them were surrounded. We're counting the wreckage in this area west of Rochefort now, and we've already counted lying there, derelict and abandoned, 81 German tanks, seven assault guns, 74 other guns, and 405 vehicles. In this action the Germans lost the bulk of one Panzer division and the westward thrust towards the Meuse was finally stooped.

Since then the Germans in this sector have been driven back 12 miles. Since then we have held the initiative, and now the Germans' northern flank is being heavily attacked. With the British on the offensive as well, the attack now extends along a 25-mile front, from Marche almost up to Stavelot.

Attached to the 30th Infantry Division was the Eighth 23rd Tanks Destroyers Battalion, whose number included George Wichterich:

We went into this town and we knew that there were Germans in there so we went in, house-to-house, trying to find if there was anybody in these houses. We got in this one house and a shell hit the barn in the back of the building, knocked the whole wall down on top of us and cut my neck in the back, knocked the barn down, killed the cow in the barn, but this was a gun that they took a Tiger Tank and they put a 15-millimeter gun, big mortar gun on it to fire, you couldn't, there was no turret so you couldn't shoot it with a turret, you had to turn the whole Tiger Tank around about an eighty-ton tank and you could just about see the shell coming and that's how I got wounded. Usually artillery, you could hear it whistle, you could hear different whistling sounds, except for a mortar, a mortar is just like a piece of stove pipe and put a shell in it and you drop it down and it goes out . . . it's a deadly thing cause you don't know it's coming, you can't hear that like artillery. Artillery, the mortar sounds like a bird taking off like a flutter, and all of a sudden a big explosion, and there's many a guy got killed because of that . . .

When they [the Germans] came back with the tanks they overtook our infantry and a lot of our infantry killed some of them and as I said with my gun squads they chased them out of and I was already out after having my Jeep shot out from under me. That infantry was almost wiped out in that counter-attack . . . we went into an area on the outskirts in a town . . . there was snow all over the place about waist deep and we got chased out of there, because another instance of coming in the fog and you could hear the German tanks coming, because of the *clinkitty-clinkety-clink* coming in and all of a sudden they would appear on the road. Well, we knocked the first tank out and eventually they overran the infantry and we were able to dismantle our guns . . . so we got out and left the guns there and we went back, we got in the Jeep and drove back.

In the fog, aiming was hit and miss. Equally, there was always uncertainty about what the enemy would do:

Lieutenant Springfield on the other side of town, he did a lot of wiping out of the opposition with the position he had, because they were coming around the hillside and didn't know he was there, they came through there with a truck a half-track full of ammunition with a red cross on the side of it, supposedly an ambulance, but it didn't work out that way, it was loaded with artillery shells . . . we shot it with the three-inch gun and the whole thing exploded . . .

BASTOGNE

Like Eugene Madison of the 501st Parachute Infantry Regiment, many men were rushed to Bastogne to help the beleagured American troops:

> We left at night and they took us in these big cattle trucks up there. We drove all night and got into Bastogne about daybreak the next morning. We'd been strafed by a Messerschmitt and one thing and another. The drivers of these trucks were what you call the 'Red Ball Express' they were a coloured unit, they were truck drivers, and they pulled in those big cattle trucks, big long trucks – had sides on the trucks but they were open – it was cold, my goodness it was cold. We got strafed just after daybreak the next morning, a Messerschmitt came over and our driver disappeared. Never saw him again. One of the boys in the truck said he could drive it and he got back in the convoy and we came on into Bastogne . . . never saw that driver again . . .
>
> We got in there about 8 o'clock, unloaded and went on down into the town. It got colder and colder, it was foggy in the morning when we got there – we had a dense fog and we got in a fight with some Germans on the way down into town. One of the boys in the platoon was killed there on that first morning . . .

By this time the 101st Airborne Division was confident of holding Bastogne, aware that tanks from Patton's Army were close to them, and encouraged by General McAuliffe's holiday message: MERRY CHRISTMAS! This is how the news reached US troops in the pages of *Stars and Stripes* on 4 January:

101st – TREATED ON COGNAC AND COURAGE
GOT McAULIFFE'S ORDER ON YULE EVE

Stars and Stripes *Paris Bureau*

Brigadier General Anthony C McAuliffe's own story of how he replied 'Nuts' to the Germans, who demanded the surrender of his outnumbered, surrounded 101st Airborne Division, was revealed yesterday.

Told in a dramatic order of the day, the General's fighting explanation was hectographed on the battlefield and distributed to men of the 101st Airborne on Christmas Eve, after the division had been fighting with ammunition dropped by parachute and treating its wounded on cognac and courage.

A copy of the order was brought back by a glider pilot evacuated when the siege was lifted, and obtained by the *Stars and Stripes* last night. The text follows:

'What's Merry about all this, you ask? We're fighting – it's cold – we aren't home. All true but what had the proud Eagle Division accomplished with its worthy comrades of the 10th Armored Division, the 705th Tank Destroyer Battalion and all the rest? Just this: we have stopped cold everything that has been thrown at us from the north, east, south and west. We have identifications from four German Panzer Divisions, two German Infantry Divisions and one German Parachute Division. These units, spearheading the last desperate German lunge, were headed straight west for key points when the Eagle Division was hurriedly ordered to stem the advance.

How effectively this was done will be written in history; not alone in our Division's glorious history but in World History. The Germans actually did surround us, their radios blared our doom. Their Commander demanded our surrender in the following impudent arrogance:

December 22, 1944 – To the USA Commander of the encircled town of Bastogne:

The fortune of war is changing. This time the USA forces in and near Bastogne have been encircled by strong German armored units. More German armored units have crossed the River Our near Ortheville, have taken Marche and reached St Hubert by passing through Romores-Sibret-Tillet. Libramont is in German hands.

There is only one possibility to save the encircled USA troops from total annihilation: this is the honorable surrender of the encircled town. In order to think it over, a term of two hours will be granted with the presentation of this note.

If this proposal should be rejected, one German Artillery Corps

To save the infantry, Allied tanks of the US 3rd Army move relentlessly towards Bastogne during the final drive to relieve the town. Despite the pleas of the enemy commander, McAuliffe refused to surrender, rebuffing his advances with the famous riposte of 'Nuts'.

and six heavy AA Battalions are ready to annihilate the USA troops in and near Bastogne. The order for firing will be given immediately after this two hours' term.

All the serious civilian losses caused by this Artillery fire would not correspond with the well-known American humanity.
(signed) The German Commander

To which the reply was made
22 December 1944 – To the German Commander:
NUTS!
(signed) The American Commander

Allied Troops are counterattacking in force. We continue to hold Bastogne. By holding Bastogne, we assure the success of

the Allied Armies. We know that our Division Commander, General Taylor, will say: 'Well Done! We are giving our country and our loved ones at home a worthy Christmas present and being privileged to take part in this gallant feat of arms are truly making for ourselves a Merry Christmas.
NAC McAuliffe
Commanding Officer

As Captain Don Witty wrote a few days later:

A trip over the road into Bastogne would convince anyone of the determination with which the 3rd Army soldiers are fighting. Across France you became accustomed to seeing the debris of last stands or particularly bitter fighting, but such piles of rubble were usually scattered at intervals. Not on the road to Bastogne. The narrow dirt-track is pockmarked yard by yard with shell-holes, and the ditches and fields littered with personal equipment and with battered and burned-out vehicles, both German and American. Belgian civilians wander about their shattered farm-buildings, dazed and uncertain by the speed and fury of the fighting. Dead animals cover the ground, and you are almost surprised to see a live and healthy pig trotting up the road.

After the event, McAuliffe himself, writing on 3 January, had plenty to say about his defence of Bastogne and the conduct of the troops. Most of all he resented the idea that he and the 101st had been 'rescued':

It didn't occur to us, until it was all over, that the eyes of the world were on the 101st Airborne Division and the attached armour during the defence of Bastogne. The first thing we heard was that we'd been 'rescued' by the 4th Armoured Division. Now I, and everyone else in the 101st, resent the implication that we were rescued or that we needed to be rescued. When General Taylor arrived on the 27th the first thing he asked me was what kind of shape we were in. I told him, 'Why, we're in fine shape: we're ready to take the offensive.' General Taylor said: 'I should have known it, but all that stuff I read in the newspapers was beginning to worry me just a little.' The fact is we were thinking

As the battle progressed, towns such as Wiltz in Luxembourg were reduced to ruins that became ideal hiding places for enemy snipers and shelters for the wounded. Lightly armed search patrols scoured empty buildings looking for people, spare food and other supplies.

about what a tough time the Kraut was having. We weren't alarmed about our own position at all. After all, we'd deliberately jumped into that kind of position in Normandy and Holland.

For the first three days of the battle of Bastogne there was fog: on the fourth day it cleared. After that, 'terrific' was the only word that described the air support we got from those Thunderbolts. Those are the 'gutsiest' fellows I ever saw. The Air Support Officer we had was a captain named Parker. He really knew his stuff and ran a great circus. He called himself Maestro. He has a fine gift for salty language, and when he was telling those airplanes what to do there was always a big crowd of soldiers standing around just listening to him talk. Finally it got so bad we had to ripe him off. But Maestro Parker and those Thunderbolts really did a job for us.

For the first three days we gave the Germans the licking of their lives . . . the Troop Carrier Command did a great job on the supply end too. They brought us all the ammunition, rations, and other equipment that we needed. Our morale was always tops. Good morale is just as contagious as panic can be. We had several thousand reinforcements – attached troops – and they caught the infectious courage of the old men of the 101st right away. Airborne Divisions always have good morale. We were fortunate enough to have been associated with the First and Sixth British Airborne Division up around Arnhem. They don't come any better. No one should be surprised at what the 101st Airborne Division did at Bastogne. That's what should be expected any time of airborne troops. With that kind of troops I, as a commander, can do anything.

OTHER GALLANT STANDS

One of many gallant stands was made by an American infantry regiment near Stavelot, where on 20 December they succeeded in stopping a crack SS armoured column:

When night came, the wreckage of 17 German half-tracks lay crumbled along the village road and through the fields, and each half-track had its quota of SS dead. But in the night the Panzer Division sent out its pincers to outflank the infantry and by morning they were almost encircled. Only one free road was open to enter or leave their line and that was a narrow winding road and it was under machine-gun fire. In the morning I was guided down that narrow road to see the SS spearhead being blunted. There was a heavy mist lying on the moors, and for a time it was impossible to see more than ten yards ahead or ten yards on either side of the road. Hidden somewhere in the mist, tanks and anti-tank guns were barking at each other. If it was visualised, firing it must have been very close. We pulled up at a small farm-house about half a mile from the fighting. A sentry stepped up and his eyes roved over our uniforms bit by bit – battle jacket, trousers, boots badges, then there was a slow, thorough inspection of our papers. We went into the farm-house where the colonel was sitting by a red-hot stove. 'Sorry about the hold up,' he said, 'but there are so many Germans around in American uniforms – four of them came past the command post just ten minutes ago and got away in the mist. By the way, which road did you come?' I told him. 'Um,' he said, 'so it's still open.'

We went over to a map standing on an old-fashioned sideboard and he lit a candle so I could see it. 'He we are,' he said, 'and here are the Germans so far as we know – here and here and at the bridge down here and two of his tanks were seen over there, and a machine-gun post fired on one of our Jeeps just here.' He smiled. 'Looks like they're trying to get all round us, but getting round us won't get rid of us, and maybe that's something they haven't figured on.'

By the New Year, the US First Army at the Meuse was sufficiently recovered from its pounding by the Panzers to go on the attack. In this offensive action the infantry, working as ever with the armoured divisions and artillery, played a critical part:

The Fifth and Sixth Panzer armies chose the US First as their attacking point and hammered a 50-mile salient in its line. Technically they tore the Army's front line apart, they hit its communications, overran its weak divisions, threw overwhelming weight against its best divisions, threw paratroops and spies behind its lines, and set its operations chiefs and its divisional commanders a most serious situation to face.

Every man and every officer stood the test – some by quick thinking, some by swift improvisation, some by good planning, some by just sheer bravery, and some by guess and by God; but they all came through. I know. I saw it.

For 18 days they took the most savage pounding that SS divisions and Panzer corps could inflict, and then they returned to the attack.

It went in at 8.30 in the morning under a heavy snow-cloud that deprived the men of air support or even air observation for the guns that began to fire on them. It went in through snowdrifts and up hillsides and through forests. It went in down ice-bound roads on which tanks slithered and slipped; it went in against an icy wind that froze your fingers and made chilblains on your face.

Infantrymen, their wet clothes freezing on their bodies, slogged their way through the snow, and uphill – always uphill – to drive the Germans from their observation posts; while the tanks slithered and slipped down the roads to drive the Germans from the villages.

The tanks would fight their way in and flush the Germans out of the villages and the barns, and force them out on the snow-covered fields so the infantry could get at them. Then the Germans' artillery somewhere back in the hills would open fire on the village and we had no air observation to spot the guns. When the fire got too heavy, the tanks would be forced to withdraw. When the gunfire stopped, the tanks would race in again to get there before the German infantry could get back into the cottages. The artillery fire would begin again and force the tanks out. And it would go on like this until forward observers could spot the German guns, and call for counter-battery fire. Then the tanks would slip in again, and the village would be ours.

We took ten villages like that, and by midnight that first day we had also taken 290 prisoners and gained two miles. But by midnight too the snow began again, covering the battlefield with heavy swirling flakes. The day brought the depressing news that there would be another day of hard slogging without air support, and without air observation. By dawn the snow was freezing on the periscopes of the tanks, blinding the gunners and the drivers. It made the advancing infantry white and invisible. It covered the minefields and the enemy pillboxes. By afternoon it became apparent that these American soldiers who had just faced the heaviest 18-day battle that two Panzer armies could provide must also face the heaviest slogging match that winter could force on them.

Ernest J Rooke, a private in 9 Para Regiment, not only endured the harsh conditions of the winter and the battle, but witnessed one of its more horrific incidents:

We later took up defensive positions in various locations in the area of Rochefort and Marche-en-Famenne around the Brussels-Luxemburg highway, usually holding high features with access to the many roads in the area which branched off from the main highway and the town of Marche. The ground was frozen hard beneath the snow and in many places the ground was more rock than earth. Digging-in – a necessity for self-preservation against enemy shellfire and attack – was extremely difficult. At night we went out on patrols for which we were issued with snowsuits which we wore over our full kit. I felt like an Arctic explorer. Our role on patrol was to check out enemy positions, movements, etc, but not to engage the enemy on these occasions. It was quite eerie to be out in the fields on a moonlight night, freezing cold, wind howling, and suddenly see a half-track vehicle appearing out of the blue, keeping fingers crossed until it passed by. I had one bright spot of relief. January 3rd 1945 was my 21st birthday and such was the efficiency of the service that I received a cake from home (not on the day – that would be expecting too much). Cake-making was not mum's forte – it was like a large rock cake but it went down well with a mug of cha in the trench.

A few nights later I was woken in the middle of the night as I was sleeping in my trench. 'Rookie, the line's gone' said the Sergeant. At this stage sections were posted out perhaps 500, 600 even 800 yards or more in front of our main position, communication being with cable and telephone handsets. With a two-man escort I moved out trailing the cable in my hand. After slow progress on rough ground and thick snow I eventually found the break. I handed the end of the wire to one of the escorts instructing him to hold on tight and not to move while I tried to find the other end of the cable in the snow. I was lucky. Having none of the more sophisticated equipment I had to join the two sections of cable with a normal joint bound with tape. I had bared the ends of the wire, made my joint and was just about to tape up when some idiot at the other end decided to test the line. A charge surged through my damp fingers – I was not too pleased. Wow! I could have wakened the dead. I secured the line, checked OK and we returned to our base position. The NCO in charge of our little section was somewhat dilatory in identifying us. Fortunately our comrades were a little dilatory too. It was quite a night, but we didn't see any of the enemy.

By now the Germans were retreating, and we were plugging

some of the gaps in the line. Some of our comrades a little further to our right had some hard fighting and suffered many casualties. For us the patrolling went on for a week or more. One thing I do recollect – our cooks saw to it that we were well-fed under very difficult conditions. Never was hot stew so welcomed. It couldn't have been fun slaving over a hot burner – with your backside freezing. It was very, very cold in the Ardennes in the winter of 1944–45.

For infantrymen like Rooke, the massacre at Bande was an event that would never pass from the memory.

The highway from Brussels to Luxemburg (route N4) passes through Namur, Marche-en-Famenne and Bastogne. Bastogne had of course been very much in the news, and in our thoughts, as we followed the accounts of the heroic stand of the 101 US Airborne Division. Some five miles south-east of Marche-en-Famenne and 17 miles north-west of Bastogne the village of Bande straddles the highway – a few buildings actually fronting on the road with the remainder of the village a few hundred yards north of the road. Following our arrival in Belgium on Christmas Day the Battalion had gradually moved eastwards across the River Meuse to the area of Rochefort and on towards the main highway. About one week after my 21st birthday the Germans were retreating and we moved into Bande.

There were no cheering crowds to greet us – nor was there any noticeable evidence of flagwaving or banner-flying – in fact none of the recognisable signs of liberation. The reasons soon became obvious. As we made contact with the villagers we became aware of their deep distress. As we drank their welcoming hot drinks and exchanged a few words in our schoolboy French we listened in horror to their stories. Gradually as the hours passed and over the following day we learned of the previous two to three weeks.

A week after the start of the German offensive in the Ardennes, German troops arrived in Bande, a few days before Christmas. On Christmas Eve (which was a Sunday) all the male residents of Bande and the neighbouring village Grune were round up by the SS and taken away for questioning. The younger men aged

17 to 30 years, about 30 in number, had been taken away to a place apart from the older men. One young man escaped from his captors and made his way back to the village with the news that the young men had all been shot.

We were taken to a building where we saw the victims – rows of young men laying on the straw on the floor. The bodies were frozen stiff – it was a gruesome sight. Every man had been shot at the back of the neck behind the ear. It looked as if the murderer was probably standing just alongside the victim when firing the fatal shots. I was deeply shocked by what I saw, as were my comrades. Most of us had seen other victims of war – we had seen crushed bodies, men who had suffered severe injuries, but this was callous, calculated killing of young men – civilians.

As we talked with the villagers we tried to show by gestures and the few words of their language we knew just how we felt. We could only shake a hand, put an arm round a shoulder. Even if we had had a command of their language we would have found it impossible to find words to express our feelings. After the bodies had been identified (and this must have been a most distressing task for the relatives) soldiers from our Battalion placed the dead young men in coffins draped with the Belgium flag. A few days later the coffins were taken in our transport to the village church and then to the little cemetery on the outskirts of the village. Sections of our battalion acted as pallbearers, others followed the relatives in the procession; others carried the coffins into the cemetery. The victims were buried together; later their bodies would be transferred to family graves.

A few days later our Battalion was on the move to Roermond in Holland to hold a defensive position on the River Maas.

THE TURN OF THE TIDE

The US 82nd Airborne, meeting the Nazi thrust, turned the enemy's own guns on them and went on to retake the village of Cheneux. Their story, told in *Yank* magazine, typifies the courage and daring of the infantry:

The meeting [between B Company and Germans] took place on the hilly road that led down into this Belgian village. B Company of the First Battalion started out at 15.00 to look over the town, which was reported to be lightly held by the Germans. That was an optimistic estimate. When the Americans got within half a mile of the town they were promptly tied down by Jerry flackwagons which came out to greet them. Lacking artillery and tanks destroyer support and armed only with M-1s, light machine guns, flak grenades, and bazookas, B Company was in no position to start trading punches. Regimental headquarters was notified of the situation, with an urgent request to send something to get the German flackwagons off B Company's tail. Just about that time somebody hit on the idea of sending a previously captured Jerry half-track, mounting a .77, in as a pinch-hitter until our own T-Ds and artillery arrived. A hurried call was sent out for five volunteers to man the German vehicle.

For three hours the Americans operated their one-vehicle armoured patrol up and down the hilly road that led into the German-occupied village. Seven Jerry flackwagons, mounting 20mm guns, and several heavy machine guns, were deployed around the edge of the village, well-hidden by thick underbrush and a heavy ground fog that reduced visibility to 100 or 200 feet. Most of the time Kelly, who was at the sights of the .77, was firing almost blind, aiming in the direction of the spot from which the 20mm came. And machine-gun tracers were coming. Once, however, the men on the half-track saw a column of German infantrymen coming down the road toward B Company. Kelly raked their ranks with his .77, forcing them to abandon the attack. Another time Hoover, the BAR man, spotted a Jerry machine-gun nest and silenced it.

Just before dusk, a blast from a 20mm hit the brace of Kelly's gun. He got several pieces of flak in his lower lip and chin. At that point, Snow, the guy who used to clerk for the board of education back in Los Angeles, started doubling in brass. He maneuvered his vehicle into position against the tracers coming from the enemy 20mm or machine gun, then moved back to take Kelly's place on the .77. A roaming German half-track got into Snow's sights on the crossroads just outside of the village and went up in flames and there were two probables on machine-gun nests but Snow couldn't be certain because of the bad visibility.

Finally, with his ammunition almost gone and Kelly in need

of medical attention, Snow turned the captured Nazi vehicle around and headed back to the CP to resume his regular duties as regimental clerk.

While Snow and Kelly were running interference for them, elements of B Company moved up for a closer look at the village. A lieutenant leading a squad on a wide swing around a German strongpoint was hit by sniper fire, leaving his outfit without either an officer or a noncom. Cpl Curtis Aydelott, an S-2 section leader from Clarksville, Tenn, had joined up with the patrol squad when he was separated from his own outfit in the battle confusion. So Aydelott stepped into the lieutenant's spot. Aydelott's usual duties are not with a line company; he ordinarily goes on patrols or follows in after an attack to roll Germans for identification papers. He went along on this deal to bring back any Jerry prisoners but instead was thrown in a spot where he had to double as a line noncom.

Ordering a machine-gunner to cover them, Aydelott and a bazooka man skirted a house on the edge of the village and flanked a flakwagon parked there. The GI with the bazooka opened up on the Jerry vehicle, setting it on fire, while Aydelott sprayed it with his tommygun. None of the five-man Nazi crew escaped.

Aydelott's helmet was shot off his head during the advance but he was uninjured. He got another helmet from a sergeant who had been shot in the chest. The sergeant told him he didn't think he would be needing it again very soon.

After determining the strategy of the German occupying force, Lt Col William E Harrison, the battalion commander of San Diego, Calif, ordered an attack on the town that night. The battalion kicked off at 22.00, after a ten-minute artillery barrage with two T-Ds for support.

As so often in the Ardennes, bad weather intervened and hampered progress, but the men of the Allied infantry were undeterred:

It had started to snow and a thick veil of white covered the huge fir trees which lined the hill road leading into town. B Company, advancing on the right side of the road, yelled over to C Company on its left: 'The last ones in town are chicken. Get the lead out of your tails, you guys.'

C Company made contact first, taking on a column of 100 German infantrymen who were supported by 19 flakwagons, several tanks and an assault gun. The first wave was pinned down by murderous fire from Jerry advance machine-gun emplacements. But then when our second wave came up, it overran the enemy positions and wiped out both guns and crews. S/Sgt Frank Dietrich of Detroit emptied his tommygun on a machine-gun crew and when the last Jerry started to break and run for it, Dietrich threw the tommygun at him. The shock of being hit by the gun slowed up the fleeing German just long enough for another C Company man to finish him off with a BAR burst.

Meanwhile B Company had attacked the flakwagons with their bazookas and hand grenades mixed in with spine-freezing Texas cowboy yells and self-exhortations to 'get those bastards.' One B Company man finished off a Jerry flakwagon gunner who wouldn't surrender. The Kraut was injured but he still leaned over his gun, firing at the advancing Americans. Suddenly one tough battle-maddened GI made a direct break for the flakwagon, yelled, 'You German sonofabitch,' jumped up on the vehicle and stabbed the Jerry with a knife until he fell over dead. Another B Company man, a staff sergeant, had sneaked up on a flakwagon ready to throw a grenade inside when he was hit in the left arm and side by small arms fire. Unable to pull the pin, he called to another GI to do it for him. Then he turned and hurled the grenade into the flakwagon.

The battalion got into the first building on the outskirts of town that night, set up their CP there and dug in. The Jerries launched a five-hour counterattack supported by flakwagons and a tank. The counterattack finally failed but only after the tank had hit the CP three times.

As elsewhere, the 82nd encountered Germans disguised in American uniforms. They were very nearly taken in by the deception:

During daylight hours the Yanks and Jerries traded punches

at long range with nothing particularly startling save for the experience of S/Sgt Edgar Lauritsen, a headquarters company operations sergeant from Limestone, Maine, and Pfc Theodore Watson of New York, a medic. While a German tank was shelling the CP, two Jeep-loads of soldiers in American uniforms – a captain and eight enlisted men – pulled up in front, got out and started walking around the other side of the building toward the German lines. Watson hollered to them that they were going too far but they ignored his warning. That aroused the medic's suspicions. He demanded to know what outfit they were from.

'The Ninety-ninth,' said the captain, continuing his route.

Sgt Lauritsen, who had just come out of the CP, caught the tone of the conversation, got suspicious himself, and shouted, 'What outfit in the Ninety-ninth?'

'Headquarters,' was the captain's slightly guttural reply as he continued walking toward the enemy lines. The accented answer convinced Lauritsen. He hollered, 'Halt!' and the eight American-uniformed strangers started running, Lauritsen opened up with his M-1. The captain staggered, shot in the back, but his companions grabbed him and hurried toward a steep embankment which led down into the woods.

The rest of the Americans in the CP, attracted by the firing, thought Lauritsen had gone flakhappy and was shooting Yanks. They were all set to drill Lauritsen himself when they realised what had happened. By that time the eight fugitives had escaped into the woods, presumably making their way back to German lines.

But the payoff on the entire spy deal was the deception the same German captain pulled on an American captain back at the regimental CP just before he was spotted by Lauritsen and Watson. The two Jeeps, loaded with the eight Germans who were wearing mud-spattered American mackinaws and carrying M-1 rifles, stopped in front of the CP.

'Hey, captain,' the German captain yelled to an American officer standing outside. 'I'm from the — Division. Have you seen any of our tanks around here today?'

'Yeh,' the unsuspecting American answered.

'How many?'

'Oh, about four or five.'

'Good. Say, how far is it to such-and-such a place?'

'You can't get down there. The bridge is out.'

'Thanks. By the way, how are things going around here?'

'Aw, they're all screwed up.'

'Well, I've got a good piece of news for you,' the German said. 'I just came up from corps where I heard Patton had driven a spearhead through the Jerry lines yesterday, captured 11,000 Krauts and 230 enemy vehicles.'

'Good,' the American said.

'By the way, Captain, do you have a cigarette?

'Sure,' replied the American officer, pulling out a pack and offering it to his visitor.

'Thanks, Captain,' the English-speaking German in the American uniform called back as he started his Jeep in the direction of the front lines, followed by the second Jeep.

The American officer still insists his visitor spoke perfect English without an accent, used US idioms, and slurred his suffixes like a born New Yorker. He claims most anybody would have been taken in by the imposter.

Regardless of the information the phoney US soldiers carried back to the German lines, it didn't do the Nazis who were here much good. That night the Third Battalion came up the valley and joined with elements of the First Battalion to clear the village. In doing so, they were credited with the destruction of one Mark IV tank and seven flakwagons. The regiment was also credited with the first town in this sector – and possibly along the entire front – to be retaken from the Germans by assault since von Rundstedt's offensive began.

REINFORCEMENTS, REPLACEMENTS AND PRISONERS

Like other British forces, the men of the 1st Battalion the Queen's Royal Regiment were called to act as reinforcements in the battle. Soon after arriving across in Belgium Royston Gumbrell suffered from a bout of malarial fever, but recovered in time to play his part:

Boxing Day dawned with the weather closing in on all fronts, fog descended so thick that anything outside the hospital ward was hardly discernable . . . even the wireless news was one of gloom and despair as we heard that the Germans had broken through on a broad front . . . it was this event that was to change the events of my hospital experience. When approached by the Medical Officer on his morning rounds and the high-ranking commander of the area, who asked all and sundry how they were feeling, etc, I remarked that I was a lot better than I was when admitted three to four days ago. 'Good' was the reply, 'you, you and you can all get up and get dressed. You're discharged. We need all men we can lay hands on.' Whatever jobs we were trained for – head cooks and bottle washers, etc – our job now was to help stem the breakthrough in the Ardennes region of Bastogne.

Within a few hours we were packed into army trucks for the long and tortuous journey from Ostend. Passing through Brussels we eventually arriving [sic] in the City of Louvain, some forty-five or more kilometres from the capital. Throughout the journey, the snow fell quite thick and fog impeded the progress of the convoy. With freezing temperatures, the inactivity in the back of the lorries and although closely packed in, even with heavy army overcoats, heavy woollen army footwear and thick leather army boots, it was so cold I could not feel my feet.

We eventually arrived at the [RHU] known as the Reinforcement Holding Unit . . . the Sergeant Major at our dispersal unit, which was at one time a barracks for German troops, asked why I was so slow in getting down out of the transport lorry, I remarked that I could not stand or move. I told him that my feet felt as if they did not belong to me at all. I was lifted off the tailboard and taken to the medical room whereupon my boot laces and tongues of my boots were cut away to release my swollen feet which seemed to look rather black and blue.

By the morning of the 1st January 1945 I was back on duty, the weather had improved and the Air Force was once again in action on the Ardennes and the German armour was at last pushed back. The 101st American Airborne Forces were relieved and the original front line restored. In a number of towns and villages, a large number of German troops had penetrated masquerading as American forces in uniform with American accents. These were apprehended by various groups of military police and patrols.

On a patrol, late one evening, with a small section of men, we arrested and disarmed four of these infiltrators. My last active patrol took place across the open countryside outside Louvain. A last final fling by German fighters caused heavy damage to our airbase in the Brussels area. Quite a few planes were destroyed on the airfield. Crossing the fields in single file, well spaced out we suddenly heard the unmistakable drone of a German fighter; we were just near the entrance to a farmhouse but how we had the good fortune to escape the plane's machine guns firing at us I shall never really comprehend to this day. I dived with another fellow of the patrol into the rather small doorway with my right foot a few inches out of the doorpost, I suddenly felt a stinging pain in my heel. After the plane had departed, I realised part of the heel of my boot was missing, resulting in a badly bruised heel on one side for a day or two which soon healed . . .

The enemy fought to the bitter end, with heavy fire - often from well-camouflaged positions - constantly holding up the progress of the recovering Allied forces.

To get to Les Tailles, the men of the 84th Infantry Division had to . . . cross some more woods. The German positions were well-camouflaged. The enemy's fields of fire and barrages were well planned to catch us as we came out into the open. At 8am, January 12, Company F and Company G jumped off. As they came out of the woods north of Les Tailles, they were met by very heavy fire and were held up. At 3 in the afternoon, they began to move again. Ten minutes later, Company G and tanks were entering Les Tailles but the opposition was so sharp that the village was not cleared until 9 o'clock. About 140 prisoners were taken.

This happened again and again - we had to fight hard for a place but when we took it we gathered in batches of prisoners . . .

Petites Tailles was a striking example. To get to Petites Tailles, the 1st Battalion had to move across relatively open ground down the Houffalize Road. The enemy was able to bring direct and observed fire on our troops all the time. A continuous effort was made to approach the village from the flanks, but the open terrain made the maneuver difficult. The 1st Battalion jumped off at 8 in the morning, January 12, but the enemy's heavy weapons and tanks held it up all day and inflicted heavy casualties. Under cover of darkness, however, we tried again. The fighting was hard, but Petites Tailles was ours by 9 in the evening. By chance, both Les Tailles and Petites Tailles were cleared at the same time.

In Petites Tailles, we picked up 70 prisoners. Most of them were non-German. The German officers and noncoms had got out while the getting out was good. The others were left to their own fate without orders. By the time they fell into our hands they were meek indeed. In some instances, they would walk in squad column on the street asking for an 'Amerikaner' to surrender to. In at least one case, a group of 20, completely equipped with rifles and machine guns, tacked on to one of our platoons. In the dark, it is not so easy to surrender successfully.

What had happened? In this little village, which cost us so much blood to take, the prisoners were very deceptive. The German officers and noncoms had fled to fight from another village another day. The prisoners we picked up were the 'expendables'. Any one of these prisoners behind a machine gun under tough, experienced German officers or noncoms in the middle of the day was one man. That night, in a prisoner cage, he was another man.

At 8 in the morning, January 13, the 333rd's 2nd Battalion jumped off from Les Tailles for the third time in two days. After taking Collas, a little village southwest of Les Tailles, at 10 o'clock it struck out for the woods. Immediately the terrain became worse than the enemy, though the latter did its best to help. The roads were terrible, barely more than trails. Under the snow, which now had ten days to accumulate, they were invisible. By 12 o'clock, the enemy's activity became more stubborn. By the end of the day, we had penetrated only 500 yards.

The problem of getting through the woods was faced that night. Two narrow trails ran through the woods to Dinez and two special task forces were formed to get through those trails. Both started out at 8 in the morning the next day, January 14.

The woods, snow, cold, and narrow trails made supply,

evacuation, contact, control, and communication a battle of nerves. The only supplies came in by half-tracks. Mortar ammunition had to be carried by hand over two miles. In Odeigne, the 333rd's 2nd Battalion had captured a horse and sled. It held on to them and in these woods the horse and sled were its only means of evacuating the wounded. Radios would not work in the woods and it was impossible to lay wires. Visibility was so poor that it was always like night in the middle of the day. Since a small group of five or six infantrymen worked with one tank, it was hard to put a company or even a platoon together – a troublesome problem for the infantry whenever they worked with armor.

Companies F and G rode light tanks part of the way but progress was too slow that way because the tanks were held up all the time. By pushing themselves to the limit, both task forces were able to move through the entire woods by 4 o'clock in the afternoon. Without stopping once the woods were cleared, Company F attacked Dinez and Company E attacked Wilogne. Surprise paid off again. Both were captured before night was over and about 100 prisoners were taken in Dinez. Most of our casualties resulted from shellfire and frostbite. We were about 4,500 yards from Houffalize.

Meanwhile, on the right flank, in the 84th Infantry Division zone, the enemy was wedged in between the Laroche Road and the Ourthe river. On the whole, progress was much easier, but one minor crisis resulted in perhaps the most unusual experience of the campaign.

The first important objective was Berismenil. At 7.30 in the morning, January 13, the 334th's 1st Battalion moved out from the Laroche Road to take a hill about 1,500 yards [away from] Berismenil. Only sniper fire was encountered and the objective was taken by 11 o'clock. At 2.15 in the afternoon, it went forward again to take another hill about 750 yards northeast of Berismenil – the 334th's 2nd Battalion Commander, Captain James V Johnston, once said wistfully: 'Every time I see a hill, it's going to be our next objective.'

By 6 o'clock in the evening, the 1st Battalion had taken its second hill against light resistance. Nevertheless, the situation was confused because orientation in the dark was difficult. When

a patrol carrying blankets was fired on from the rear, it was clear
that the battalion was almost entirely surrounded by the enemy.
Later that night, a reconnaissance patrol was sent to investigate
the enemy's position south of the hill but failed to return. At
that, the battalion commander, Major Roland L Kolb, decided to
see for himself. Leading another patrol, he suddenly observed a
German command car pull to the base of the hill and halt. Two
men stepped out and began to walk up the hill. When the pair
approached near enough, the patrol jumped out of hiding.

Berismenil itself was captured by the 335th's 2nd Battalion. It
covered 3,000 trackless yards, thereby achieving a considerable
degree of surprise but giving up all possibility of using any
vehicles to back up the attack. Berismenil was captured almost
without opposition. By the end of the day, January 13, the enemy
had been cleared out of approximately half the 84th's zone.

The other half was rapidly cleared out the next day. Nadrin,
a village about 1½ miles southeast of Berismenil, was occupied
by the 334th's 1st Battalion at 11am, January 14. Only some
machine gun and small arms resistance was encountered. At
the same time, the 334th's 3rd Battalion attacked Filly, about
a mile southeast of Nadrin. Tanks and tank destroyers could
not use the roads because they were heavily mined and the
infantry went on alone. Filly was entered at 3.30pm without any
artillery preparation and fully occupied a half hour later. The
3rd Battalion went on to take the last two objectives, Petite-
Mormont and Grande-Mormont, by 7.15pm.

By this time, the bulge was practically a memory and the chief
interest of every commander – company, battalion, regiment, and
division – was now to send out patrols to make the first contact
with the Third Army.

On 29 January, Richard Hottelot of CBS also reported on the virtual end of
the battle, and the infantry's part in it:

On the Western Front this morning the biggest thing is the
infantry attack in the First Army sector in which about one
division is involved. This gives you a good idea how the Western
Front has calmed down. Only two weeks ago this kind of an

attack, in which we advance a few thousand yards and take a few small villages, would have been only a tiny part of the day's operations. One reason for this is the snow – inches of snow that have fallen on top of the already deep drifts. Quite apart from the bitter cold, the snow wears men out when they have to move; loaded down with their heavy winter clothing, their weapons, and their ammunition, it's a great physical strain to mount an attack. Men who lead a column and break a path through fresh snow have to be relieved every hundred yards or so. That's one reason for the lull. The other, and probably the main one, is that the divisions that fought so hard and so well during the German counter-offensive can use a rest. They're drawing extra winter equipment and brushing up on new tactics: the higher staffs are making strategic dispositions, preparing to resume our own winter offensive. Until it comes, it's probable that the Western Front will remain much the same as it is today from the Rhine to the North Sea: constant patrols; short, sharp fire fights, and here and there a larger attack to get more favourable positions.

Almost the final 'fling' for the 84th Infantry Division came in the middle of January, as their history records:

Houffalize was made completely untenable on January 15. At 11.00, the 333rd's 1st Battalion jumped off from Dinez and captured the village of Mont, midway between Dinez and Houffalize, by 14.00. Tanks, infantry and artillery worked together smoothly. At 16.00 the advance was renewed to Hill 430, overlooking Houffalize. It was taken by 17.30 without opposition.

A 33-man patrol, representing all the battalions of the 334th Infantry, left Filly at 11 in the morning, January 15. They crossed the Ourthe in two 400-pound rubber boats, which they carried, at 11.45. The rest of the afternoon was spent in an old mill on the other side of the Ourthe. Just before dark a small patrol went forward as far as the village of Engreux, about 1,000 yards from the Ourthe, where they expected to meet a patrol from the Third Army. They found the village free of the enemy but found no sign of the Third Army's patrol.

Late that night, the patrol received word that the rendezvous had been changed. Starting off again at midnight, the patrol moved out across some more woods and over a 1,200-yard ridge. At 2.30, January 16, in the dead of the night, they stopped at a small Belgian farmhouse. The whole family, papa, mama, a son and a daughter of 22, turned itself into a reception committee. There was bread, butter and hot coffee. The patrol had decided the rendezvous had been changed for a good reason.

That morning, at 9.30, Pfc Rodney Himes, second in command of the patrol, spied a soldier walking outside the farmhouse. Since the patrol had been ordered to stay inside the house, Pfc Himes began to 'bawl him out' and asked him 'what outfit he was from.'

The answer was Troop A, 3rd Platoon, 41st Cavalry, 11th Armored Division, Third United States Army.

The junction was officially achieved at 9.45am, January 16. The bulge was wiped out after 13 days of hard, continuous fighting.

The battle was on the way to being won, and the infantry had played their part. That it was worthwhile was poignantly summed up in this letter from Hershell Scolf to the family of Vernon Leroy Francisco of Company F, 2nd Battalion, 505th Parachute Infantry Regiment, 82nd Airborne Division, who was killed in action on 4 January 1945:

Vernon said to me when we went into the battle on December 18th that he believed it would be the end for him. He wanted me to stay with him when they came. Of course I told him he was just thinking crazy and to stop it because we were going to New York and see all the things that he had told me about and there was no more said. Then after his death, a shell went off too close to me and I lost my memory. Things are coming back to me little by little. It is hard for me to remember. Vernon was shot 15 times by machine-gun bullets. The last thing I heard him say was tell Mother that I died for her so that she would not have to say 'Heil Hitler'.

7
MEDICS!

In the heat of the battle the cry would go up – 'Medics! Medics!' Forward would run the stretcher-bearers, the corpsmen accompanying the troops, to take the wounded to an aid station, often a farm building commandeered for the purpose and marked by the prominent display of a Red Cross flag. There, the doctors and nurses would assess the extent of their injuries and their likelihood of recovery. From the battlefield, wounded men who were thought to be treatable, but who were too badly injured to return quickly to action, were collected, usually by truck, and taken farther back for treatment and, eventually, evacuation.

The weather in the Ardennes often made it difficult for help to get to the injured before they were killed by the cold. As well as 'genuine' casualties, the medics had to deal with conditions exacerbated by the weather, notably men with foot disorders and colds and, inevitably in battle, cases of self inflicted wounds. And there was always the hope of a 'blighty one', a relatively minor, non-fatal wound serious enough to assure a return home.

The story of Eugene Madison of the 501st Parachute Infantry Regiment paints a picture repeated dozens of times over in the Ardennes:

> We were attacking through the woods on the 2nd or 3rd of January
> when I became a casualty and got shot. I was left there in the snow
> about a foot deep and I stayed there about five hours before a
> medic Jeep – one of the boys in my squad when he left me there,
> he said, 'We'll get a medic to you.' It was five hours – I could hear
> it [the medic Jeep] coming through the woods. I attracted their
> attention and they got me out. They said 'We're sure glad we found
> you. That paratrooper down there said he was going to kill us if we
> didn't get you.' He said 'We've been looking for you for a while.'

We were attacking through the woods. An artillery shell came
in and got me in the legs. I had a pair of overshoes on over my
boots. And this boy came back and checked my legs and he said
'You're not going anywhere' – this boy, Pate – so they went on.
Pretty soon he came running back. He didn't have overshoes – we
only had a limited number of them – he said, 'You don't need
these any more' and he took my overshoes off and took off again.
But then later on that evening I got picked up by the medics and I
ended up just outside Paris in a hospital there . . . I was scheduled
to go back, to be evacuated to England but he was an airborne
Lt Col, he was a doctor there in that hospital . . . he told the nurse
'Keep this man here I'll work on him myself right here.' So I
didn't get to go back to England but he got me fixed up.

Private Lester Atwell was a stretcher-bearer who found himself in the thick
of the action, which he describes with graphic detail:

After dinner, there were many casualties. All three litter squads
were rotating on the hauls, and every now and then the walking
wounded came in under their own power, with an arm, or a
leg or a hand bandaged. Preacher and Charlie Heydt, the two
technicians, working under the lantern light, removed the
bandages, shook [sulpher] powder into the wounds, applied
splints and rebandaged, while Warren Troy bent over the litter in
the midst of the work. 'Could I have your name, please? And how
do you spell that last name? What's your rank? Serial number?
What company are you with?' The captain would be standing
there, supervising, giving the diagnosis which Warren wrote on
the tag before tying it firmly to the man's field jacket. That man
was carried to one side, to make room for the next litter under the
glare of the lanterns. Contrary to what I had read and expected,
there was seldom a great deal of blood; the technicians were never
drenched with it, nor was the floor ever slippery because of it.
As soon as the bandaging was done, I moved in, picked up the
equipment and carried it outside. If there was time, I'd quickly
sweep up the pieces of torn and bloody clothing and bandages,
swabs, Carlyle bandage boxes, and burn them in the stove. The

litter cases were attended to first, then came the patients [who were] walking wounded.

'Well, what's the matter with you?'

'Got shot in the ass.'

'Take down yer britches, and le's have a look.'

There were few tears, few big scenes, seldom any cries even when the pain must have been outrageous. When, as frequently happened, the litter-bearers brought in compound fractures, sucking chest wounds, shattered backs, shoulders, necks and so on, Captain Stetner gave over his supervision and worked on those cases himself. In a respite he sometimes delivered a short, clear explanation to the two technicians on the nature of the wounds they had just dressed. During the little lecture, he kept up the roaming back and forth . . .

When the ambulance drove up, I'd lift one end of the litter and carry out the wounded man with anyone who happened to be standing about. As soon as the four litter cases were in, the walking wounded were led out and crowded in along the floor of the ambulance.

Day after freezing day Atwell and the other stretcher-bearers would be ordered to the front, and ever-younger, raw and apprehensive replacements would be brought in to cope with the numbers of casualties:

Finally Sergeant Campbell had his way. In his usual quick, low voice, he gave the orders for the litter-bearers to go out with the companies that morning.

Cursing Sergeant Campbell up and down, carrying extra stretchers, they set off in the snow. I got up and stood looking out the window at the double file of infantrymen going past the door in the great blowing clouds of snow. There came the long wild scream and crash of German 88s, and the double line, thin-looking without overcoats, indistinct in the swirling snow, wavered and sank down flat, then struggled up and went on, heads bent against the wind.

This was 'jumping off' – this cold, plodding, unwilling, ragged double line, plunging up to their knees in snow, stumbling, looking back at the last farmhouse in sight with the Red Cross flag printed in front of it.

While the two thin lines surged forward against wind and snow, a Jeep drove up before the house and deposited a small figure burdened down with the new heavy pack that replacements were given. Lopsided, he carted it up the path, knocked on the door and came in. 'Medics?' he asked.

'Yup,' said Preacher. 'What kin I do for yuh . . . ?'

'I'm – I was told to report here,' was the glum reply. 'I'm a replacement.' He was a small, thin-faced, pimply boy with a pinched, cold, lugubrious face, light hair, and red rims to his eyes. 'Name's Jenkins,' he said in answer to the question. 'No, I just come over. They tol' me to come in here.'

'Guess he better go out with A company,' Sergeant Campbell said in a quick, business-like tone. 'Jenkins, you jes throw your stuff over there in the corner. Jes wear your fiel' jacket, gas mask, helmet, brassard—'

Jenkins was shivering. A hopelessness, a great weary disgust, held him in thrall. 'No, I never done none of this,' he answered listlessly. 'I always worked in a General Hospital. I just come over.'

'Preach,' said Sergeant Campbell, 'better check over his supplies, see he' got everything he needs.'

'All you got to know, Jenkins,' Preacher said, looking through his bag, 'is how to put on a Carlyle bandage and give a shot of morphine. You know how to give morphine?'

'N-n-no. I never gave it.' This I didn't believe, but Preacher showed him how to use the syringe, gave him a supply of ampules, cautioned him about keeping them on his person, secret, tied the brassard on his sleeve for him, shook his hand, and off Jenkins went into the snow.

That night in the aid station he told me he had just caught up to A Company and had only gone a few feet with them when a German 88 screamed in and exploded nearby. There was almost at once the long cry, 'Me-e-ed-ics!' He waited, and when no one appeared, he got up, shaking, ran over through the snow and saw a man with most of his back blown away. Not knowing whether he was going to faint or vomit, Jenkins sank to his knees, and when he did neither, he began in a daze to apply bandages; he then gave the shot of morphine. Before he could get to his feet, there came another explosion and there was another casualty. 'I didn' seem like myself,' he said. 'I got sort of in a daze, putting on bandages, stickin' the needle in.'

Jimmy McDonough's initiation on the frontline was similar to Lester Atwell's experience. 'The first shell comes in and blows a guy's legs right off ... I nearly die. Then after I get him fixed up with one of the other guys, someone yells, 'Eighty-eight!' an' believe me, by that time I knew. I starts diggin' in the snow like a bastid. I didn't know whether to keep my helmet on my head or stick it on me ass.'

Like other troops, Atwell and the other stretcher bearers needed to be aware of enemy action, and of the confusion of battle.

> We went through woods, walking on either side of a winding path. Occasional shells sounded and everyone stiffened, ready to hit the ground. 'Is that ours?' They'd ask. 'Yeah, that's ours. That's goin' out.' Then one would crash much nearer. The men would droop into a crouch, wait a little and go on. We came out into clearings and plunged back into the woods again. The day turned mild; the sun brought out the scent of the pine needles and of the dead leaves that were stirred up.
>
> We came into a square, open place, its walls formed by trees. The grass was tall and we started to move through it on a diagonal ... there was a stamping and crashing in the underbrush that bounded the clearing, and a furious red face emerged, the eyes strained and protruding. 'What company are you?' it was Colonel Mauck, the commander of our regiment. 'C Company Sir!' 'Well, who the hell is leading you? You're supposed to be going this way, not that way!' The diagonal line wavered in indecision. 'Tell that goddam lieutenant to swing – lieutenant! Get your men over here!' Lieutenant Ellis was leading off in the wrong direction. Someone told him and he turned in surprise to meet Colonel Mauck's oaths and shouts. 'Goddam it, you're leading these men straight into the enemy! Get them in here, over this way!' 'Oh! Yes, sir, yessir!' came the singsong nasal voice. 'This way! Follow me-e-e.'

The line started to swing around, when there came at the end of a loud fast whistling scream a tremendous deafening explosion, perhaps two of them. Everyone thudded flat to the tall grass. There was stunned silence for a moment, and then from almost at my elbow came the repeated cry, 'Medics! Medics! Med-i-ics!'

I scrambled up shaking. Little Louden, the ammunition-bearer of our BAR team, was lying on the ground, rolling in pain, grasping one leg. I could hardly believe my eyes. Two men bent over him and the aid man, Farron, came running up.

'Don't crowd up! Stay apart! No bunching up! Louden's hurt!'

'Hey!' Astonishment. 'Lieutenant Ellis is hit too! Hey Lieutenant Ellis is wounded!'

Lieutenant Ellis was some distance from me, near the screen of bushes and trees. With unbelievable quickness, both his and Louden's wounds were dressed – Lieutenant Ellis had been hit in the back – and both men were placed on litters.

'So long guys!' Louden's tough little voice was calling as he was carried off; and then Lieutenant Ellis came by with: 'A million dollar wound! I got a million dollar wound! I'm out!'

Early in the battle, as it became obvious that many men were being lost, and not just from battlefield wounds, divisions such as the 84th Infantry had to act accordingly, ignoring pre-ordained plans:

The doctors also had to improvise. After the first few days of fighting in the Ardennes, it was recognised that the division was losing more men than were coming in. The reinforcements were not available to compensate for our losses to hospitals. The only way to meet the deficit was to send out fewer men. Roughly half the admissions to the 309th Medical Battalion's 'clearing station' were non-battle casualties and it was decided that many of these men could be salvaged without evacuation from the division. The largest group of non-battle casualties were foot disorders and colds.

The Medical Battalion was hampered in the efforts to meet the problem by a 'table of organization' which was obviously not drawn up with the extraordinary situation in the Ardennes in

mind. Nothing could be allowed to interfere with the evacuation
of the wounded, the battalion's primary mission. The clearing
station had a normal bed capacity for 25 cases only. Army policy
allowed the clearing station only three days to return to duty
those patients who did not have to be evacuated. The battalion
was unable to divert any equipment or personnel, which were the
minimum necessary to care for battle casualties, for the special
treatment of non-battle casualties.

'On the spot' training was also necessary, in this case for unsuspecting
bandsmen, with great success:

> In a large castle in Durbuy, Belgium, a provisional 'convalescent
> Center' was set up. The officers in charge were taken from
> the clearing station but the personnel was made up of the
> division band. The members of the band were given a complete
> course in medical aid to enable them to take over the wards.
> A mess sergeant, two cooks, and kitchen equipment were
> borrowed from other units. Mess equipment was obtained by
> Military Government. The Ninth Army furnished additional
> blankets and cots. Everything else was improvised. As a result,
> the convalescent center was able to care for 300 patients at once
> and the clearing station was able to return as many as 40 per cent
> of all admissions to duty. Had these men been evacuated, the
> interval between their treatment and their return to duty would
> have been much longer.

Medics themselves were often also in great danger, as this report in *Stars and
Stripes* of 29 December highlights:

NAZIS SLAUGHTER 61 CAPTIVES –
HIDDEN MEDICS ESCAPE SLAUGHTER
By Hal Boyle, Associated Press Correspondent
With American Troops on Siegfried Line Dec 26 (delayed)

For 12 hours, 30 American medics, who had been caught in a
street battle for a small town, hid in a church listening to Nazi SS

Panzer troops outside in the night shooting captured US truck and Jeep drivers without mercy.

Sgt Joseph Colella of Rochester, Ta, told his story today: 'We had charge of some stretcher squads. We had withdrawn six miles from another village and we hid in this church when the Germans came in and began shooting up the town. We could hear the Nazi tank commander stopping our trucks and ordering drivers and helpers out. Then we would hear shots. Next morning we swathe bodies of our men lying where they had been killed.'

During the fighting, Colella continued, one German SS trooper came to the church door in the darkness and called out 'Is everything all right?' One American who could speak German answered in the affirmative and the German left.

By morning some of the men who carried no arms – as protected personnel – were considering evacuating the church under a white flag, but were fearful that they would meet the same ruthless fate dealt to the drivers.

At that point they saw some American troops skirmishing in the streets.

'We knew then that part of the town was still in American hands and we made our way out of the church,' concluded Colella.

HOSPITAL DUTIES

Lieutenant Mary Louise Carpenter, a graduate of Vassar and Massachusetts General Hospital School of Nursing, worked for the American Red Cross and was assigned to the 13th Field Hospital in March 1944. Writing home to her family, she says:

December 22, 1944 – We had got used to the fact that this winter campaign was going slowly and that what had been nibbled off by our armies one day was often lost the next, but eventually regained. We at a field hospital had become used to moving into an area where during the first few days we were sometimes literally shaken by our own artillery going off right beside us. Then gradually we'd get less booms from big stuff near us until only distant rumbles would be heard and at night only distant, heat-like flashes would be seen.

It should have been more disturbing to us than it was when big artillery near us started up again. Then followed two noisy nights with the often described hornet drone of single enemy airplanes and the many assorted booms of large and small ack-ack. We wondered about this resumption of enemy air activity. The first night we nurses were all tired from working hard and found the interruptions to our sleep annoying. However, we sensed that something was going on when at breakfast next morning our cooks told us that they'd been challenged as they crossed the square from their quarters to the mess by American guards on the lookout for German paratroopers.

The next morning the wards were so busy that keeping the ward running and making rounds with the doctors seemed more important than the air-raids, or rather dogfights, going on quite heavily several times, although once when the machine-gun type of ack-ack seemed to come from right under one side of our building and then suddenly to have added to it another even louder spray coming up from right behind us, I found it a little hard to devote all my concentration to the abdominal dressing I was fixing. Soldiers outside in the square reported seeing several planes shot down that morning and that the sky had become black with flak.

Before the onslaught the air of 'R&R' permeated throughout the forces in the Ardennes, including the medical staff. Capt JJ Mihalich, serving in the 107th Evacuation Hospital, was one of the first medics to be called into service when the German attack began:

Life became a bit more comfortable, too comfortable to last long. An advance party was dispatched to Caserne, near Aachen, to find a new hospital site. When they came back with a negative report it was decided on December 16 to unload all supplies and equipment, and return the truck borrowed for this anticipated move. Were we settling down for a long stay?

'Guess we'll be stuck in this mud-hole till the spring,' all disputants admitted resignedly. 'And it's only December 16 now.' To which people in the know added that we could afford to do so quite safely even though there were very few American troops in this sector. The Nazis couldn't possibly attack though the impassible Ardennes that lay between us. Medical and surgical teams were organized and placed on detached service with the 44th and 67th Evacuation Hospitals at Malmedy, Belgium. Thus the little tent city, amidst the rolling hills and ghostly grandeur of the Ardennes forest, prepared to hibernate for the winter.

At 22.30 warning orders were received for movement. The transportation officer was sent to draw 30 trucks from First Army (to which the hospital was assigned October 22nd). Things began to happen fast.

Throughout the day of December 16th one could hear the distant crump of shell-fire, seemingly getting louder by the hour. 'Sheer imagination,' some said, but before long the lethargic atmosphere became charged with electric tension. Early the next morning the personnel was awakened by the 1st Sgt. Instead of his usual calm, gentle, gravel-like voice, he said very excitedly: 'Get the hell out of bed, throw your cots on the trucks, grab some chow and be ready to move at a moment's notice.' The shelling had become very intense. The sky was lit up with the flash of artillery, search-lights and ack-ack fire.

Soon reports started coming in about street fighting in Clervaux, 3½ miles away. Stragglers were now streaming in with the most horrible tales. Some had just escaped the Our river after Jerry paratroopers in US uniforms swooped down on their batteries. 'The Kraut is taking no prisoners,' they replied to a question as to what happened to the rest of the battery.

Now came the most unbearable hours of all; waiting for transportation to arrive; waiting while the shells were crashing all around, while the unit faced the imminent danger of being engulfed by the Nazi tide. At last, after five hours of waiting, the trucks arrived and the 107th departed at noon. Staying behind was a detail to take care of part of the equipment . . .

Then came the stark contrast between superb surroundings and the treatment of horrifying injuries:

Late that afternoon the 107th arrived at the palatial hunting lodge of the Chateau with its elaborate grounds, mirrored walls, gilded chandeliers and magnificent marble stairways. The poor litter-bearers (and practically every able-bodied man gave a hand) who hauled the wounded up those four flights would gladly have traded all this splendor for a second-hand elevator. Day and night these men labored hauling the wounded to the wards and to the operating theatre set up in the rose and pearl-gray banquet hall.

The hospital began receiving patients at midnight. The building's capacity was 250. Before long 450 wounded were crowded in and more kept coming all the time.

Wounded were pouring in from all armies and all sectors of the front. The confusion was great. Commanding Officers came to the hospital looking for members of their units and enlisted men came looking for their COs. 'What divisions is your hospital supporting,' a stray Major asked the Registrar. (Normally the hospital supported between two and four divisions.) 'Christ, looks like you're supporting all the divisions of all the Armies of the United Nations,' he exclaimed as he looked over that day's records of admissions.

One platoon of the 42nd Field Hospital arrived at the hospital minus all their equipment. The other platoon had been surrounded at Wiltz. As more units were being overrun more stragglers were appearing in the 107th chow line. Reports kept coming in of rampant Nazis appearing in groups on the highways surrounding the hospital – killing whoever came along.

But the 107th personnel, working 24 hours a day without let up, was too busy to worry about all these reports. True all contact with army was severed and it was rumored that for ten days the hospital was listed as missing. Right now the 107th wasn't concerned about these reports or about Army connections. Being the only Evacuation Hospital so far forward in the fighting zone, the sole concern of these dog-tired medics was to face their additional responsibilities in as calm and courageous a manner as did the doughboys on the line.

The Commanding Officer seemed to be at all places at all times, but he particularly worked with the operating theatre where 388 operations were performed in an 80-hour period.

Although the number of operations does not seem spectacular, a review of the statistics reveals a much greater volume of very serious operations were performed than at any other period. There especially was a large number of abdominal, chest, maxillo-facial, brain and serious extremity cases. This is understandable when it is realized most of the casualties came from the Battalion Aid Stations, since the chain of medical evacuation was greatly disrupted.

At times it almost seemed as if the unit would crack under the strain but the pressure, fear and tension only welded the personnel together even more firmly, single in purpose and spirit.

Men worked 12 hours at their usual assignment and then continued to work as litter-bearers for hours more. No one slept if they could help in some way. The mess personnel fed more than 1,500 people at each meal. The spirit was magnificent.

News arrived that the 101st Airborne had been surrounded and that Bastogne had fallen. On December 21st, just when it appeared as if the hospital was beginning to emerge from this chaos, a message arrived that Nazi patrols were observed a few miles down the road heading for the hospital. It was no longer possible to ignore the fact that at any moment a bunch of Nazi paratroopers might walk in the front door.

'Clear out in ten minutes,' came the order. 'Everything, yes everything – what you can't carry on your back must be left behind.' All patients that could be moved were speedily loaded on ambulances and trucks. Volunteers were needed to care for those that could not be moved. On all sides hands went up. 'Do you realize what it means?' they were cautioned. Yes, they did and all hands went up again. No one was thinking of being a hero. Just doing one's duty. Of the 400 patients in the hospital 300 were evacuated further to the rear and the rest were carried in ambulances to the hospital's next location.

The next 'home' was in a school at Carlsburg:

The caravan of assorted vehicles jolted to a halt at the St Joseph's

School in Carlsburg, Belgium, at noon of December 21. The hospital was at once opened to the patients awaiting admission from the clearing station as well as the hundred patients carried along in our convoy. The men were hungry and thirsty; but no one could drink his precious water; all canteens went to the patients.

There was one consoling thought: at least they were away from mortal danger. Then came the cry for volunteers to go back into the lion's den to salvage the rest of the equipment. Before long 50 men had boarded trucks and were heading back to the Chateau amid the flash of guns and the roar of revitalized Luftwaffe. 'Hell, that's one subject they never taught us in basic,' the men kidded as their trucks dashed down the Nazi-infested roads. Upon arrival at the Chateau the men witnessed the grim testimony of the timely get-away of the hospital – a German bomb had caved in part of the roof.

No sooner had all the patients been unloaded at Carlsburg and most of the equipment assembled when the frightening news arrived that savage Nazi paratoopers had broken through in this area and were killing and looting as they went along. This was the time of the Malmedy massacre. At noon of the 22nd of Dec orders arrived to proceed at once to Sedan, that ancient fortress city of France. Arriving towards evening the men were greeted with the news that the Germans were 20 miles away and advancing towards Sedan as the gateway to France and one of the most important communications centers. The men and women were too exhausted to worry any longer.

The personnel was quartered at the College Turenne and the hospital was set up at the Textile School then occupied by the FFI. Before long patients started rolling in in a steady stream. A block or so from the hospital was an important bridge spanning the Meuse river, and about 200 yards to the left of this bridge was the College Turenne. The Luftwaffe had orders to 'get that bridge', and came over nightly to bomb and strafe it and everything else along the way. A heavy concentration of ack-ack would answer. As this grim nightly duel commenced our battlewise patients would dive under their beds. This situation was particularly hard on the men suffering from combat exhaustion, and there were many such among the 1,200 patients that were brought into the hospital after the siege of Bastogne was lifted.

After a barely noticed Christmas, cheered by the arrival of better weather and the appearance of the air force overhead, the dramatic and bloody year of 1944 was on the point of ending, but not the danger to life and limb:

Even New Year's Day might have slipped by unnoticed had it not been for the intervention of the Luftwaffe. On New Year's night all off-duty personnel had crowded into the mess hall to see a Frankie Sinatra movie. It was bitterly cold outside and everyone tried to generate as much heat as possible.

While the audience was watching a news-reel of the bombing of Helsinki, the bombing suddenly seemed too realistic. The projection machine crashed to the floor. Glass and shrapnel scattered all over the place. After a deafening crash came a series of smaller explosions. A Jerry bomber had dropped some 50 anti-personnel bombs. Everyone threw dignity to the winds and dived under the tables. Before anyone dared to rise 'Bed-check Charlie' was back. This time one could hear the spluttering of his machine guns as they cut a path across the mess hall windows and poured a hail of bullets into the crowded hall. Despite the fear in the hearts of those men and women, outwardly everyone was calm and collected. In the operating theatre the surgeons, technicians and nurses remained at their stations and continued to work. It was truly a miracle that so few casualties resulted, since only one man was seriously wounded and five slightly wounded.

Even as German defeat was imminent, the casualties kept on coming:

That Von Rundstedt's all or nothing gamble was lost became quite clear toward the middle of January . . . once again the doughboys were swinging into the offensive. And this time they had many a score to settle.

But defensive or offensive, a heavy stream of casualties continued to pour in. And when on the 15th of January the hospital closed its doors at Sedan, it had completed the busiest month in its history. It had cared for 2,700 patients.

BACK UP

As British troops arrived to help the counter-attack against the Germans, medical corps were, of course, included in their number. Among them was DH Clark, Lieutenant, RAMC. He arrived on the Meuse, having travelled all night in a truck from Calais:

> My section and I found ourselves in a small Ardennes village in a requisitioned café . . . there were a few British troops, mostly lines of communications men, who knew little about what was happening – except that everything was 'SNAFU' (situation normal, all fouled up). We wondered and waited.
>
> Not for long; we were ordered forward, and I was told to set up a dressing station in the village of Resteigne. The Germans were in the next village, Bure, and were to be attacked the next day. Companies and platoons of the 13th Parachute Battalion, many of whom I knew personally, came marching through the village for the assault, full of cheerful confidence. Sherman tanks rumbled through, massive and effective-looking; the drivers were Hussars who had fought them all the way up from Normandy. The tanks looked like tinkers' caravans, with cooking pots, wine flagons, bed rolls and miscellaneous loot dangling from the camouflage netting.
>
> We took over a café as our dressing station. This was the first time I had set up a post in action, so I left it to the veterans in my section. They rapidly smashed the plate glass windows, then cleared the furniture from the rooms, either by piling it up against the windows or throwing it into the street. Shells were beginning to fall on the village and a building opposite was hit and collapsed. Our first casualty was a middle-aged Belgian woman screaming continuously in French (until the morphia took effect). Others soon came in – at first civilians and soldiers from our village, then casualties from the battle area just up the road. We soon learned that things were not going well: the village was held by SS Panzer Grenadiers, experienced troops backed

Death and injury visited troops on both sides. In a last-ditch attempt to get help for a wounded comrade a German medical corpsman holds aloft the white flag of surrender. His battle over, his fate was to be picked up by US infantry and become a prisoner of war.

by a Tiger tank. This enormous tank outgunned the Shermans easily and set several of them alight; burned and wounded

tankmen were amongst our early casualties. The 13th Battalion
men had approached the village across the snow covered fields;
the experienced Germans had let them get well out into the open
and then opened up with mortar fire which proved devastating
on the frozen ground. Many of those who had chatted with us
that morning were now dead or severely wounded. The casualties
poured in, walking, carried by their friends, slung across Jeeps.
We had to sort them out, bandage their wounds and pack them
into ambulances to go back to the main dressing station. All
were injured badly, bleeding and shocked. Most were stoical,
grateful for the cigarettes and tea we gave them. Many were
severely wounded, shattered and broken limbs; injuries that would
probably cripple them for life. It was here that I had my first
experience of acute battle breakdown. A stretcher was brought in
with a parachutist lying on his face. I went to examine him and
found him shaking all over; his eyes were tight shut and he was
moaning and whimpering. I said to the stretcher-bearers 'What's
this? Where are his wounds?' They replied, 'Oh, he hasn't any.
He's got the twitch!' I look at the casualty card; on it the battalion
medical officer had written 'Acute Battle Exhaustion: Evacuate'. I
tried to speak to him or to comfort him but got no response, only
further shuddering. So I ticked the card and told them to put him
on the next ambulance. I still have the record of that night, written
on the pages of a French hotel register in Harry Abbott's clear
architectural gothic hand. There were 118 of them in 36 hours,
all sent back except for a corporal who died slowly in the middle
of the café floor. By the end, my hands and clothes were stiff with
blood and I was dizzy and exhausted. But we had coped.

The efforts of the medical teams were not always confined to treating the
troops. Civilians caught in the middle of the battle also benefited from
their care and expertise:

[As the Germans pulled back, the medical section] advanced
into the pathetic villages of the Ardennes where the people were
shattered, starving and frightened. They had thought the war
was over for them; then the Germans had come storming back

and the SS had wreaked heavy vengeance, executing resisters and deporting most of the men.

My section spent a week in one village. We arrived in the village very soon after the Germans had pulled out; indeed we took over their aid post and a good deal of first aid equipment – far better than that issued to us! The following morning a young woman came to our door asking if we had a doctor. Summoning Harry to help with translation (he had excellent, if scholarly French, and I had little), we asked what she wanted. She was the village nurse; the Germans had shot the village doctor; many people were sick; would we come and help?

There followed a strange period as I went twice daily to do medical rounds in the village. I saw elderly men and women with ankles grossly swollen from sitting for days in makeshift air raid shelters. I saw children with rheumatic fever. I saw many injured by air raids and accidents. Where we could we gave first aid. We had few drugs and none to spare.

In a letter home to his mother on 15 January Lieutenant Clark wrote:

At present I am in a fairly recently liberated village where there are no doctors. Consequently I have a large civilian practice with whom I struggle as best I can. My French is improving rapidly perforce: luckily many of the medical terms are much the same. It called for many things, from removing German hand grenades to calming a lady who was having a nervous breakdown because her husband had run away with another woman. I have also had a few very serious cases, especially a small boy with cerebrospinal meningitis. I wish I knew some more medicine.

In Bastogne, where medical supplies could not be delivered direct, they were dropped in, though this was of only partial help. Writing on 29 December, immediately after meeting the men who had been besieged in Bastogne, the reporter Cyril Ray wrote:

They missed only one meal all the time they were there. That was on Saturday before dropping began. They had eaten all their food and were down to eleven rounds of ammunition per gun. Since then they have been almost over-supplied. All that has worried them has been their wounded. Their field hospital and medical detachment had been captured on Tuesday, the 19th – a day before complete encirclement. They had had medical supplies dropped to them, but they couldn't look after casualties properly. They're being looked after now, however.

Brigadier General McAuliffe himself also gave his men who were injured at Bastogne special mention:

The worst part of it for me was the loss of the hospital and the division's surgeon and the surgical teams. On the first day the Germans captured the divisional hospital and took prisoner every divisional surgeon. After that we couldn't give the wounded the care they deserve, but the wounded were magnificent – not a word of complaint from them. We commandeered some cognac and gave them about three ounces every night – that helped. I went up to one lad lying there with a compound fracture of the femur. I said to him, 'How're you doing?' He looked up at me and said: 'I'm doing fine, General.' You know we've got a new name for ourselves. We call ourselves the Battered – well, let's call it 'buddies' – we call ourselves 'the Battered Buddies of the Bastion of Bastogne.'

THE DARKER SIDE
Self-inflicted wounds were commonplace in the Ardennes as elsewhere throughout the war:

In Tillet, a wave of self-inflicted wounds broke out. Time after time, men were carried into the aid station from nearby houses, wincing with pain, shot through the foot. Each swore it was an accident. 'I was cleaning my rifle.' Sometimes the wounded man would say, pointing to a friend, 'He can tell you. He was in the room with me.' And often on the face of the friend there would be a look of duplicity as he backed up the story. The circumstances were almost always the same: the man was alone in a room, or a foxhole, and at most in the presence of his best friend; there would be the one shot, the cry for help, the wound always through the foot. Everyone naturally wondered why there were so many of these accidents in Europe when men were thoroughly accustomed to their weapons, whereas in the United States, on firing ranges, such accidents were almost unheard of. There had been so many self-inflicted wounds that word was read out that every man similarly injured would have to face court martial charges.

Meanwhile, the dead needed treating with due care and respect. Francis J Moloney, a member of Patton's 3rd Army who was blind in one eye and 'practically had to beg' to be drafted, was assigned to graves registration. His job, performed with dignity and pride, was to evacuate the dead from the battlefield – both Allies and Germans – and identify and bury them:

The only positive identification was the two dog tags. One around the neck; if the two were in the pocket we had to find something else to match him. Then if they didn't we had to fingerprint them. In the bitter cold winter over there we had a tent with a big fire where we had to thaw the bodies out to fingerprint them. That was always not a very pleasant job. But anyway we did and we did it with precaution and pride. One dog tag would be placed in the soldier's mouth and the other would be put on the cross or the Star of David what would be at the grave . . . the 3043rd Graves Registration Company; we were the only company that had a cemetery in Europe with no unknown soldiers buried in it. For that we received a meritorious service plaque and a title to wear on our uniform.

8
COUNTER-ATTACK

Once the German attack had run out of momentum the Allied forces advanced from all round the perimeter of the Bulge. Many German vehicles were stranded having run out of fuel, and their crews joined the infantry walking back to the east.

The American counter-move from the south was the quickest and strongest, led by tanks. A rapid advance always makes those involved vulnerable to ambush, as discovered by Private Gerard Rossignol, of the 68th Tank Battalion, serving under the command of the 6th Armored Division.

On the twenty-ninth of December we moved before daybreak to a new assembly area. It was a very large field. I had never seen such a massive amount of trucks, tanks, Jeeps, and tank destroyers in one area. These vehicles were all stopped.

We kept moving to the center of them, in a narrow lane, passing by everybody. I looked at Montana, and made a motion as to ask where we were going. He looked at me and shrugged his shoulders. He did not know. He was taking a radio communication from the company commander. We even passed our company, and the spearhead of the task force. Colonel Reed had assumed Combat Command responsibility of several units in his sector. Again Lt Colonel Davall became the Commander of the 68th Tank Battalion. Company B, being the Combat Team to spearhead the attack. As I look back, this seasoned team had certainly proven themselves under fire. We prepared to attack, but due to heavy traffic, coupled with ice and snow on key roads, some of the units of other sections were delayed until late afternoon, subsequently the attack was postponed. On December 30th, Company B launched an attack at about noon. It was a fun

In deep snow, tanks with steel tracks were practically uncontrollable and even without enemy interference could only manage to cover about 60 miles in ten hours. Even so, Allied divisions made steady progress, with men sleeping in their tanks by the roadside if needed.

day for us, because being the point, we overran the enemy, and they surrendered. We knocked out trucks, personnel vehicles, communication lines, and high buildings, which could serve as observation posts.

The enemy had large deep holes, usually occupied by half a dozen men. We drove very close to the edge of the hole, and Resnick would fire a couple of high explosive rounds, directly in the area. It always amazed me to see so many men climbing out without a scratch. They were dressed in white, and well-camouflaged against snow. We destroyed many machine guns, and artillery pieces in this wooded area. We established our defenses for the night. We didn't get much sleep because the enemy was close by.

New Year's Day was a slow day for us. We attacked the town of Mageret, late in the morning and then again in the afternoon. As a result the town was secured. We serviced the tank, and replenished our ammunition supply. We were somewhat hampered by artillery, and mortar fire, but another company was doing most of the fighting with very little progress. We withdrew for the night at the edge of the woods, high on a hill, but did not receive much damage.

Mageret was one of the villages earlier occupied by the 10th Airborne Division as part of their defence of Bastogne. On 2 January the American advance was supported by airpower.

The next morning, we saw the rising sun. The air force had not been able to give us any support for days, due to low ceiling clouds. Finally the sky was clear. We heard the humming sound of planes. We looked at each other in silence, hoping it was our US Air Force. As the noise grew louder, we could feel the ground shaking. The planes were our planes. It was a heavenly sight. They were at very high altitude, and we could see their vapor streams. We anxiously observed the fighter planes maneuvering through the bomber formations. There must have been hundreds of planes.

The Air Force came in strafing, and bombing the enemy that had been dug-in. It was impossible to see all the action due to the hilly terrain. Our view was obstructed to both our right and our left. We could hear the explosions, and see the black smoke. I thought to myself, there will be nothing left. We will waltz through them today.

The sight of aircraft in action was always impressive, and well-provided dug-in troops could survive enemy attacks from the air.

We moved out after the Air Force ended their bombing. To our left we were flanked by the 50th Combat Team Battalion, and to our right flank was the 69th Combat in our sector. The Company moved towards Arloncourt. The enemy let our Company move in close before opening fire on us. By then, we were close to the wood brush area. It was then that I realized we had been lured into a trap. The Germans demolished our tank company, with the exception of my tank and the other point tank.

It was a massacre. Some of the tankers were half way out of the tanks when they were machine-gunned before they were able to escape. Smoke was billowing from the tanks where the ammunition had exploded, and we were not in a position to see where the enemy was. We were in a cove with trees in front of us. Resnick and Frank went over to some of the company tanks, to destroy the cannons with phosphorus bombs. The bombs burned and destroyed the breech. They did this because the enemy was threatening to overrun our position. The action was standard military procedure. There was a small stream in front of us. Frank and the other tank commander decided to make an attempt to cross the stream, so as to locate the enemy. The other tank crossed over. Our tank did not make it across. We got bogged-down in the stream, unable to move, the water level got up to my navel button. We knew we were going to be the next target, but no one abandoned the tank.

By contrast, a tank that could not move was extremely vulnerable because it was a static target.

We did not have a long wait before we were fired on. It must have been an .88 armor-piercing shell, because it hit us in the front center, where the thickness was five inches. The shell came through between Montana and I. The heat from the shell, hitting transmission oil and water, caused a heavy smoke inside the tank. We could not see anything. Frank shouted, 'anybody hit?' I replied, 'I am.' My legs, my right foot, and my head hurt. Montana opened his hatch door. He started to get out, as I saw the light through the smoke, I wanted to get out the same time he did, but was only room for one person at a time. I completely forgot that I could use my own hatch. All I could think about was what had happened to our last tank, less than a month before. Montana calmed me down, and assured me that the crew would get me out. When we were all out, Frank wanted to give me a shot. I asked him if it was going to put me to sleep. He convinced me it would only remove the pain. I took the shot. We then crossed the stream, heading towards the remaining tank company. They lifted me onto the tank, and laid me close to the turret, which was away from the line of fire. Montana laid on top to further protect me from the line of fire. The driver was going to make an attempt to move out, on dry ground, away from this area. I don't think we moved more than five feet, before a shell hit the turret. It came through and swirled inside, destroying and killing everyone inside the tank. I did not look. We got down from the tank and saw a half-track about half a mile away. A half-track is the size of a ten-wheel truck, with the front end of the truck. The transmission drives the rear end which is a lag track similar to a tank track, but smaller in proportion. It has more traction and therefore has an advantage over tires in snow, mud, and rough terrain. Montana then said, 'I'm going over to hold that half-track until we can get you over there.' He ran like an Olympic champion across that field. Frank and Resnick helped me hobble towards the half-track. Mortar shells were exploding, and machine-gun bullets were zinging all around us. I told the guys to let me go. We were not moving fast enough. They let go of me and I ran so fast that they could hardly keep up with me. Montana had persuaded the halftrack driver to wait for us. When I got there, I hurled myself inside onto the floor. I used so much force that my head was resting on the accelerator. The driver barked at me and said, 'Remove your damn head from the gas pedal so we can get the hell out of here!' I was so exhausted that someone had to pull me off. I could not move. My tank crew also hitched a ride.

Rossignol was fortunate that his tank did not catch fire and 'brew up' when hit by the .88.

Infantry also moved up from the south, like Paul Curtis, a recently arrived replacement serving in the 26th Division. As he went forward he found that the severe winter weather was almost as much of a threat as the enemy.

There were only two men in the squad, the Sgt and assistant squad leader. We were assigned as the BAR team. We inquired where the other men of the squad, usually eight men were, and was told they had been killed. I thought they were joking but soon found out they were serious. The Captain came down to talk to us and told us the 328th was the regiment Sgt York fought in during World War I and they believed in fighting. Seems like a pretty tough outfit. We got some more men and made up a full squad a few days later. We have two BAR teams in the squad and 2 men to each team. Cliburn and I take turns carrying the BAR as it weighs 22 pounds. One man carries the BAR and the other man carries the M-1 rifle and the ammunition. The BAR fires a clip of 20 rounds and the M-1 fires eight. We threw the tripod on the BAR away to make it lighter. We can not put oil on it as it is so cold it will freeze. We wear all the clothes we can get on. It is really cold, snow knee-deep. I wear long underwear, two wool shirts, two pairs of woolen pants, woolen sweater, field jacket, overcoat with a rain coat over that, woolen cap under my helmet, and woolen scarf, two pairs of socks, combat boots with arctic overshoes over them, woolen gloves, a pack, rifle and ammunition, with a grenade hanging in every button hole in the overcoat. We are pretty well loaded down and usually four cans of 'C' rations and extra bandoleers of ammunition. If you fall into a snowdrift, some one has to pull you out. A canteen of water is soon frozen and also your 'C' rations. We never get a hot meal on the front line. We are in Luxembourg in the last weeks of the 'Battle of the Bulge.' It is so cold in some months we had more casualties from the weather than from the enemy. It is a court martial offense not to take off your shoes and massage your feet every day to prevent frost bite. Best thing in the world for athletes foot as I have never again been bothered by it. We also throw away our bayonets as we are told the Germans are not too interested in bayonet fighting. Most also throw away their gas mask but I remember the old captain from training advising us to hang on to it.

Infantry soldiers are usually overburdened with items of equipment which might be useful, and often discard anything which is of no immediate use or inconvenient to carry. As the battle progressed, the sight of casualties became even more common.

We are on patrol one day and I see my first German prisoners. They were captured at the top of a hill and come down the hill with their hands up. We are in a line to the bottom of the hill and as they pass each man he covers them with his rifle until they reach the last man in line and they are taken behind the lines. I have heard that sometimes they never made it all the way back. I remember riding in the trucks to the front line. We would see dead German soldiers lying on the side of the road frozen, their naked feet would be sticking up out of the snow. They would be a yellow color not white at all. The other Germans had taken their shoes when they were killed. The first night on the front we are put on outpost guard and shells explode all around us. We are in one house and a GI comes in after dark and says he has been wounded and he is scared and in pain. The Sgt looks him over and he has a big bruised place on his thigh where a shell fragment hit him but did not break the skin. The Sgt tells him he is not hurt and to get back to his post. He is more scared than hurt. I have to stand guard in a foxhole. It rains and sleets all night and the Germans bring up tanks and shell us from the woods at night and retreat back into the woods in daytime. We spend the next night outside a building and it is so cold we can only stay outside ten minutes before being relieved. The Germans are firing mortars from the woods nearby. When a round is dropped into the barrel it makes a little popping sound as it is fired from the barrel. As I stand outside they are so close I can hear the little popping sound as it leaves the barrel, but they don't know we are close. We move out the next night and I fall into a branch of water and lose my bandoleer of ammunition. Have to wait until the next day to get more. We march about five miles and stay in a barn that night. One GI is so sick we have to help him walk and he coughs all night. Next morning he is unable to walk. We tell the Sgt he probably has pneumonia. He looks him over and says he has hiccups. They haul him away in an ambulance.

As the weather took effect many soldiers involved in the counter-attack, both Allied and German, succumbed to sickness.

We are supporting another company and cross a river the next day and see some GIs coming back wounded. We stay in another town for one or two days and attack the next morning. We come down a hill into the town and are shelled but no one gets hit. I see two or three dead Germans lying around. We move into another town in the afternoon. Another village is about 1½ miles away. We can see men moving around but we can't tell who they are. The Sgt picks me and two others to go with him on patrol to the village to see who they are. The road is up on a ridge with woods below on both sides. As we get about halfway, German mortars in the woods below us and to our right begin firing at us. They fire four or five rounds. The first round goes over us. The next one falls short and the next over. I realize we are being 'bracketed', as we did in training. Each shell as it explodes throws mud and snow on us. I think one more round will probably be on top of us, but they never fire that round. Maybe they ran out of ammunition or maybe some one was looking out for us. The troops in the village are ours. A piper cub comes flying over and the Germans begin shooting at him. He is so low I can't see how they can miss him, but he is unharmed and flies away. You can see puffs all around him as the shells explode. When we get back one of the boys has blood on his chin, where a little piece of shrapnel hits him. He is put in for a Purple Heart. We attack a town the next morning and capture some snipers. My squad has to clear some houses on the street and the sergeant and I enter the first house. He tells me he will go upstairs and for me to search the basement. Daylight is just breaking and as I go down the steps into the basement, I see something white lying on the floor. I call the sergeant and we go down into the basement. We find a GI who has been wounded the day before. He has been hit in the head, and has his head bandaged and is wrapped in a blanket. He can't speak and can only move his eyes. His bazooka is lying outside the door in the street all broken up. We got the medics for him and move on. We saw the medic later in the day and they told us when we left the basement a German medic was in the basement and surrendered to them. He had bandaged the GI and stayed with him all night. He probably saw it as a good opportunity to surrender but he never showed himself to men with rifles. I saw a German in one building who had been burned up. Both his hands and feet were burned off.

By this stage of the battle many German soldiers were disillusioned and demoralized, and anxious to surrender if they could do so safely. Equally, frontline troops often developed a sinister sense of humour as a reaction to the rigours of combat and a means of coping with the horror.

At this time there were so many casualties, cooks, office workers and others were being placed in the infantry. One GI had just joined us and he asked someone to tell him how to operate his M-1.
We were in the woods near Wiltz, Luxembourg one day. Snow was knee-deep and two Germans were lying there frozen stiff. One GI was a cut-up, always anything for a laugh. He began telling us 'look here'. He had one of the Germans by the legs and was pushing him through the snow like a wheel barrow using his legs as handles. We laughed but it was a pretty grim sort of humor.

If it was possible and allowed, troops always preferred to live in buildings rather than in the open. They usually traded with the civilian population to mutual advantage.

January 28 – We were loaded into open trucks and rode for hours. I was sitting on the back of the bench on the truck and thought I would freeze. When we stopped I just turned loose and fell off the truck to the ground as I could not stand. As near as I ever came to freezing. I believe sometimes some of the GIs would be wounded and would lie in the snow and when the medics found them they would be dead. The wound didn't kill them, they just lay in the snow and froze. We were in Alsace Lorraine, a little country between France and Germany, we were here to rest a few days. Clibura and I were assigned to a home of three people. A couple and a little boy of about ten. The little boy would build us a fire every morning and we got to sleep in a bed. The Germans were there before and the little boy did not like the 'bosch'. We stay in the kitchen where it is warm and try to talk with them. A pot of potatoes is usually cooking on the stove as this is about all they have to eat and black bread. As we go through the chow line we bring them some of our white bread. The old man has a pig he is going to slaughter and is looking forward to sharing his meat with us. The army has dumped a load of coal at the end of the street. They have a guard and no one can get the coal but a GI so we load him up with coal. He has no extra clothes, just what he is wearing and wears a pair of rubber boots. We are issued some new clothes and we give him a shirt and pair of pants and give him some shoes. We are issued some boots that are made like sportsmen wear. Leather uppers and rubber bottoms. The very thing for snow. Those old combat boots are undoubtedly the coldest you could put on your feet. We are also issued mittens instead of gloves. The mittens look funny as they only have one finger to be used as a trigger finger. We have to leave before the Frenchman can kill his pig though.

In the Northern sector the 30th Division was still fighting in late January and also enduring the hard weather. Private Dennis C Racicot recalled:

Company F was located in the small town of Rodt, Belgium. The weather was bitter cold and at night men were only required to man a post for an hour. It had dropped to 10 below zero at times and to keep men from freezing their feet, an hour was about all a man could stand. This night, I stood guard on an outpost that called for a short walk back and forth on the porch of a town building. I was grateful for the walk. Some outposts were standing in a doorway or manning a machine- or an anti-tank gun at a road block. In any case, everyone was cold.

My platoon was lucky, for upstairs in this building was a wood stove and it was kept going full steam. When one would come back from a guard post, that hot wood stove felt like a million dollars. The room with the stove was also our sleeping quarters. Actually, we were in seventh heaven compared to some of the places we had been, digging foxholes in a snow-covered forest, holing up in an old barn. This situation was a luxury.

Rumors about this time were that the Germans were well on the run, and that we might just be finished with our part of the Bulge offensive. Not so, for as we began the day of January 24, 1945, the word came down that we had another town to take.

Although the German offensive had failed and many German soldiers were willing to give up, some carried on fighting hard to defend the approaches to their homeland. As they withdrew they carried on ambushes and blocking actions to reduce and delay the advancing Allied troops.

We were up early on January 25th preparing ourselves for the attack to come. Our Company assembled just after dawn. It was still cold and there was about two feet of snow on the ground. This would slow us down. Our platoon started its move towards this small Belgium town in a three line approach, single file. We had about 3,000 yards to cover across open fields and we moved as fast as we could. I was surprised that there was no artillery preparation. Our Sergeant told us that it would be better without the artillery. The Germans would not know we were coming. This seemed foolish to me. Any German with even poor eye sight could spot us a mile off in that white snow.

Our first objective was a railroad embankment, and in particular an underpass. I was again surprised and relieved that we encountered no opposition in reaching that underpass. No German artillery, no German mortar fire, nothing. I expected the town to be vacant of any Germans; however, this was not the case.

We reached the underpass, and just a short way on the other side of the railroad tracks, we began to encounter buildings, but still no opposition. The street we were now on had less snow cover so we broke into a run, hollering as we went and shooting our guns in the air. I guess this type of activity was supposed to frighten the Germans who might be there. As we moved along the street two men would check out a building. As my turn came, a buddy and I entered a residential home. As we entered the front door and moved through the house, we came to the kitchen.

There was a door that led to the cellar. As we opened the cellar door, we could hear a voice coming from the bottom of the stairwell. The voice was that of a female and she was speaking the Belgium language.

We called down to come up, but we were still not convinced that the people down there were all civilians. An old man and a woman came up the stairwell. The woman could speak a little English, and we made out that there were some Germans down there that wanted to surrender. When the old man and woman returned to the cellar at our bidding, some six German soldiers came up the stairwell and surrendered. None had weapons and all were scared to death that we would kill them. They had good reason to be scared, for we had been told before the attack that we did not need any prisoners.

We took these guys out of the house and marched them down the street where we met our company Sergeant who had set up a company CP in an old barn. He bawled us out for bringing in prisoners, and asked us why we did not grenade them when they were in that cellar. I told him, 'Sergeant, there were also civilians down there.' It was only then that he laid off of us.

I should explain here in my story that my company had discovered the massacre at Malmedy, Belgium, where some 100 American GIs had been gunned down after they had surrendered. After that discovery, we did not take many prisoners. However, as for me, I could never bring myself to take another life unless it was to save myself or others in my outfit. To do the same as what the SS troops had done at Malmedy would make me their equal. I did not want that on my conscience.

Not all American soldiers were so governed by humanity and conscience. As news of the massacre at Malmedy spread, many stopped taking prisoners in revenge for the German atrocity.

After unloading our German prisoners to the good Sergeant, he told us to keep moving up the street and to catch up with the rest of the platoon that had been searching out homes and other buildings. We hurried along and soon caught up to some guys.

A side street had not been checked out, so my buddy and I moved ahead and began searching out buildings. This was a farming town, and many of the dwellings were a home, a chicken pen, cow pen, all wrapped into one setting.

As we came to the end of the street, there was a big barn. As my buddy opened the big barn door, I stood ready for anything. As soon as the door was open, there was a lot of chatter that came from a number of civilians that had taken refuge there. We asked them, 'Germans, Germans, are there any Germans?' No, no, came the answer, all is gone from an old man who could speak some English.

We moved through the barn to the rear cow pens and horse stalls. By this time, we were taking occasional mortar rounds. As I looked out the window of a stall, I could see a German tank parked some 300 yards away in the middle of a field. With the white snow for a background, it stood out like a sore thumb. As we watched that tank, a German climbed out of the turret and started to walk across the field away from us. My buddy and I both took aim and fired at him, for we felt that he might have been the one directing mortar fire upon us. To our left from outside the barn, there was a great deal of automatic fire going on from some GI's BAR. Someone hit the man in the field for he went down and stayed down. From this point on, the mortar fire ceased to come in. It has always been my hope that it was not my bullet that put the man down.

Our good Sergeant received orders to check out a street to the east of us, so he took me and several others and we took off. We walked down a snow-covered trail. Both sides of the trail were lined with cottonwood trees. We soon ran into several Belgium homes and found them unoccupied. As we started our return to the CP, our Sergeant decided that we should establish an outpost where two men could watch a field to our north and also the small street that the homes were located on. Another man and I were selected to man this outpost for the first hour.

We found an old foxhole half-filled with snow. We improved on it a bit and used it as our outpost headquarters. It was mid-afternoon by this time and it was growing colder by the minute.

As we sat in our hole, my feet began to suffer, so I would take off a boot and rub my feet like crazy. I alternated taking off one boot and then the other. My buddy did the same thing. After some two hours had gone by, we decided that our good Sergeant had forgotten about our relief. We drew straws to see who would go to the Platoon CP and find out what was up. I won the draw and took off for the CP.

Arriving at there, I found everyone was cozy, sitting around keeping warm. I finally found the good Sergeant and, of course, he was embarrassed that he had forgotten about us. He decided that we did not need that outpost now and told me to hustle out and bring in the other man. This I did.

Being forgotten and left on the ground without being relieved was always a depressing experience, especially at night or in severe weather.

We had just returned to the CP when someone at a window post hollered, 'Some Germans are coming in from the north!' As I looked out a window, sure enough, there was a column of German infantry coming toward this little town. They had two self-propelled artillery tanks with them. By this time we could hear the roar of their motors. Word was passed around to stay put and be quiet. An artillery observer from our Battalion was with us and he called in a fire order. The salvo soon came over, but not on target. We never knew where those rounds went. Our observer studied his map again, called in another fire order, and this time he was on target. Facing artillery explosions, the German column broke up. One of the German tanks went to our right and poured on the coal. This was a mistake for the tank came in direct fire range to an American Tank Crew, who had parked their tank next to our building. This tank crew put two rounds into that German tank and disabled it. It also caught on fire. As I watched out the window, I could see men crawling out of that burning tank. I could not bring myself to shoot at them.

By now it was growing dusk and things settled down. The Germans had withdrawn behind the line of cottonwood trees and we could see nothing to shoot. The last we could hear of those

Germans was the sound of that one tank still alive as it moved off into the distance. The attack had been repelled, so we thought. We found out later that this column of Germans had been kicked out of a small town by elements of the 82nd Airborne Division and all that they were doing was looking for a place to hole up for the night. They had no idea that we had taken this small Belgium town. They walked into a fire-fight that they certainly were not looking for.

There were many such small encounters as the shattered remnants of the German armies in the Ardennes tried to find their way back.

THE COLD CONTINUES

British troops moving into the Ardennes for the counter-attack were also badly affected by the terrible cold. It was bitterly cold. Norton, an interpreter with the British Army recalled that . . .

> . . . it was so cold that the DRs – the Dispatch Riders on motorcycles – they would go from one little village to the next, stopping at a bistro for a drink . . . and then falling off their bikes.

For Hans Behrens, a wireless operator in a 5th Panzer Army tank unit, it was faintly amusing that

> . . . the Americans . . . came amiss . . . they had rubber pads on their tank tracks. And as the roads were either in snow or icy they just slid all over the place.

The 23rd Hussars, a tank regiment in the British 11th Armoured Division found that steel tracks were no better when moving forward to Wellin.

> . . . the roads were getting into an appalling state, and our awkward, top-heavy Shermans skated about on their steel tracks like a stampede of drunken elephants.

Another British regiment with Shermans, the East Riding Yeomanry, were advancing in late December from the northern side of the Bulge and found . . .

> The roads by this time were almost impossible. A slight thaw had followed the first snow, then came a succession of white frosts and three or four inches of solid ice were everywhere on every road. One saw an unending succession of lorries that had crashed out of control. Tanks with steel tracks were practically uncontrollable, Jeeps and scout cars with four-wheel drive were just possible with the greatest care . . . the tanks made sixty miles in ten hours . . . Further on, things got worse . . . the snow in the hills here was several feet deep even on the by-roads. The main roads were different; they were just six inches of solid frozen gleaming ice . . . in darkness down similar filthy roads . . . in a blizzard in all its fury . . . a terrible cold drive . . . with the sound of gunfire booming out over the howling of the bitter wind. [Contrary to Behrens, they found that up an icy precipice] it was only those tanks with rubber that could make any headway – on the camber of a road two men could slide one sideways by merely pushing it. [As wheeled vehicles could not reach them to replenish,] we had to have Buffaloes, amphibious craft with special 'spud' tracks that would grip on the snow, to bring up petrol and ammunition.

Sometimes more traditional means were used. When the vehicles of the 61st Recce Regiment could go no further,

> Lieutenant Spreag . . . transferred himself to a horse . . . with two Belgian woodmen he rode to the outskirts of St Hubert, then straight through it. The Boche had just left.

In the field in the Ardennes survival was at stake. The 23rd Hussars' Regimental History records:

> . . . there was no question of camping out in a field, or 'bedding down' in a barn, or perchance 'kipping' inside our tanks. We would all have frozen to death . . . life in the open in defence was particularly hard near Bure in place on 'Chapel Hill' almost two

thousand feet high . . . it had one windowless building . . . and a young pine wood which covered the last few hundred feet – and snow which covered it all. It was in view of the enemy, so no fires could be lit. The ground was frozen solid and no shelter could be dug . . . perhaps the worst part . . . were the feeding arrangements. As no fires could be lit, and all visible movement had to be avoided, the food had to come by cook's truck before dawn and after dusk. But the tea froze faster than one could drink it, and the stew turned into iced jelly.

Allied Commanders had been concerned by the combined effects of harsh weather and a lack of suitable clothing and footwear. Bradley stated in his memoirs that on 16 December his main preoccupation was with a shortage of manpower caused in part by '. . . a wholly unexpected onslaught of trench foot caused by late-arriving, ill-designed cold weather footwear. Trench foot had cost us an additional 12,000 non-battle casualties.' Poor boots inflicted more losses during the fighting, Hans Behrens, noticed:

> When I was later wounded and in American hospitals, Americans had a lot of frostbite because they had rubber-soled boots and of course that attracts the cold . . .

According to Edward Norton, British boots were no better, but the American soldiers appreciated British battle-dress:

> The Americans had officer-type uniforms and they were very light and they were not suitable for these conditions, so as the Airborne Division was taken out of the line, we were told that we were getting new uniforms and we could dispose of our old ones, so we did an enormous trade with the Americans, and traded our old uniforms for whatever they had that we fancied. Now I found I could change my boots – and it is a well-known fact that British Army boots were lousy because they let the water come in – so I traded mine for a pair of galoshes.

The British boots were not designed for these conditions and did not keep the cold out either. Whilst in the Ardennes Norton saw that . . .

US infantrymen ride to the 1st Army front. En route there were villages to clear; this brought battles which, for the men of the 84th, were 'just as hard, just as bitter' as the bigger conflicts. 'Men died, dug for cover, ducked .88s, bandaged up buddies if they could, the same way.'

> . . . the weather conditions were shocking . . . freezing cold. It was so cold that the Military Policemen on duty, they were wearing straw round their boots, up to their knees for protection. And they were on point-duty, and their face was completely caked in ice. Even armour plate was no protection especially in some of the Shermans.

And the men of the East Riding Yeomanry had comments to make on conditions inside their tanks:

> The Sherman tanks with aero engines were air-cooled, and the cooling air was sucked in through the turret by the large fans cooling the crew to virtual numbness on its passage.

The German troops were reduced to ineffectiveness by the sort of weather they had needed to protect them from the Allied Air Forces. Von Manteuffel remarked of his sector:

> We knew its narrow, twisting roads and the difficulties, not to say dangers, they could cause to an attacking force, particularly in winter and in the bad weather conditions which were an essential prerequisite to the opening of our operation.

As the operation developed the weather deteriorated from von Manteuffel's point of view, 'Snow fell, the temperature dropped, the scanty mountain roads were sheets of ice.' The German Chief of Army Staff, Guderian, commented 'Heavy congestion on the narrow, ice-bound roads, belated switching of the rearward, blocked units to Fifth Panzer Army's sector caused this army to lose mobility.'

Prolonged exposure to winter conditions demoralized the German soldiers in the field. Sergeant Norman Kirby, serving at Montgomery's HQ, had interrogated a German straggler and concluded that:

> His compatriots were in the open, in woods from which they would soon be driven out by the extreme cold.

As time went on, German troops in large numbers opted for capture rather than stay at liberty in the open. Not far from Dinant a mixed body of American and British tanks found a panzer column in the snow:

> Well over 40 tanks were captured . . . most of them out of petrol. Tank crews and infantry also surrendered in large numbers, frozen and hungry and exhausted.

As the snow and the fighting continued . . .

> Miserable grey-clad soldiers coming out of the woods, filthy, unshaven and badly frostbitten, to give themselves up . . . nearly all hospital cases. These were the pathetic victims of Hitler's blind optimism, neglect of logistic necessity and arrogant assumptions about the absolute physical and mental superiority of his soldiers.

It was on the 27th that the German thrust reached its extreme western limits and with some difficulty and much gallantry was finally held by the American Armies. It was on this day, too, that the Allies began to hit back. It so happened that the Fife and Forfar Regiment was very near the tip of the German bulge. They were thus destined to become involved in the task of holding, and finally rolling back, the enemy.

Temporarily held up by the absence of the enemy, which nonetheless made its presence felt by 'the banging of heavy artillery' and by bad weather – including a blinding snowstorm which 'literally froze the war to something like immobility for a short time' – the Yeomanry were soon in action again. On 3 January . . .

> . . . another severe day with icy roads, extremely uncomfortable, indeed dangerous, for tanks and transport . . . the enemy were known to be very close at hand and the Yeomanry soon discovered them. As they crossed the ridge south of the hill, the leading tank was fired on and brewed-up at once.
> Lieutenant David Reid recorded that . . . retaliation for this unfriendly reception was swift: the Troop commanded by Lieutenant JW Samson stalked the self-propelled gun which had caused the trouble, discovered it lurking in the lee of pinewoods which crested the hill and knocked it out. A second self-propelled gun was later found abandoned.

The Yeomanry were working in support of two units of the 6th Airborne Division, who had arrived . . .

> . . . breathing smoke and flame against von Rundstedt. They had come out from England to help tackle the ugly situation and had missed their Christmas fun and games.

Chapel Hill, their objective,

> . . . was not finally captured until well after midday, and the attack by the Parachutists down in the valley had to be postponed

until the hill was cleared. The Parachutists then formed up in the wood to the south-east of Bure. 'A' Squadron gave the promised support from the heights from which they lashed the enemy with fire. As soon as the airborne troops were in Bure one tank Troop started to join them, but when they neared the village gunfire broke out and accounted for two of the leading vehicles. This annoyed the other members of 'A' Squadron who were still on the hilltop and they promptly brewed-up three German self propelled guns.

'C' Squadron were now ordered to send up a Troop into Bure and a very lively time was had by all. The weather had now become positively savage. [Sporadic] blizzard reduced visibility often to a matter of yards, deepening snow made ground conditions nearly impossible, and the cold was most searching. As if these conditions were not enough to be going on with, heavy enemy shelling had to be endured, especially by the airborne troops.

There were mines stopping their progress, too:

Meantime, the Troop from 'C' Squadron that had been sent off to support the attack on Bure was making an adventurous approach to that disputed village. The tanks slithered from side to side on the glassy road. Two hundred yards short of the village the leading tank went up on a mine and this gave the remainder of the Troop some cause for thought. However, a diversion was found, the village was entered from another quarter and another of the tanks was hit, this time by an armour-piercing shell. The unfortunate airborne troops were also meeting trouble from a strong and determined enemy. Major RL Leith, who had come up with the 'C' Troop, made liaison with the OC Parachute Battalion, and as darkness was falling the attackers could not hope to make any further progress that night. So, with the British holding one-third of the village and the enemy the rest, a halt was called to the fighting. One Troop of 'C' Squadron remained with the infantry throughout the night, while the remainder of the Squadron proceeded by a series of intoxicated slithers back along the snow-filled road to Tellin.

If a competition were held among the survivors of 2nd Fife and Forfar Yeoamanty today to decide which was the most perishing period of the whole of the European campaign, 'A' Squadron, Regimental HQ and 'F' Company Rifle Brigade would certainly vote for the nights which were spent on Chapel Hill. This feature, one-thousand feet high, was a bastion vital to the success of the operations around Bure. With snow showers howling through the tree, not a solidly built house anywhere in sight, the country was at its mid-winter worst. The men were soaked by their continuous work among snow, and supply vehicles could only be towed up the slopes to a 'thus-far-and-no-further' point, after which they had to be manhandled by exhausted troops.

Now the action really began to hot up, but within a couple of days it was obvious that the Germans in this area were in retreat. Between times, the men much appreciated the hospitality of the local civilians:

From early light on 4th January there was enough excitement to satisfy anyone. All three tanks which had been left in Bure were knocked out by well-directed enemy fire, and when 'C' Squadron, now in position to the south-east of the village, pushed another Troop forward with the intention of out-flanking the village, another tank was lost. There, for hours, the situation remained deadlocked. Each side resorted to heavy shelling. It was certainly remarkable that relatively few casualties were incurred by the Yeomanry, for their position was simply plastered. There were times when it seemed as though the whole Squadron must be out of action. The vehicles looked so shrapnel-scarred and mud-bespattered that they had the appearance of being knocked out. Corporal Gorman and Trooper Lines were killed in this action and Lieutenant Jones and several troopers wounded.

At nightfall 'C' Squadron was withdrawn to Tellin. This village, though right on the edge of the war zone, and frequently under German fire, had still a good many civilians in it. And hospitable ones, too! Particularly memorable was the kindness of the nuns who gave food and wine to the tired and shivering tank crews until a direct hit on the convent put an end to the meal. On the 5th of January the 23rd Hussars were ordered to relieve, while the Regiment moved back to Wellin. There they remained in a defensive role for the better part of a week during which, thankfully, the progress of the Ardennes battle got firmly into reverse gear . . .

The diary of William Steel Brownlie, Lieutenant in the Yeomanry, paints a vivid picture of the tank action, the essence of which was shared by Allies and Germans alike:

2 January

We put two tanks over the bridge into positions where they could see the countryside ahead. This took a couple of hours, as we had to spread brushwood on the ice-covered roads to give them a grip. I then received a shock.

The Germans were holding Bure, six miles up the valley, and we were to attack them from a favourable direction, perhaps by way of a ridge running east on our left front. I was to be taken by a small force of 61 Recce Regiment, in bren-cariers, to see if there was route suitable for tanks. I should explain that it was a horrible experience to go into action in vehicles or with weapons to which you were not accustomed. No infantryman would ever get inside a tank, for example. Here was I in a small-tracked vehicle, out of my element. The officer in charge gave me a Bren, said I was his gunner as well as his guide. I wished I was back in Ypres, even in Chanly.

We motored through a Christmas card landscape of snow, pines and glades, except that at one point I was out on foot and a small shell exploded nearby. There were signs of German patrols, also the tracks of wild boar, which didn't matter so much. The important thing was that there was no covered approach for tanks on the left and right of the ridge, as the country was too thick. So we veered to the right, ended up in a village. The bridge was blown, the locals said that the Germans always occupied the place by night. Suddenly a shell crashed right among us, bowling us over. When the smoke cleared there was one carrier less, its crew of three blown to pieces. We scattered, but nothing more came over.

I had to get word back that there was no covered approach for the tanks, for the way ahead was in full view of the enemy, but had to use the carriers' wireless, having no direct communication of my own. There, control promised to pass the message, he added that we were to stay there all night and try to keep the Germans out of the village. I also learned from the very nice platoon commander that they had no rations . . . I decided that this was no place for me and resolved to walk back to Chanly, hoping not to meet a German patrol on the way. Hm, seven miles. To stay, or to go?

A sudden alarm, and four small vehicles were seen coming up the road from the direction of the enemy lines. They were special Air Service Belgians, who had been dropped in weeks before and operated beyond the front in Jeeps. Their leader agreed to take me back to Chanly. Their way of crossing the river was quite simple. One Jeep drove into it until it stalled, then they all waded in and manhandled it across; and so on with the other three. Off we went, myself sitting in a pile of ammunition, grenades and explosives, the others continually smoking and holding Sten guns. We were still in enemy territory, and I did not enjoy the ride. But they got me to Chanly. The Squadron had moved forward a mile to Resteigne, I hitched a lift there, collapsed in the door of our Mess, asked for and was given some whisky, had a ham and egg supper, then had a talk with the boys and our friendly hosts. One was a girl who had left Antwerp to get away from the Buzz-Bombs, only to find herself in the front line.

3 January

I do not know if my report that there was no covered approach towards Bure by tanks had any effect, but certainly the decision was to move direct to high ground, with no element of surprise, overlooking Bure. From there we were to support by fire Paras who had been flown from England. They were to attack up the valley to our right, while we took on targets ahead of them. When they got to the edge of the village, we would come and join them.

We moved at first light, the snow having stopped, and could see the whole area over which the battle was to be fought, a panorama of black and white. It was a dominating position. We ourselves were overlooked only by the top of our own feature, where there was a thick wood almost enclosing a church of some sort. We called it Chapel Hill, and were assured that it was occupied by friendly troops. It was not.

As we settled down waiting for the battle to begin, there was a roar and Guy Wilkes' tank was hit by an AP shot from the Chapel. We scurried round, looking for positions giving us both cover from Chapel Hill on our left, and still a good field of fire to our front. Jimmy Samson's 3 Troop was sent to deal with Chapel Hill, while the main attack was postponed by 30 minutes. Meantime the unfortunate Paras sat in the woods down to our right, being heavily shelled. Our Desmond Chute was with them as liaison in a scoutcar, and kept urging us to clear up the nonsense on our flank, so that the attack might start.

Easier said than done. The Chapel was guarded on three sides by thick woods, and the SP or whatever it was had a field of fire down the avenue on the fourth side. Eventually Cpl Dave Findlay motored into the open gap with his gun already traversed and it [shot] out at a range of 200 yards. He knocked out the SP, but received a hit that bounded off his turret, showering him with fragments and wounding him in the face. This High Noon encounter earned him the MM.

Now the airborne advanced from their Start Line, and we saw small black figures running out of the line of trees across the white expanse of snow, one or two dropping here and there, the rest soon disappearing into the jumble of houses and garden of the village. There were little puffs of smoke as the Germans tried to keep back the flood, but we kept a stream of fire on them, and they were gradually pushed back from house to house.

Geoff Hales' Troop was sent down the track in front of us, to go into the village and give close support. He had gone about 300 yards when . . . own tank was hit. Sgt Robinson took cover in a hollow. Geoff and his two crews came struggling back up the slope. Amazingly none was injured, while only one man in Guy's tank had been hurt, hit in the leg by a second shot as he was baling out. Geoff had rescued nothing from his tank but a large carton of Mars Bars – he had a friend in the factory in Slough.

The battle in Bure raged furiously, and the Airborne were in danger of being pushed back. Desmond still with them in his scoutcar, reported a Tiger at the far end of the street which was proving unassailable. He did not sound happy in his work, and then fell silent, so we found it difficult to continue our fire support, not knowing who was where.

However, on the hill south of the village, down which half the Paras had come in the first rush, there came a counter-attack. Three SPs followed by bunches of infantry were mowing a patch through the Airborne, who were scattering in all directions. We hit the leading SP with our third shot, range about two miles, and it halted. The second was soon also stopped and the third, having been hit three or four times, disappeared. The counter-attack was over, and we felt that we had done our job. We were shelled, with no damage.

With darkness we harboured near the Chapel, which was in ruins. A body lay in the brushwood, apparently the commander of the SP. We sat and ate in the tank. There was no wind, no more snow, but it grew colder and colder. The ground was too hard for digging, so we decided to sleep in the tank. Jock McKinnon (driver) and Mackenzie (co-driver) in their seats down front; Buck Buchanan (gunner) on the deck below the gun; Norman Ingram (operator) on top of the gun; self on the floor with feet in one sponson and head in the other. Sleep? Within minutes the icy cold of the metal seeped through your clothing, and the breath froze on your lips. I lit a candle in a tin lid, and a fat lot of good it did.

4 January

Out at dawn to our previous positions, just in time to avoid a tremendous stonk by enemy Medium guns on our harbour area in Chapel Hill. I sat chewing my fingers to keep them from freezing up. Jimmy Samson walked over to discuss some point or other, and I hardly recognised him. He seemed to have shrunk to half his normal size, face black and blue, encrusted with dirt, icicles and beard. But then, how did I look? We later invented a story that he blew his nose, and half of his moustache broke off. Not true, but credible.

Dick Leith's Squadron joined in further attempts to push through Bure, coming in on a flank along with a unit of tank destroyers. These were anti-tank guns mounted on tracks, designed for defence, in which we did not have a lot of confidence as on some occasions they had refused to fire in case they gave away their positions. Dick has a dispute with them, on the air, saying that they were just getting in the way . . . his flank attack failed, but one Troop penetrated up the main road into the village, where it was knocked out by the Tiger, if that is what it was. One tank did not brew, but ran against a house with engine running and gear engaged, where it scraped away with its track for 12 hours until the petrol gave out.

Meanwhile we sat and shivered, with no word from Desmond. His scoutcar had in fact been destroyed by a shell while he was out conferring with the Paras. Three miles away on our left front was a huge round hill, code-name Orange, all white except for a wood on the summit. There was discussion about who was occupying it, but in the afternoon I saw a platoon of infantry advance up its lower slope in arrowhead formation, the size of ants at that range. A grey snout emerged from the trees above them, there was a flash of flame and a white puff among the little figures, who ran back the way they had come. The snout fired again, and one little black figure seemed to leap into the air, and fall back into the snow. He lay there until we left the area of Bure. I was able to report that Orange was not helped by our troops, and hoped that the information was useful to those who gave us orders and controlled our destinies.

Back at last light to Chapel Hill, where Pinkie Hutchison cheerfully announced that he was going on leave, and would I take over the Squadron till he came back. He got into a scoutcar, waved, and disappeared. The Squadron was now down to nine tanks, out of a possible 19, one a non-starter which had to be towed to and from its daytime firing position. My crew were rather pleased, reckoning that a Squadron Leader was supposed to keep himself safe and secure, with others doing the fighting. There was only a small grain of truth in this. Another miserable sleepless night in the turret.

5 January

Out to the same positions at dawn, frequently shelled, but things quieter in the village. We were told that the enemy were pulling out, so I sent Jimmy Samson's Troop round to the far side of Bure, to take on any enemy withdrawing. His Sgt Robinson blew up on a mine, but the rest [moved] round to the rear and spent the day firing at odd packets of Germans.

Colonel Alec came up in his tank, and said that we would probably be relieved by 23 Hussars. They arrived late in the afternoon, and haggled about where they were to position themselves. I finally told them that we were leaving anyway, and that they could leave the line undefended if I followed their tracks cross-country. The ground was churned up, and at one point I cleverly laid my newly-acquired Squadron in a short-cut over virgin snow. Unfortunately this concealed a frozen pond, and three tanks bogged. We tried brushwood under the tracks, towing with a long rope, no use . . . finally three Armoured Recovery Vehicles were sent back to help, and Colonel Alec ordered me to come on back 'in any vehicle available'. I suppose that this was typically kind on his part, but I felt an absolute shit leaving my crew and the others: Brian Jule in charge of the ARVs and Jimmy Samson, whose tank I took to get back. It did not have rubber treads, unlike mine, and when we got from the muddy tracks to the icy roads it kept slithering, at one point crushing a 15cwt truck against a wall – nobody in it.

In Wellin I saw the troops settled in their billets, and searched for the Mess. There I had the first shave for almost week, a drink, a hot meal and a talk with the others about recent events. Finally Desmond Chute and I (acting OC and 2i/c of the Squadron) collapsed into a huge bed upstairs and went to sleep.

Steel Brownlie modestly concludes:

> This was the small part we played in pushing back von
> Rundsted's 'bulge' in the Ardennes. We had been suddenly
> wrenched out of the comforts of Ypres, at such short notice that
> some of the troops went in gym shoes, having no time to get their
> boots, never mind their bedding. My abiding memory is of the
> tiny black figures labouring in a white landscape, while we did
> our best to support them. That, and the cold.

FINAL DAYS

As January neared its end, the battle drew to a conclusion, though the
fighting was hard until the finish.

For the 84th Infantry the final push came after they had taken Houffliaze.
Their last mission, equally as hard and as meaningful to the outcome of the
battle as the ones they had already completed, would take them from Beho
to Gouvy and then on to Ourthe:

> We rested five days and on the sixth day we went into battle again.
> This time we moved up north to do our part in the drive to take
> back the last bit of the ground which the Germans had seized in
> their December offensive. The big objective was St Vith.
>
> This drive was actually begun on January 13, soon after
> Laroche fell and the German withdrawal all along the line was
> well under way. The 30th and the 106th Infantry Division came
> down toward St Vith from the north, from the direction of
> Stavelot. Two days later, January 15, the 75th Infantry Division
> attacked from the west, from the direction of the Laroche Road,
> and Salmchateau fell. On January 19, the 30th Infantry Division
> took Recht and the 1st Infantry Division cleared a defile on
> the 30th's left flank. The next morning, January 20, the 7th
> Armored Division launched the final attack at St Vith, also from
> the north, but it was held up at Born which did not fall until
> nightfall the next day, January 21. From Born to St Vith were two
> more miles. As the 7th Armored was preparing to close the last
> gap, the 84th Infantry Division was preparing to clean out the
> area to the south midway between Houffalize and St Vith.

Still on the look out for German vehicles, a tank destroyer of the US 90th Infantry Division rolls past snow-covered ruins in Berle, Luxembourg. Even buildings such as churches and monasteries, which were often used as shelter by the enemy, were not immune from attack.

Our objectives were the villages of Beho, Gouvy and Ourthe. As operations went, it was not a major operation. After taking all there was to take in our original zone, we were helping out in the last stage of the action in the zone next to ours. But to the men who fought for those three villages, the battles were every bit as important as any other battles anywhere. Men died, dug for cover, ducked 88s, bandaged up buddies if they could, the same way. It was still cold. The snow was three or four feet deep. Vehicles still could not get off the roads without staying off permanently. There were many bridges in our new zone and all were down. Tanks, heavy machine guns, artillery and rockets were still at the enemy's disposal. As far as the man in the line is concerned, war is funny that way. There are big objectives which make big headlines that are relatively easy to take. And there are little objectives which nobody notices that have to be bought yard by yard. For the man in the line, the big battle is the little one.

From our lines to Gouvy was a distance of approximately 2,000 yards, but approximately 5,000 yards separated us from Beho. On our right flank, the main enemy strong points were the village of Gouvy and the railroad station about 1,000 yards east of the village where the enemy was prepared to throw in tanks, anti-tank guns, and infantry. At 8 o'clock in the morning, January 22, the 335th's 2nd Battalion jumped off toward Gouvy. At first the advance was slow and difficult because weather conditions were so trying and the enemy was able to take advantage of observation from the front and high open ground to the southeast. But continued pressure forced the Germans to withdraw east of the railroad. At 12.50, Company G entered Gouvy. In the woods north-east of Gouvy, however, the 2nd Battalion met heavy resistance from dug-in infantry supported by tanks.

Beho was attacked at the same time from both flanks. The 334th Infantry came down on the right, the 333rd Infantry on the left. Two battalions worked different routes for both regiments. On the right flank, the 334th's 2nd Battalion started out near the village of Halconreux to the south-west and had to cross about a mile and a half of thick woods to get to Beho. The 3rd Battalion came down the road from Bovigny to the north-west. On the left flank, the 333rd's 1st and 2nd Battalions came down on both sides of the road from Rogery to Beho, a bit farther to the north-west, the 1st Battalion on the left hand side of the road, the 2nd Battalion on the right side.

The chief resistance was encountered by the 334th's 2nd Battalion. At 6.30am, January 22, the 2nd Battalion jumped off from the edge of woods west of Halconreux. Company F went through the village 20 minutes later, meeting no opposition. It was planned to get the whole battalion into the woods between Halconreux and Beho before daylight but the snow and hilly ground made this impossible. At about 7.30, as the battalion was approaching the railroad at the western edge of the woods, enemy small-arms fire, supported by mortars and at least three tanks, opened up. This burst of resistance held up the battalion until 1.30 in the afternoon when a way was found to bypass the opposition and the battalion succeeded in pushing forward into the woods.

Meanwhile, the 334th's 3rd Battalion was moving down the Bovigny-Beho road. By 4 o'clock in the afternoon, it had reached a point on the eastern edge of the woods from which to launch the final assault on Beho. In the original plan, the 2nd and 3rd Battalions were going to make a co-ordinated attack on Beho, but the snow and the dense forest were slowing down the pace of the 2nd Battalion. At 5.15, when it seemed clear that the 2nd Battalion would be unlikely to participate in the joint attack before dark, the 3rd Battalion was ordered to take Beho alone.

After a heavy artillery concentration, the 3rd Battalion moved into Beho. The village was occupied by 8 o'clock that night. At this, the enemy force in Beho tried to withdraw to the north, only to find itself in the direct path of the 333rd's 1st Battalion which had meanwhile been coming down from Rogery.

At 8.15 that morning, January 22, the 333rd's 1st Battalion had jumped off from Rogery and had pushed on to the high ground about 400 yards northeast of Beho by 5.30 that evening. Two hours later, when the enemy force in Beho tried to withdraw to the north-east under pressure of the 334th's 3rd Battalion, it ran straight into the 333rd's 1st Battalion. For more than an hour, the fight raged. Some of the heaviest action of the day took place north-east of Beho as the enemy was driven to the east by artillery and small-arms fire.

Meanwhile, the 7th Armored Division was pushing down towards St Vith to which the enemy was still grimly holding on, the last prize of his Ardennes adventure.

THE LAST MILE

The next day was spent securing Beho and Gouvy, our primary objective, from enemy counter-attacks.

To secure Gouvy, we had to take the village of Ourthe. At 7.45 in the morning, January 23, the 335th's 3rd Battalion moved out along the Gouvy-Ourthe road. As the leading elements of Company K advanced to the edge of Ourthe, the enemy on the high ground to the east and south-east opened up with automatic weapons, heavy mortars and small arms. The advance was halted. Company I was sent to attack Ourthe from the north but came under the same fire. Our artillery was then called on to soften up the enemy force in Ourthe. Under the cover of smoke, artillery and mortar barrages, Companies K and I, with the support of Company C, 771st Tank Battalion, started forward again at nightfall. This time, Ourthe was ours.

At Beho, the problem of securing our gains turned out to be the problem of repelling a strong enemy counter-attack. Once more it was demonstrated that the enemy, far from resigning himself to permanent loss of initiative in our zone, would try from time to time to wrest it from us.

At 6.30 in the morning, January 23, the 334th's 2nd Battalion renewed the attack from Beho to seize the high ground and crossroads about 1,000 yards east of Beho, between Beho and Audrange, and the high ground about 2,000 yards south-east of Beho. By 7 o'clock, Company E had surprised the enemy outposts at the crossroads and had occupied a near-by monastery. By 8.30 Company G had taken the other objective without resistance and had begun to dig in. But the day's fighting for Company E was not over.

At 8.30 a force of 200 men from the 20th Panzer Grenadiers, 9th SS Panzer Division, supported by three tanks, approached from the direction of Audrange. The tanks began to shell the monastery. Fortunately, the walls were exceptionally thick and the fire had little effect on our men. At the same time, the German infantry closed in. Backed by tanks, this threat was more dangerous. To meet the critical situation, Company E called for artillery on the monastery itself. When our shells began to land with deadly effect in the very yard of the monastery, the tide began to turn.

Meanwhile, Company F had been sent out to relieve Company E. When Company F arrived on the high ground southeast of the monastery, as many Germans as were alive beat a hasty treat to

Audrage. By 9 o'clock, the crossroads was quiet again. In effect, our share of the battle of Ardennes was done.

It was still vital to keep alert for enemy action, but troops were also becoming aware of – and notching up – their successes, and were cheered by news of conquests elsewhere on the battlefield:

25 January 1945 – The great white-painted Shermans swished through the snow and cut across the open country under heavy gunfire from German 88 millimetres . . . and on into a belt of woods. As we entered the wood the tank radios began to chatter about the position of enemy infantry – enemy 'doughs' they called them – who were dug-in in foxholes [and] about enemy tanks they were knocking out. There was a short silence on tank radios while German 88s shelled the woods . . . and then the German gunfire stopped and an elated tank commander came on to talk about some 'big boys' he captured. What kind of 'big boys', he was asked. He snapped back about a piano . . . about octaves, and in the small frontline Command Post where his back-chat was heard there was a chorus of 'octaves . . . 8 . . . 8 . . . 8 . . . Oh, 88s.' He'd captured the 88s . . . how many? Seven of them, he said, intact and complete with ammunition. Could he have engineers along to demolish them? Well, what he said was . . . could he have some doughnuts. But the doughnuts couldn't get down in time. So . . . instructions on how to demolish them with his own tank resources were sent.

The excitement of the battle increased as a new piece of chatter was radioed from tank to tank . . . in front of the leading tanks German infantry were running in disorder . . . without helmets, some without rifles . . . and there was the battle-wise request: who should fire on them . . . whose pigeons were they?

Then came the news from observer planes that a great column of German vehicles retreating eastwards from St Vith had been caught by our aircraft and were being bombed and strafed.

On the same day, Captain Wilfred B Crutchfield, USAF, witnessed the Germans in full retreat:

We'd come in on the road that leads north-east out of Prum. To our surprise, this road, and others we could see, were jammed with German vehicles of all kinds. Double columns bumper-to-bumper. The concentrations were all retreating towards Prum, stretched ahead as far as the eye could see (in my 118 missions I've never seen so much enemy equipment).

As I led the squadron down I found myself headed straight for a flak-gun. I gave it a burst – and knocked it out. Then I took a quick look at the situation and decided to bomb first on a curve in the road. I dropped my two wing bombs on the curve, tore big holes in the road, and knocked out six trucks. This stopped the whole column deader than a duck. Then we really went to work: bombed and strafed the columns of tanks, half-tracks, cargo-trucks, and horse-drawn vehicles over an area of about five miles – knocking out flak at the same time.

Hundreds of the Jerries jumped from their vehicles and ran for cover; others started pulling their vehicles off the road in an attempt to hide them in the trees. But the ground was snow-covered so it didn't do them any good. We followed the tracks and bombed and strafed them in their hide-outs. After our bombs were all gone, we worked back and forth on the column – and all hell broke began to break loose as we'd knocked out all the flak in the area and they were helpless. I've never seen so much confusion. The Jerries would run into the woods and then out again. They were like chickens with their heads cut off.

When most of our ammunition had gone we took stock of the situation. By a careful count we could see from 85 to 90 vehicles of all kinds either completely destroyed or burning and shattered.

AFTER THE FIGHT

The battle ended sooner for some troops than others, but as the report of Lieutenant Colonel AW Brown of the 3rd Royal Tank Regiment concluded:

The American US 2nd Armoured Division now took over the whole area. The enemy were completely disorganised and most abandoned their vehicles for lack of petrol or other reasons. There were still a large number of enemy lying up in the woods and valleys but all that remained was to mop this up and this was to be carried out by the Americans.

Even so, it was impossible to relax completely, for a number of reasons:

Desmond and I reorganised the Squadron, wrote William Steel Brownlie on 6 January, in light of the men and tanks we still had. It was my main job, helped by L/Cpl Taylor, to redistribute the available clothing and equipment, so that there would be as little hardship as possible if we went into action again. No stories had been brought, no-one had a clean change of clothes, soles were coming off boots; frantic messages were sent, with little luck.

On the other hand the billets were good, there was rum and hot food, and a piano in the Mess. The host was Monsieur Colette, the local inspector of Eaux et Forets . . . an unpleasant affair was the possible court-martial of a man who had baled out of his tank, without orders, on Chapel Hill. Cowardice in the face of the enemy was a serious charge. Colonel Alec ruled that it be dropped. Admin problems having been dealt with as far as possible, we recced the country to the east in case of another break-through. This was on foot, except that a new officer, McNamara, took out three tanks for practice, and bogged the lot. I drove one home, skidded off the road and demolished two or three trees. Steel tracks and solid ice don't go together.

The Fife and Forfar Yeomanry, after its 'first shave and hot meal for nearly a week' took the chance for some relaxation and . . .

. . . the Recce Troop became a little boastful about their prowess at wild-boar hunting. A lucky party had the chance to explore the famous Grottos of Han, a sight which peace-time tourists never fail to visit.

The week of relaxation contained one threat of organised action when plans were made to continue operations with the 6th Airborne Division as they followed up the retreating enemy. This plan, in the end, was cancelled. The great German offensive which had at one time sent a seismic quiver of anxiety through the Allied countries was now petering out in failure and exhaustion. The wild German gamble of 1944 had failed just as the vast offensive of March 1918 had failed . . . in Eisenhower's words, the enemy had given the Allies the chance to turn his greatest gamble into his worst defeat.

On their return to Brussels, the Regiment was somewhat sheepish at its joyous reception:

> As the procession of battered tanks, still white-washed and camouflaged, returned to the Capital they were received with great enthusiasm by the population. For many unhappy days the Belgian people had been apprehensive of the possibility of another spell of ruthless German occupation. And they were inclined to treat as heroes those who had helped to spare them that fate. The Regiment didn't seriously object to being treated as heroes, though they know that the Americans had really surmounted their own troubles.

Robert Watt, RSM in the 3rd Royal Tank Regiment, had the highest regard for those who had fought this decisive battle but a matter-of-fact view of the continuation of the conflict:

> With the defeat of the German forces in the battle of the Ardennes Bulge, the war moved on, leaving us far behind and we continued to turn out a constant supply of that human fodder necessary to keep those churning tank tracks moving ever forward. To me, their departure was another stage in the training schedule. I had given them the benefit of my bitter experiences and long since ceased to shoulder the burden of the destiny of those noble soldiers. As they climbed aboard the truck, destination unknown, I knew by the loud-mouthed jokes and banter and the tremor in their voice that the show of bravado was just an act to hide the fear of uncertainty churning in their stomach. As I waved them off and wished them well I wondered how long it would be before they asked themselves, 'What the hell am I doing here?'

As January 1945 ended, the battle was virtually over, but there were still shocks in store. The bodies of these soldiers from the US 28th Infantry (the Bloody Bucket Division), found on 1 February, all had bullet wounds through the head – evidence of an enemy atrocity.

The battle also ended in injury, and the ignominy of being treated in an enemy hospital for wireless operator Hans Behrens:

> My tank commander was going off to the headquarters to
> get new information. I was left alone with Hans, the other
> wireless-operator and machine-gunner in our little half-track.
> In the front we had about inch and a half armour-plating but
> at the back – we didn't expect to be hit in the back – it was only
> about ten millimetres. And I was sitting just doing my paperwork
> for the code, decoding of a message, and suddenly there was hell
> let loose and sparks inside and I felt pain . . . in my legs, then
> I heard voices which I could not understand I thought it was
> the Russians [Ukranian volunteers with the *Wehrmacht*] talking

in their own language, and the door was ripped open and there was standing an American with his sub-machine gun. This sub-machine gun had some armour-piercing bullets there which went through the back of our doors, and through the first-aid kit, and there was I sitting right in front of the wireless-set, and feeling pain in my legs, and a terrible fright, terrible fright.

I do remember pulling the plug out of the wireless-set and ripping the top cipher paper off my communication-pad which I put in my mouth and swallowed, as an obedient soldier!

And the pain got more intensive in my legs, and the American beckoned me out, you know, 'Come on, come on, let's go, let's go,' and I virtually fell out because my legs couldn't take me any more. There was more fright perhaps than . . . the actual wounds. And then . . . an American sergeant came up in his . . . battle gear, [he] spoke in reasonable German, and all he was interested in . . . to go and see his grandmother in Brunswick. He obviously was of German descent, and that was his aim, to get to Brunswick to see his grandmother.

And [Hans] said to me, 'Let's have a look at your legs, and it was bleeding of course, and then the American very kindly gave me some toilet-paper, which I needed badly, which was pink – in the front line, it's unbelievable today.

. . . One of the American soldiers then helped me . . . just in front of our own tank . . . through on the other side of the woods there was an enormous assembly of armour . . . and our orders were, of course, next morning to attack. Thank God I never made it because I wouldn't be sitting here now.

And . . . I was loaded on a Jeep, and of course I still had my full uniform on . . . and taken to the First Aid Station. And at the very moment, the only German plane I ever saw in the last few weeks came down and started to machine-gun fire along this road . . . so I said 'For God's sake get out . . . it's no use coming now.' And I went to the First Aid Station and they looked me over . . . and re-bandaged me again and I was sent back into a more luxurious field hospital. I was the only German among them . . . because across the bed where I was laying in red letters 'German' across it . . . and I do recall that . . . an American Red Cross lady came, and

she sort of had a word with each one on the bed and threw
a packet of cigarettes and candies as they call them – sweets –
on their beds and when she saw me she passed by and at that
moment they were playing the Ave Maria by Schubert one of my
favourites and I swallowed for a few times and I said, 'Well what
did Papa say.' 'We're all the same, we're all Christians, we're all
the same people' . . . and the Red Cross. That hurt me, that hurt
me very much . . .

9

THE BATTLE REPORTED

Allied press reporters were witnesses to events in the Ardennes, and as well as reporting events, the bloody action and the bravery of the men, commented widely on the progress and implications of the battle. All the major agencies were represented, and many reporters employed to file copy for military newspapers and magazines, such as *Stars and Stripes, YANK* and *Soldier.* They shared all the hardships of the troops, sleeping in foxholes and spartan billets. Many were also trained in the basics of combat – both theory and practice.

> [The recruits of the BBC's War Reporting Unit came] from the various departments concerned in war reporting, and in the following months went through an intensive course of special training. To begin with, a physical training instructor toned up what he called his 'BBC Commandos' for life in frontline conditions, and they were instructed in gunnery, signals, reconnaissance, aeroplane and tank recognition, and map reading. They went on assault courses, they crossed rivers on ropes and ducked under live ammunition. They learnt how to live rough and how to cook in the field. They ran cross country against men maybe 15 years younger, and they finished the course. They often finished last, but they finished – and the army didn't like them any the less for that.

Even before the battle began, newsmen were aware of 'rumblings' in the Ardennes region, and of the fact that, despite what was to follow, American troops were on the alert, searching day and night for signs of the enemy, whatever that meant in terms of civilian casualties. Early in December, Robert Barr wrote from the region:

> I went into Groasshau down a squelching, muddy road that

shelves steeply out of the forest. An infantry platoon was
approaching the village . . . crouching watchfully in the ditches,
then moving forward to the next turn in the road and crouching
again. Three riflemen lay flat in the thick mud on the road itself,
rifles to their shoulders, watching the wrecked village for snipers.
In stops and starts the platoon edged its way in and fanned
out right and left to search the cellars for anything the forward
platoon might have missed. A German with his leg swathed in
bandages came limping out with his hands well up. Three of his
comrades lay dead and mud-splashed beside a garden wall.

Behind the garden wall the debris had been pushed aside to
clear a coal chute which led down to a cellar. One of the soldiers
pulled back from his peep-hole and pointing his thumb at the
coal chute said: 'Go down there and mind your feet.'

The cellar was dark and filled with dust and broken masonry
from the grenades that had blasted the Germans out. In the
thin shaft of light that slanted down from the coal chute an
officer was crouched, marking his map. A soldier with a walkie-
talkie lay beside him speaking quietly into a microphone. In the
darkness behind, some 40 soldiers were lying in groups of three
or four around fires made from the grease-soaked cardboard of
their ration boxes. Over the flames they were heating water to
make coffee. One Joe began to fidget with an over-heated can of
pork loaf which he was trying to open – and which was burning
his fingers. This firelight pantomime inspired a few unhelpful
remarks. But most of the men sat around with eyes half-closed
getting a bit of rest. In the next cellar an officer was crouched
over a small table talking on a field telephone. He was covered
in mud, his cheeks were grey and hollowed and his eyes were
sunken and red-rimmed from lack of sleep, and from peering at
his maps in this dark cellar. He was reading off map references
into the telephone. How he could see the small figures in the
dark I don't know. While he talked a dull boom . . . *boomp* . . .
could be felt in the cellar. Somebody said; 'They're mortaring the
road again.'

The signaller, lying curled in the shaft of light, went on
muttering his code-words and jargon into the microphone,
the infantrymen had let the fires die down and were drinking

hot coffee from their canteen cups; the officer laid the field telephone down and called: 'Who's here from —?' and he mentioned the name of an infantry company that was flanking him. A soldier rose from the darkness and came over to the table. Quietly an officer outlined his plans for the evening advance and indicated where his patrols would operate during the night. The soldier repeated the message slowly, saluted, and scrambled up the cold chute into the daylight.

The officer looked round. 'Who's here from —?' and another soldier stepped forward in the dark. Up above, the smoking wreckage of Grosshau was still being searched for snipers and enemy wounded. But down in the cellar the next advance was being planned.

Travelling with the First Army, and cabling via London, Richard Hottelet captured the urgency of the situation, but also the false optimism of the Allies in the early hours of the German offensive. At 1.45pm on December 17th he reported:

The Germans have begun a major counter-offensive on the 1st United States Army front, 30 miles south of Aachen. They are attacking and advancing westward into our lines in the area of Monschau. By noon today they had penetrated several miles into our lines and were still advancing and fanning out. The German counter-offensive is being carried out by a number of divisions, including infantry and Panzer divisions. During the night and this morning, scores of paratroopers were dropped behind our lines to cut communications. This German counter-offensive is on the largest scale they've tried since Morlain, in the Normandy beachhead. There's no doubt that it's their major effort but there is no reason to believe that it will seriously endanger the 1st Army Front.

The purpose is obviously to take the pressure off the Roer river front, farther north, where the American 1st and 9th Armies are threatening the approaches to Cologne.

Though we were taken by surprise, swift counter-measures were taken to bring the German advance to a stop. Right now, fighting is still going on with several German spearheads and, fortunately, the weather improved slightly during the forenoon so that our fighter-bombers could go in and attack. The German attack began at 7 yesterday morning. Our reconnaissance have spotted additional movement behind the German lines in this area, but there was no other indication that any major operation was being prepared. Then, night before last, German artillery all along our front opened up in an extremely heavy barrage, laying thousands of shells into not only our forward positions and supply lines up toward the front, but into communication centers many miles behind the front. The barrage was heaviest south of Monschau.

At 7 yesterday morning the Germans began their offensive drives. The first of these were small, sharp counter-attacks in company or battalion strength. For a few hours it became apparent that they were all being pushed forward vigorously and it also became apparent that on such fronts from six to seven miles south of the town of Monschau something much bigger was in progress. There, in the first few hours of fighting, our forward elements were either overrun or pushed back. The enemy followed with tanks as well as infantry. After eight hours we saw that the enemy was attacking with divisions, including Panzer Divisions, because the pressure on our lines continued more heavily than before.

Into this attack the enemy poured his men and his tanks with convoys of literally scores of tanks and long columns of vehicles. He could afford to do this because weather over both the front and over airbases yesterday completely cancelled out our airpower. The attack continued without meeting any effective American resistance until we stopped it after darkness had closed down. But the Germans had another trick up their sleeves. Beginning at about 7 o'clock last night, they sent an unusually large number of airplanes over our lines. I was up at the front, at the 1st Army's northern flank, and even up there they had air alerts all during the night. At first it seemed that they were reconnaissance planes because they dropped flares through small breaks in the clouds, but, then, others came over, dropped bombs, and straffing. It was only hours later that it became apparent that the enemy's main intention was to drop paratroopers. He dropped them at widely scattered points along more than 50 miles of the 1st Army Front. They were not saboteurs in civilian clothes; they were scouting paratroopers dropped in combat sticks. Their mission was to occupy road-junctions, set up road blocks, attack some of our headquarters, and, in general, spread confusion behind our lines, which would delay us taking counter-measures against the main offensive.

Special American details went out immediately and took many of them prisoners. The mopping-up is still going on today. Then, early this morning the enemy's armoured infantry pushed off again. This time he began to fan out in several directions, but, by this time, counter-measures were beginning to take hold and the German progress was slowed down. Our fighter-bombers got up, too, and bombarded one column on the road, a column of at least a hundred motor vehicles, 50 tanks, and self-propelled guns, and even horse-drawn wagons heading west. Our bombs hit the columns heavily and knocked out a number of the tanks and guns.

Although the situation is certainly not clear, there's no doubt that this German offensive will be continued and contained. We are suffering losses, but so is the enemy. If he loses now in this sector, he will not have to help defend the Rhine.

What does this mean as a military threat?

At 2.30 in the afternoon of the same day, Major George Fielding Eliot was already pondering the reason for the attack:

This attack was launched in a sector which has long been quiet; the Belgian and Luxembourg frontier region on the eastern edge of the great Ardennes Forest . . .

The German reason for launching this counter-attack is perfectly clear. It is a normal German reaction whenever the German High Command believes that it is about to be attacked in force. The Germans always do it when they have the means. It upsets the plans of the attacker by forcing him to switch his reserves from his proposed offensive area to the area where the counter-attack is in operation. Thus, it may gain days, if not weeks, of time as well as giving the Germans valuable positions from which they have to be ousted at great trouble and expense before the original plan can be resumed.

Air bombardment continued day after day, as long as the weather was fine enough, but clearing snow from planes was a vital part of the preparation for flying in freezing conditions. By this stage in the war, many of the pilots were young and inexperienced.

The German Commander-in-Chief seems to have taken the Americans completely by surprise . . . German elements are across both the Belgian and Luxembourg borders and German pressure is continuing, though progress is slower than yesterday, this is the largest German counter-attack since the one which tried to pinch off the Allies breakthrough east of Avranches, in Normandy, way back at the end of July.

The Germans chose well-wooded and difficult terrain for the attack. The reasons were undoubtedly to hamper the Allied airpower and to provide opportunity for the withdrawal of the German forces under cover in case they are finally stopped. The Germans are hardly going to risk the loss of their most important mobile reserve forces just to gain a few days' delay. Their idea would seem to be, so far as it can be guessed now, rather to upset our plans by a hard blow and them pull out their vitally important armored units before gathering resistance can involve them in a fight from which they cannot escape.

The major result for which the Germans might hope, if everything goes well with them, would be a penetration into the communication zone of the1st Army in the area of Liege-Verviers. This would have the affect of turning the right flank of the 1st Army and might occasion us a good deal of trouble. However the Germans are nowhere near this area as yet . . .

Next day, from first Army headquarters at 9am, Hottelet was beginning to realize that this was no push-over for the Allies:

. . . The enemy has poured more infantry and more tanks into the battle this morning, after a pause of about 12 hours. The entire front, stretching about 20 miles south of Monschau is in motion. On our side counter-measures are being taken. On the enemy's side more strength is being thrown in. The weight of his tanks has already given him a penetration of a number of miles deep into our front. When I left the front two hours ago the situation was still fluid.

He's still pushing at several points farther up and down the front. He starts to make it hard for us to assemble troops to meet the main threat. There's no doubt about it that this is the major German effort. Some of the best units in the German Army are involved in the penetration. The Panzer Division spearheading the main thrust is a crack division that's been on the most important sector of half a dozen fronts since it was formed.

Before the Germans launched this counter-offensive, von Rundstedt, German Commander-in-Chief in the West, issued an order of the day to the troops under his command. It read; 'Soldiers of the West Front, your great hour has struck. Strong attacking armies are today advancing against the Americans. I need tell you no more. You all feel it; everything is at stake. You have the sacred duty to give everything and to achieve the superhuman for the Führer and the Fatherland.'

That order of the day about says it. This big offensive in the west is intended to be a serious threat to our whole army position and to break the back of our winter offensive towards the Rhine. There's no hit-and-run character about this. After tanks and infantry made the initial breach the enemy moves his artillery in. He means to consolidate and hold everything he takes and to sustain the offensive.

Behind the front right now he has more divisions ready to follow up. The preparation for this offensive took weeks. Paratroopers have been dropped. I have revealed that they were alerted and formed into special combat teams for their push three or four weeks ago. The gasoline alone he had to accumulate was prodigious, and must have drained his operational reserves.

Our bomber and our artillery have been hitting the German ground force hard last night and our night fighters and anti-aircraft destroyed another 91 of his planes. The enemy right now is matching us strength for strength, and there's no question in anybody's mind, no matter how fluid the situation is right now, that we can outslug him in the end.

All the drama of unfolding events was captured by Richard Hottelet in a report for CBS on 20 December, not least the elation of the taking of the first German prisoners:

They told of the feverishness of the night before the jump-off. They told of American soldiers standing by their guns until they were literally overrun by tanks. They described how they had captured American supply dumps, and fought for the food and cigarettes and gasoline we left. Some German prisoners described how their officers gave them strong propaganda to emphasize the importance of the operation. They were told that the recapture of Aachen would be a Christmas present for Adolf Hitler.

Every one of these prisoners says that this is the big effort. If this succeeds, things will go well. If it fails, there'll be no chance of launching another drive. They said that their intention was to cut lines, capture so many of our supplies, and inflict so much damage that our own offensive to the Rhone will have to come to a stop . . . but we know our own power, and we know that we can beat the enemy down.

The news came thick and fast, with reports of American counter-attacks to the first German onslaught, and of the vital role that the weather was playing in the battle:

NAZIS SAY PATTON HITS ON LEFT

An indication of General Eisenhower's strategy to smash Field Marshall Gerd von Rundstedt's great winter offensive into Belgium and Luxemburg came last night from German News Agency, which interrupted its program with a 'flash' that Lieutenant General George S Patton's Third Army had struck on the Nazi's left flank and succeeded in slowing down the drive into the First Army's lines.

There was no confirmation at SHAEF of this enemy report, only hinted it in previous German broadcasts, which claimed that the Americans were hitting at both flanks of the Nazi penetration along a 60-mile front stretching from Belgium to southern Luxembourg.

Telling of the fighting, Germany News Agency said: 'A particularly grim struggle is being waged on this southern flank, where the German spearheads, heading south-west, had to defend themselves against increasingly furious counter-attacks by several divisions of the US 3rd Army.'

Dispatches from the 21st Army Group HQ had disclosed earlier that the Germans' deepest penetration of the line was 40 miles, but did not mention a specific area. Thursday's reports, however, had told of a drive to Habiemont, south-east of the Allies' communications center of Liège. Last night's dispatches said the German push had been appreciably slowed in fighting on Thursday and yesterday.

Rundstedt has already cut the chief lateral supply road in eastern Belgium, and military commentators speculated that the purpose of his counter-offensive was to set up a winter line along the Meuse, north-west of the salient which reached Habiemont by noon Tuesday.

Weather boon to foe

Weather conditions have served Rundstedt's purposes. The front has been shrouded for days in swirling fog, which barred Allied fighter-bombers from carrying out destructive forays.

Yesterday, with the weather clearing somewhat, Allied tactical fliers made more than 100 sorties on the northern sector, following up British heavy bomber blows against Cologne and Bonn on Thursday night.

German broadcasts said Rundstedt's troops in the northern area were 35 miles from Namur which, like Liège, is on the Meuse, and about 60 miles from Brussels.

Battles in this general area were said to have cost the Germans SS tanks, smashed by US armour and tank destroyers.

Some reports told of German tanks having been stranded when the enemy failed to capture needed oil supplies, the Yanks having moved back these supplies before the enemy reached them.

An American staff officer said casualties were considered light in view of the vast scale of the battle. German claims were that 25,000 Allied troops had been made prisoners and that figures for killed and wounded were greater.

The effects of the battle on citizens back home was clearly pointed out in this article in *YANK* magazine, though many might have thought at the time that it was too late in the day to be talking about doubling the draft:

COUNTEROFFENSIVE

Not since D-Day have US citizens listened so intensely to their radios or so closely read their newspapers. The German counter-offensive in Belgium and Luxembourg was a blow that was felt in every town. To most Americans it was one of the greatest since Pearl Harbor. It completely reversed the high optimism of last August. But it was a healthy pessimism that now pervaded the country, based on a sober re-evaluation of the war's cost in men and materials and a realization that now nobody could accurately guess as to its duration.

The unexpected display of German strength had an immediate effect on Government planning for the war effort. Chairman JA Krug of the War Production Board announced in Philadelphia that the WPB was now operating on a theory that the war in Europe may go on indefinitely. He stated that new factories are to be built to meet the enormous demand for trench mortars and other munitions. The German counter-offensive, he said, is causing heavy losses of American equipment and it may be necessary to re-equip the entire First Army. All this means a boost in American production requirements.

Even more significant, however, was an order doubling the draft rate for January and February from 40,000 to 80,000 men.

Production of civilian goods was frozen from current levels and allotment of tires for civilian use was sharply cut, reflecting an increasing shortage in rubber for military vehicles on the European front.

No attempt was made to disguise the extent of the tactical surprise achieved by the Germans and this resulted in open criticism of military intelligence for failing to give adequate warning of the German movements along the Belgium-Luxembourg front.

The reporters did not hold back from describing unpalatable events, nor, as their profession demanded, from commenting on events as they unfolded. The shock of the attack, and the reasons why the Allies had been caught unawares was also the subject of John Hall's hard-hitting report for the *Stars and Stripes*:

I HAVE COME BACK TO THE BEWILDERED ISLES

Two stock questions have been flung at me – 'How did it happen?' and 'What went wrong?'

I cannot give a simple answer: because of security I cannot give a completely full explanation. But I can explain a number of points which may help you get a better perspective on von Rundstedt's giant offensive.

No thinly-strung army could have held against the weight of men, armour and explosives which Rundstedt hurled into the Ardennes. When the full story can be told, the world will learn how many Americans stood there and died rather than retreat or surrender.

Cling to illusions

Many here still cling to two dangerous illusions – one that American military power is limitless, the other that Germany has been left with very little of anything. These are the evils of propaganda and shiftless thinking.

Rundstedt looked for the sector he thought weakest. It had been quiet for weeks on that front. Measured against vital spots like the Ruhr and the Saar, nothing in front of us there was worth fighting for.

Anyone who has spent time 'out in front' in this war knows that in quiet sectors it is the easiest thing in the world to drive into the other fellow's lines – yes, the German lines – and, if you're lucky, to go a long way without a shot being fired at you.

Well, it was on that sort of front that von Rundstedt struck.

Paratroops had already been dropped behind our lines and had been at work several hours, cutting telephone lines, attacking command posts, and doing everything possible to create confusion and prevent the American leaders from fighting an orderly defence.

Stealing US equipment

Added to that was the enemy's new 'weapon' – the trick of using vehicles and armor exactly like American equipment and putting German soldiers into American uniforms.

They got through – tanks, men, and self-propelled guns. They rode west. Pulled off the highway or lane into the forest covert and fired, say, a dozen rounds at American battery positions. Then, before counter-battery attack was possible, they packed up and hared to another covert.

Part of Rundstedt's plan – an important part – was to paralyse the direction of defense measures. He ordered some of his American-dressed and civilian-clothed 'infiltrators' to attack headquarters, to kill full colonels and upwards, with special directions to kill generals. They were 'brass hat killer squads' – and they were a failure.

Some of the enemy's gun units had orders to shell headquarters in the hope of dissipating the battle direction at high level. They, too, failed. Then the Luftwaffe took up the task.

Once the enemy had got his mobile units roaming behind our lines it became a war of hide-and-seek on roads, lanes, and in narrow forest paths.

Then there was the weather. German meteorological experts 'gave' Rundstedt perfect weather – fog and mist so thick that aircraft could not move. And it stayed like that long enough for the 'wildcat columns' to scatter within call of the Meuse and give the enemy time to pour exploiting troops through the gap. It gave the enemy so much help that when the weather did clear and the combined Allied Air forces went in he could afford to stay in these forest coverts – out of sight.

Can't praise fliers enough

I cannot praise enough the brave young American fliers who went into the Battle of the Ardennes. I watched them actually scraping the tree-tops to search for hiding enemy tank units. They were superb.

And those 'wildcat columns' brought their own ack-ack with them, Rundstedt forgot nothing. In spite of everything that has been said to the contrary, I have seen no evidence that the Nazis are short of men or materials. The German dead and prisoners were all men of good physique, and most of those alive were full of pep and convinced of Germany's final victory. The enemy's artillery barrages show no marks of shell rationing, and he appears to be well supplied with fuel for tanks and transport. I talked with a captured German officer who claimed that while we were fighting in the Falaise pocket, all the best German motor transport was busy evacuating food, ammunition and fuel supplies that had been cached in France and the Low Countries. He claimed that they had enough material cached to fight a full-scale war for 12 months. One powerful factor which induced the Germans to begin the Battle of the Ardennes was the knowledge that every hour we were able to use to the port of Antwerp made Germany's doom more certain.

Fought, died bravely

I have seen enough to [testify] that the great majority of the young Americans fought and died bravely. It was a curious experience to be with the Americans these last ten days and to see, when they realized what had happened, the stunned 'it can't happen to us' look on their faces.

In a way, since the Normandy breakthrough, the Western Front had been too one-sided. They had been a winning team too long. None of this affects my admiration for the combat GIs, the way they fight and the way they are led. In my view the strength of the American front-line troops lies in the middle senior officers – the majors and lieutenant colonels. They are magnificent.

Nothing of what has happened these last two weeks can be blamed on the American combat troops. They did, and are still doing, their duty, and are fighting well. I referred to the 'it can't happen to us' bewilderment that struck many Americans. But now I must point out they very quickly snapped out of it. We saw remarkable feats of swift American organization. The Hun captured very little that was of immediate use to him.

American supply columns were ordered to make certain evacuations. Hundreds of motor trucks appeared as if from nowhere. In a few hours thousands of tons of ammunition, food and fuel were on their way back to safer areas. In half a dozen ways American mobility outsmarted the Hun blitz in this affair – but the telling of those stories will have to wait.

There was more dramatic news to come with the liberation of Bastogne, described in this vivid report, made more telling by the personal stories it told and the emotions conveyed:

WOUNDED COME OUT OF BASTOGNE – THEIR BODIES AND MINDS SEARED
By Jimmy Cannon, Stars & Stripes *writer*
With American Forces, December 29 – Detroit shouted, but all you could hear was a smeared whisper through the bandages. 'I'll never forget that town,' he muttered. 'I left a piece of my nose in it.'

The convoy of the wounded came out of Bastogne in a slow trickle. The day was beautiful, if you like Belgium in the winter time. The snow on the hills glittered in the sun and the planes towed vapor trails across the big clean sky. The wounded sat stiffly in the trucks and they rose tacitly when they came to a rut in the frozen road. The dust of the road had made their hair gray, but it did not look strange, because their faces were old with suffering and fatigue.

'We're all 4Fs in here,' said Chicago, to the guy who had climbed into the truck. 'A healthy guy like you better look out, you'll get drafted.' Detroit's neck was swollen as he yelled, but his voice was still small and remote. 'We were standing around a mess truck,' he said, 'waiting for some hot cakes, when they let go with everything they had. We were in a field and they were up above us and all around us and what a going over they gave us.'

'Who won the Christmas football games?' asked New York.

'We did,' said another Detroit, who had a slab of shrapnel in his back. 'Anyone who is alive is a big winner.'

Tocono Mountains who sat curved over with a blanket over his head, said these hills reminded him of home.

'There was an outfit getting an awful going over in a little village,' he said. 'We went across an open field and exposed ourselves to keep Jerry busy. He got so interested in us, those other guys got away.'

'Give me Paris.' Brooklyn shouted. 'Give me Paris and a nice mommer who'll wash me and shave me and tuck me up to sleep for nine million years.' They all laughed, but you couldn't tell they were laughing by looking at their faces. Anyway, they made the sounds of laughter.

'Find me a girl like that,' said Illinois, 'and I'll marry her myself.'

'We are good in the hospital,' said New Mexico, who is a full-blooded Indian, 'but those poor bastards in the line didn't have nothing to eat for four days, some of them.'

The convoy slowed down in the street of a town and a girl came out and gave them hot coffee. St Louis gave her a crumpled deck of Camels, which she didn't want to take, but he insisted. The convoy moved again, rocking through the beautiful day. St Louis bummed a cigarette because he had given away the last one he had.

Come the New Year, and the clearing of the weather, good news began to come in from other sectors of the battlefield:

FOE STOPPED; RHINE BRIDGES HIT
3rd Parries Thrusts; Bombers Hammer Arteries to Salient

With the Germans in the Ardennes bulge digging in for a defensive and attempting to build up strength for a possible second lunge into the Allied lines, the war in the air assumed added significance yesterday as some Eighth Air Force heavies struck against bridges over the Rhine and Moselle rivers, which form a triangle where they meet behind the Belgian-Luxembourg battle zone.

The attack on the Rhine bridges was the first reported such assault by Allied bombers other than one isolated attack on a single span in the Cologne area several weeks ago. Apart from operations along the southern flank of the enemy salient, where German attempts to cut the corridor into Bastogne were beaten off, there were no radical changes in the battle line, according to dispatches which covered activity 36 hours old at the time of release through censorship.

With reports from SHAEF and the fronts indicating that a renewed German counter-offensive was not to be discounted, the Eighth Air Force continued to strike to prevent the enemy from massing more troops and material in the breakthrough area west of the Rhine and Moselle. At a recent press conference, Gen Eisenhower declared that it was in the area west of the Rhine that the main battle for Germany probably would be fought. Not only were bridges targets for the Eighth, but rail centers in this region were also hammered.

What proportion of the 2,000 Eighth Air Force bombers and fighters employed yesterday was over the enemy's rear areas was not disclosed. Targets for the heavies – 1,300 were in action, escorted by 700 Thunderbolts and Mustangs – included Hamburg, Harburg and Misburg, as the Eighth carried on its first strategic mission in nine days, as well as continuing its tactical support.

Realising the danger in the drive by 3rd Army troops northwards from Bastogne toward Manhay, on the northern flank of the enemy bulge, the Germans tried hard to sever the corridor feeding Lt George S Patton's men from doughboys holding on the north.

Among other disclosures yesterday was the news that the 82nd Airborne Division had been engaged in the attempt to stem the Germans' drive into Belgium. These veterans of Sicily, Italy, Normandy and Holland were used as infantry, dispatches said, and helped to stop the 1st SS Adolf Hitler Tank Division; made contact with two other US units nearly trapped around St Vith and then fought off counter-blows by three enemy divisions. The men had been in a rest camp before going into the line.

German units slamming into the corridor from the east lost 25 tanks in an all-day fight, and other troops coming from the opposite direction, also met with defeat.

On the western tip of the enemy salient, Rochefort was recaptured by the Americans, whose pressure forced the enemy to evacuate this city, 16 miles east of the Meuse. Northeast of Rochefort, a small German pocket near Grandmenil was surrounded.

The Germans apparently were seeking to find out just what changes might have been made along the Allied front to meet their thrust into the Ardennes. One example of these tactics was a German stab into the town of Tripsrath, three miles above British-held Geilenkirchen. This is in the region along the left flank of the positions last reported held by the US Ninth Army.

The Germans, two companies strong, were thrown out by a British counter-attack. A subsequent attempt to take the town was broken up by artillery.

As the Germans were beginning to be pushed back, the news became a little more heartening, but there was still the realization that the enemy was far from defeated.

INTO THE VALLEY OF NAZI DEATH –
AND OUT – SNEAKED HOGAN'S 400

By Ken Dixon, Associated Press Correspondent

East of Marche, Belgium, Dec 31st – Their faces blacked, their helmets and iron horses left behind, the fighting 400 of 'Task Force Hogan' came out of the woods through ten miles of enemy lines Wednesday morning.

Isolated and encircled, far from help, they had been given up as lost. All but about 20 returned, led by Lt Col Samuel Hogan of Pharr, Tex. This what they had done:

Penetrated enemy lines more than 30 miles; been trapped by three panzer divisions outnumbering them hundreds to one; until their gas ran out, fought a mobile, cagey battle that kept the encircling Germans confused and at bay; dug into a village highpoint; and, as 'forward observers', radioed information from the midst of the enemy that enabled American artillery to smash a major counter-attack along the whole sector.

Refused to surrender

They refused to surrender despite almost certain annihilation; rendered their armoured vehicles useless to the enemy and made a bold Christmas night escape afoot, just as the German trap was being sprung; hiked over timbered hogback ten miles to safety.

They jumped off one afternoon with 60 vehicles, ranging from medium tanks to Jeeps. After 30 miles of easy, swift going, they hit a road block and tangled with anti-tank and small-arms forced, they cleared it that night, and next day were forced to draw away from armoured infantry shooting down from a mountain precipice.

Probing north and south, they found they had been sucked in between overpowering enemy forces. After trying again and again to break out, they finally spotted a village perched on high, barren hill-top. They uncorked their reserve punch to hammer through tough opposition to the village, where they used their last gas to roll tanks, half-track and artillery to the seven-road entrances.

During the next two freezing days they beat off attack after attack, meanwhile directing American artillery by radio on the German below. The artillery also attempted to fire medical supplies in and failed.

Planning the escape

When the Germans asked for the unit's surrender, the colonel refused. He was planning the escape.

Lt Harold W Randall, of Whiteoaks, Kan, led a patrol to see how the land looked. After he reported back, everyone blacked his face with soot or axle grease, and helmets were discarded because of the possibility of tell-tale silhouettes.

The task force crept out into the darkness. Three medics and their captain insisted on remaining behind to care for 12 wounded. One of the wounded held a tommy-gun on 17 Germans until the force could make its getaway.

As the men topped the hogback's first peak, a terrific barrage thundered against the trapped town. The group brushed silently by German sentries and got into the American lines. A few of them were arrested by suspicious doughboys. Finally, they came in and were recognized with shouts of welcome.

The last man to return was Hogan. 'My feet got hurting me,' he grinned, 'so I just sat down and rested a while.'

The fact that there was no room for complacency, and the continued role of the weather, were also highlighted in this report of 3 January:

GERMAN ARMOR PULLING BACK
Corridor Cut More by 3rd Army

Lt Gen George S Patton's drive between Bastogne and St Hubert into the German bulge in Belgium has gained another two miles, and the enemy, with the waist of his salient narrowed to perhaps only ten miles, was pulling back his armor from SHAEF, where a 36-hour time-lag for security purposes was still in effect.

While the armor was moving eastwards, Field Marshal Gerd von Rundstedt's troops kept jabbing against Patton's forces at points along a 25-mile front running east from south of St Hubert to south of Wiltz, in Luxemburg. Dispatches suggested that the Germans were readjusting their positions within the salient, possibly for a second lunge.

On the northern flank of the bulge, US patrols probed more than a mile into the no-man's land between the lines between Hotton and Marche without making contact with the foe, who was dug in in defensive positions in this sector.

US troops moving up against the western tip of the enemy salient lost contact with one armoured division that had been in that region and met only rearguard action from elements of two other divisions.

The keys to victory: piled cans of gasoline that kept the Allies going through the battle – and which the fuel-starved German forces failed to capture. As their supplies waned, the Germans realized that they would not be able to deliver to Hitler the victory he so desperately desired.

While icing conditions slowed action on some sectors, Patton's troops scored gains both east and west of Bastogne, taking towns which have changed hands several times in give-and-take fighting. At the eastern end of the southern flank, the border town of Echternach was re-captured by the Americans. On the western end the doughboys were about two miles southeast of St Hubert.

In one of the continuing enemy counter-attacks against Patton's positions ringing Bastogne, a group of around 500 German infantrymen was flung back by troops of the US 26th Infantry Division, who made some gains in following up the defeated Nazis.

German blows against the Seventh Army sector between Bitche and Wissembourg were reported to be definite attempts to penetrate or bend the American lines, but most of the attacks have been dealt with successfully, except for one in the area south-east of Bitche, where the Seventh lost some ground.

United Press reported German counter-forces across the Saar. In Saarlautern, it said, two more blocks have been cleared of Germans.

Even before the year of 1944 had ended, questions were being asked about the lack of Allied preparedness for the surprise attack in the Ardennes.

On 27 December, the *Stars and Stripes* published this unattributed hard-hitting piece, overtly critical of the intelligence services and accusing the powers that be of over confidence:

ARMY HEADS MAY ROLL IN WAKE OF NAZI PUSH

Washinton, December 29 – Sources close to the War Department expressed belief today that the heads of some American and British military chiefs would roll because of recent reverses on the Western Front, with the primary responsibility for the German breakthrough apparently being laid at the door of the intelligence service, the Associated Press reported.

Meanwhile, in Philadelphia, JA Krug, War Production Board chairman, said WPB was operating now on the theory that the war in Europe would go on indefinitely. He pointed out that new factories to make trench mortars could not go into production until August. If the war ended before August a good deal of money would be lost, but if it didn't end by then, as probably it won't, said Krug, the new plants – costing $200,000,000 – would save many American lives.

Although it was indicated that a complete report of the circumstances leading to the German winter drive had not reached here, the finger was pointed at the intelligence service by the *Washington Post* and by two US correspondents, William L Shirer, of the Columbia Broadcasting System, and Charles A Michie, of the *Chicago Sun*.

Said the *Post*: 'The disquieting thing to the people is that our command was caught napping. Blame is attached to the intelligence service. For the mistake, both the British and ourselves must accept joint responsibility, for at SHAEF the chief intelligence officer is a Briton with an American as his deputy, the deficiency will no doubt be remedial.'

Shirer, who returned Friday from a six-week tour of the front, said the 1st Army commanders were and are aware of a German attack three weeks before it began and guessed correctly where it might come, but that events indicated G-2 had failed to appraise the high command of the projected Nazi attack. Michie said military analysts in Washington believed the Allied commanders did not know enough about the preparation for the German counter-thrust to ready adequate defenses, adding his own conclusion: 'What they mean is that our military intelligence service failed in its job of reporting accurately the movements of the enemy.'

Two other columnists commented on America's use of military manpower. Hanson W Baldwin, of the *New York Times*, said the US was 'luxurious and wasteful' in using its men and called for a more thorough 'comb out' of the Army and home front for replacements for the ground forces – 'the arm of ultimate decision.'

Drew Pearson charged that the War Department itself was responsible for 'a lot of favourable news which gave the public a general feeling of over-confidence.'

One item, he said, was that some 800,000 German troops were killed or captured in the clearup in France. 'Of these, however, about 400,000 constituted Russian Ukranian labor battalions,' Pearson said. 'Thus the American public mistakenly believed that a large slice of Germany's army was decimated.'

Pearson contrasted German and American methods of employing troops in the front line. US troops are kept in the front line, with fresh men being brought up only as replacements, Pearson said, whereas the Germans took out their first-line troops after Normandy and sent them to rest camps. 'Experienced Germans, refreshed after a long rest, are now taking the offensive against us,' Pearson asserted.

Once the Germans were beginning to be driven back, and their troops were starting to surrender, there came hard-hitting comments on the state of the leadership of men in the field.

HIMMLER, NOT AILING RUNDSTEDT, COMMAND WEST, CAPTIVE SAYS

By Jules Grad, S7S Staff Writer, with US Troops in Belgium

January 4 – Heinrich Himmler, Hitler's 'hatchet man', personally is directing the German campaign on the Western Front, Col Van der Heydte, German prisoner-of-war, has informed American officers. 'Army Group commanders now take their orders only from Himmler,' he stated. 'Von Rundstedt is a very old and very sick man. He is Commander-in-Chief in name only.'

Offering late news of Nazi leaders still in Germany, the captured colonel told army officers:

'Dietrich is still a table waiter not fit to lead a German army. His staff swarms with SS generals, but it's easy to be a general these days. He told me he intends personally to knock the American armies out of the war with his SS divisions.'

The colonel and his troops were scheduled to drop in the Mouschau-Malmedy area on Dec 16 – first day of the German attack. Due to 'inexperience' of the JU-52 pilots, they were dispersed over a wide area.

Van der Heydte and some of his troops entered Mouschau when they heard the Germans had captured the town. When he learned the report was false, he immediately surrendered.

THE PERSONAL TOUCH

By the close of the battle, as winter's end was approaching the war reporters were as weary and battle scarred as any of the combatants. Robert Barr filed this moving report on 13 January 1945:

A Tank Destroyer company had pulled itself off the ridge and was preparing to swing east to a busier part of the line. The snow along the ridge was churned by the tracks of the great tank-destroyers and by the wheels of the ammunition carriers and the trucks. And some thin scraggy trees on the edge of the wood were splintered and smashed where they had barged their way under the trees for the night. Deep inside the wood there were fires alight.

It was just coming on dark, and I could smell cooking, so I called in. In the half-light a single file of men, ankle deep in snow, their mess kits ready, were waiting patiently for chow. There were four fires in a row; on the first three great metal trays were sizzling with hot food; the men began to trudge forward holding out their mess kits. From the first tray came a steaming ladle of macaroni and tomato sauce, from the second a ladle of mashed potato, with the cook saying: 'Is that enough?' And from the third came a chunk of steak and a ladle full of gravy.

Beside the third fire a captain stood against a tree, watching rather anxiously, watching the sizzling trays and watching the faces of his men as they came into the firelight. The captain was young, about twenty-eight, and there seemed to be something special about the stew; he kept watching his men as he talked to me. 'For five days,' he was saying, 'my men have been fighting on cold rations, mostly crackers and cheese. I've been saving this stuff till we could get somewhere we could cook it. Why don't you have some? It smells good.' I said I was pushing on, but could I have some coffee? 'Sure, he said, 'sure, plenty of coffee.'

It was getting darker and the ghost queue kept filing last, each face lighting for a moment in the glow of the fires. It was a strange pageant of tough, rough, bearded faces. They were all young lads, and the captain apologized for the beards. 'We couldn't shave in the front line,' he said. 'It was too cold. Now we've got hot water, we'll be shaving them off after chow. Do you want to stay and see it?' I said I'd like to, but I'd just crept in for a cup of coffee. 'Oh, yes, coffee,' he said. 'Follow me.' We wound in and around a few trees to the prize tableau of this forest pantomime. In the darkness under a great fir-tree was a huge log fire. On the log fire there was a great cauldron, and on the cauldron a great iron lid. It didn't fit too well and steam hissed out all around the edges, and the firelight made the steam turn scarlet. And, in the midst of it all was a strange hunched figure with a long woollen cap and a long brown beard; he sat with one hand poised over the great iron lid, in the other he held a ladle.

He sat perfectly still. At his feet were the adjuncts of his profession, a bowl of sugar and a tin of cream. He said nothing. I took some sugar and I held my canteen forward. He lifted the iron lid, scooped a ladle of coffee, and banged the lid down quickly. 'He does that to keep the cold air out,' the captain explained. 'Is that enough?' I said it was; my canteen was brimming over and scalding my fingers. 'Are you sure you won't have any chow?' asked the captain for about the fourth time, and when he saw that I was staring at the coffee-man's beard he laughed. 'That old man,' he said, 'is just twenty-six years old. Why don't you wait and see him shave his beard off?'

I sipped my coffee and said that I had to go, but I'd come back again tomorrow. 'We won't be here tomorrow,' said the captain. 'We've a date with some Panzers two miles east. Why don't you have some chow, and see the beards come off. Let the war look after itself for one night like we're doing.' It was such an unusual pantomime, the dark forest, the snow, the smell of good food and good coffee, I felt I had to see the whole show. 'All right,' I said. 'If you're letting the war look after itself tonight, I'll join you.'

Also among the war reporters was Lee Miller, the American photographer who had chronicled the progress of the Allies from Normandy, through the liberation of Paris and on into the aftermath of the Ardennes, when the US Army, fighting with the Free French were pushing south from Strasbourg. With her own Jeep, she was able to move almost at will among the troops. Her article, 'Through the Alsace Campaign' for the April 1945 issue of *Vogue*, was written like a description of a series of photographs, and summed up the mood that prevailed at the finish of the Battle of the Bulge, before the final push to Berlin:

> I'll never see acid-yellow and grey again like were shells burst
> near snow without seeing also the pale quivering faces of
> the replacements, grey and yellow with apprehension. Their
> fumbling hands and furtive, short sighted glances at the field
> they must cross. The snow which surrounds innocent lumps
> and softens savage craters covers alike the bodies of the enemy
> and of the other platoon which tried before. The new craters are
> violent with black circles of clods around, the smell is choking.
> In the ditch a waxen-faced dead German was frozen in a heroic
> pose, and the new boys stamped their feet because the others did.
> They were too numb to feel the cold. Mostly they twisted one
> foot around the other, shyly . . . a lieutenant who was holding his

cut face leaned against a tree. He left a bloody hand mark and
walked on. He started down the ditch and sat on the edge, slowly,
with his hands to his belly. He sat there for a while. Soldiers who
passed him spoke. He motioned them on. One stayed and then
went back to the mill. Two guarded German prisoners came with
a litter, but he was dead. They left him covered up by the side
of the road. The guard and the prisoners saluted and returned
towards the mill . . . what kind of atavism are we creating for
hordes of people and children who peek out of their cellars
at dawn to find the strange men who were eating soup in the
barnyard before the 'noise', pale and dead in the snow?

The German offensive in the Ardennes undoubtedly caught the local
people by surprise and turned their lives into a nightmare they would never
forget. Gerard Rossignol was driving into Belgium in January 1945 when
he noticed:

It had rained and snowed, and turned to bitter cold. It was a
horrible sight. The natives were walking away from the front-
lines with whatever they could carry. Old men and women,
with small children, most of them, had their feet wrapped in
burlap or anything they could utilize to keep warm. We could
see their terrified looks. They were leaving with no place to go.
I will always remember one old man, with a small child tied to
his back, and a bag under each arm. You could almost feel
their pain.

Allied soldiers were also struck by the incongruous juxtaposition of a
superb landscape and the weapons of war:

All round Brussels and Liège it was milky fog. But when you
drove past the frozen canals and the tobogganing children up
to the heights of the Ardennes the sun broke through and it was
like a spot-lighted stage, mile upon mile of untrodden snowfields
under the clear and frosty lamp of the winter sun. If you turned
your back to the ruined villages and forgot the war for a moment,
then very easily you could fancy yourself to be alone in this
radiant world where everything was reduced to primary whites

and blues; a strident sparkling white among the frosted trees, the deep blue shadows in the valley and then the flawless ice-blue of the sky. Flying Fortresses went by, immensely high, spinning out their vapour trails half-way across Belgium.

All this was an uplifting thing to see, and it triumphed for a little in the mind until one came upon a stranded tank threshing madly in a ditch or saw a line of infantry passing over a hill. And then in the villages one met a recurring tragedy as sharp as any in this war. These Belgians had had their outburst of joy at liberation, only to see the Germans come back again. Then the shells of the Allies returned a second time. As the Germans retired they took with them the men of the villages to work in Germany. No wonder that the women stood in their doorways asking over and over again, 'Are you sure they have gone for good?'

Finally, a report of unexpected friendship, even in the midst of battle:

YANKS AT HOME ABROAD
Change of Plans
With the Ninth Army – Two riflemen of the 334th Infantry of the 84 Division wish that the Jerries they encounter could be persuaded as easily as three they shared their K rations with.

Pvt Thomas Kyle of Union City, NJ, and Pvt Edwin Olson of Badger, Iowa, both in A company, were walking up a railroad track from the little village of Leifarth, Germany, early in the morning when they were surprised by three Germans who had penetrated the American lines in a sudden counter-attack.

The Germans motioned the Americans to join them in a dug-out near the tracks. All five crowded in together. Then the Germans found that their counter-attack was sagging and that they couldn't move their prisoners back until our mortar barrage lifted. Time dragged on slowly; so Kyle and Olson began talking to the Germans and found that one could speak a little English and another a little French.

After a while, they brought out their wallets and showed the Germans pictures of their families and their homes. They had quite a collection of typical American scenes. Came noon,

and Kyle and Olson were getting hungry; so they opened their
K rations and shared them with the Germans. The afternoon
passed with more talk about the US and about how well German
prisoners are treated there. As they talked the mortar shells
started falling closer.

Suddenly, late in the afternoon, the three Germans threw down
their rifles, raised their arms and cried 'Kamerad.'

Kyle and Olson picked up the German rifles, and marched their
prisoners back to the battalion CP [Command Post].

GLOSSARY

AA Anti-aircraft

AP Armour-piercing

APC Armoured personnel carrier

AT Anti-tank

BAR Browning Automatic Rifle

Bn Battalion

Cal Calibre

CO Commanding Officer

Co Company

CP Command Post

Div Division

FA Field Artillery

Feldwebel Sergeant

FHQ Hitler's personal Headquarters

Flak German AA Artillery

GI Government Issue – all officially issued military equipment of the US Army; the soldiers who used it

G-1 Senior staff officer on American formation command staff

G-2 Intelligence Officer on American staff

G-3 Operations Officer on American staff

G-4 Supply Officer on American staff

Hauptmann Captain

HE High Explosive

HMG Heavy machine gun

I and R Intelligence and Reconnaissance

KG Kampfgruppe, German fighting group, often improvized

LMG Light Machine Gun

M-1 American infantry rifle

MC Military Cross

MG Machine gun

MG42 German belt-fed light machine gun

MM Military Medal

MP Military Police(man)

MP44 German sub-machine gun

OB West German Commander-in-Chief in the west and his HQ staff

OKW German Armed Forces High Command

POL Petrol Oil and Lubricant

PoW Prisoner of War

RCT Regimental Combat Team

RSM Regimental Sergeant Major

SABOT A type of armour-piercing shell

SHAEF Supreme HeadQuarters Allied Expeditionary Force – Eisenhower's HQ

SIGINT Signals Intelligence

SS Schutzstaffel – the Nazi security organization

Tac Tactical

Tec Technician, a category of qualified soldier in the American Army

TD Tank destroyer

VGD Volks-Grenadier Division, a German division raised in the Autumn of 1944, often consisting of older men and youngsters.

ULTRA Information gained by the Allies by decoding Enigma transmissions

Wachtmeister Officer

CHRONOLOGY

November 1944

3rd Conference at OB West. Commanders of the German 5th and 6th Panzer Armies and 7th Army are given orders to attack in the Ardennes on 25th November.

16th Start of major attacks by the US 1st Army towards the Roer dams in the area immediately north of the Ardennes.

22nd US 1st Army offensive culminates in the capture of Eschweiler close to the Roer.

25th HQ 5th Panzer Army moves forward into the Eifel.

December 1944

2nd Conference at FHQ in Berlin. Hitler briefs the German Army Group and Army commanders. Field Marshal von Runstedt refuses to conduct the offensive as ordered and is replaced with Field Marshal Model.

10th Lead formations of the 5th and 6th Panzer Armies begin to move into assembly areas for the offensive.

10–11th Conference at the 'Eagle's Nest'. Hitler briefs all commanders of divisions committed to the offensive.

13th Leading elements of the 5th and 6th Panzer Armies and 7th Army move to locations just behind the Start Line for the offensive.

15th–16th Assault infantry of 5th Panzer Army infiltrate the forward positions of the US VII corps.

16th Tanks of the 5th and 6th Panzer Armies attack with artillery support. American troops are taken by surprise.

17th In the northern sector lead elements of 6th Panzer Army make progress, but not as much as required by their plan. Schonberg is taken but Monschau is not, and the US 9th Armoured Division strengthens positions in the key road centre of St Vith. The German attempt to secure the heights north of Malmedy by airborne assault fails. Americans taken prisoner near Malmedy are shot. In the southern sector, 5th Panzer Army advances rapidly and takes many prisoners from the US 106 Division after encircling two regiments.

General Eisenhower orders the 82nd and 101st Airborne Divisions to the Ardennes – the 82nd to block routes ahead of the 6th Panzer Army and the 101st to hold the vital centre of communications at Bastogne in the sector of the 5th Panzer Army.

18th The 1st SS Panzer Division, leading the advance of the 6th Panzer Army fights hard to get through Stavelot and misses capturing the biggest American fuel dump in the Ardennes. Later attempts to advance via an alternative route are checked at Trois Ponts. Later still American troops reoccupy Stavelot. In the south the 5th Panzer Army continues to advance. The 7th Army manages to put bridges across the Our but is too slow to retain surprise. The US 10th Armoured Division moves to defend Bastogne.

19th In the north the forward battlegroup of 6th Panzer Army is delayed by increasing resistance and shortage of fuel.

In the south the 2nd Panzer Division and Panzer Lehr Division attacks Bastogne but is stopped by a part of the 10th Armoured Division. General von Manteuffel is forced to face the 'Bastogne Dilemma'.

20th In the north attempts by the most advanced element of 6th Panzer Army, KG Peiper to move west are stopped and the KG takes up a defensive position at La Gleize to await resupply with fuel. In the south Bastogne is cut off by the German advance. 2nd Panzer Division goes north of Bastogne and is pushed off westwards.

General Eisenhower appoints Field Marshal Montgomery to command all Allied Armies north of the Bulge. The British XXX Corps is deployed along the river Meuse as a cordon while the American 1st and 9th Armies prepare to counter-attack into the northern flank of the Bulge.

21st In the north the German attack is stopped and contained. An attempt by KG Peiper to break out at Cheneux is blocked. In the southern sector the American commander in Bastogne rejects a German demand to surrender. The weather improves, allowing the Allied Air Forces to give some Close Air Support and to airdrop supplies to Bastogne.

22nd As the weather continues to improve Allied aircraft fly more missions to attack the German forces and their Lines of Communications. Allied counter moves in the north build up the pressure on the 6th Panzer Army. In the south, Panzer Lehr takes St Hubert but cannot go further. The 101st Airborne Division mounts a series of counter-attacks from Bastogne forcing the German troops around the town onto the defensive. American armoured units moving north from General Patton's 3rd Army run into the left flank of the German 5th Parachute Division, part of 7th Army.

23rd The 6th Panzer Army is forced to give ground by increasing pressure from the north-west. The tempo of Allied air attacks builds up.

24th 2nd Panzer Division reaches the farthest point of the German advance; halted by lack of fuel three miles east of Dinant, they see the Meuse but cannot reach it. The German forces surrounding Bastogne make a last desperate attempt to take the town but are beaten off. Some forward elements of 5th Panzer, afraid of being isolated, begin to fight their way back to the east. In the north the remnants of G Peiper retire from La Gleize.

25th 6th Panzer Army sends its reserve formation south to reinforce the attacks on Bastogne, but it arrives too late to be effective. As tanks from Patton's 3rd Army approach, the 5th Panzer Army goes over to defence.

26th Tanks of the 4th Armoured Division arrive at the Bastogne perimeter and relieve the 101st Airborne Division.

29th The German senior officers in the Bulge conclude that they should end all offensive operations in the sector and withdraw. The Allied commanders are now intent on pursuing the exhausted German troops back to the Rhine.

January 1945

3rd The OKW agree that 5th and 6th Panzer Armies should withdraw from the Bulge towards the Siegfried Line to prepare for the last defensive battle for Germany. The German armies have to fall back in contact with Allied ground forces and under constant heavy air attacks.

13th A great Russian offensive begins; 6th Panzer Army is pulled out to be sent east.

17th Forward elements of the American 1st and 3rd Armies meet at Houffalize, north of Bastogne, cutting off German troops to the west.

23rd In the northern sector American troops of the 75th Division take St Vith.

25th The whole front comes to rest slightly to the west of where it had been on 15 December. The US 1st Army renews attacks towards the Roer dams. The British 2nd Army moves to attack towards the Lower Rhine.

March 1945

American forces cross the Rhine.

ACKNOWLEDGMENTS

Special thanks are due to Sarah Paterson at the Imperial War Museum; Betsy Plumb at the National D-Day Museum in New Orleans for finding the records of the men who fought in both Normandy and the Ardennes; to David Fletcher at Bovington Camp, Dorset for his expertise on the British participants in the battle; and to Donald Binney.

David & Charles would like to thank the following for the kind permission to reproduce material from the following sources:

Bradley, O and Blair; C *A General's Life*, Sidgwick and Jackson, 1983. p. 28, 29, 30-1, 224-5

Butcher, HC; *Three Years of Eisenhower* published by William Heinemann. Reprinted by permission of The Random House Group Ltd. p. 86, 88

Egger, BE and Otts, LM; *G Company's War: Two Personal Accounts of the Campaigns in Europe, 1944–1945*, University of Alabama Press, 1992. p. 120-1

Fitzgibbon, Constantine; *The Fatal Decisions*, Michael Joseph, London, 1956 226

Horrocks, B; *A Full Life*, reprinted by permission of HarperCollins Publishers Ltd., © B Horrocks, 1960. p. 86-7

Kirby, N; *1,100 Miles with Monty*, Alan Sutton Publishing, 1979. p. 226

Liddel-Hart, BH; *The Other Side of the Hill*, Pan, extract reproduced by permission of David Higham Associates Ltd. p. 35-8

Miller, Lee; Courtesy of Condé Nast © Lee Miller Archives, England. All rights reserved. 272-3

Metcalfe Rexford, Mary; *Battlestars and Doughnuts: World War II Clubmobile Experiences of Mark Metcalfe Rexford*, extract reproduced by permission of The Rexford Family

Norwalk, Rosemary; *Dearest Ones: a true World War II love story*, 1999, extract reproduced by permission of John Wiley & Sons, Inc. p. 137-41

Parker, Danny S *To Win the Winter Sky: Air War over the Ardennes, 1944–1945*, London, 1994. Copyright © Danny S Parker 1994. Extract reproduced by permission of Greehill Books/ Lionel Leventhal Ltd. p. 117-18

Parker, Danny S *Hitler's Ardennes Offensive*, Greenhill Books, London 1997. Copyright © Danny S Parker 1997. Extract reproduced by permission of Greehill Books/Lionel Leventhal Ltd. p. 31-5, 39, 90-2

Reynolds, Michael *The Devil's Adjuntant*, with kind permission of the author and the publishers, Spellmount Ltd., Staplehurst, Kent TN12 0BJ. p. 99-101

Story of the 23rd Hussars, The, written and compiled by members of the Regiment, reproduced with kind permission of the The King's Royal Hussars Museum in Winchester. p. 40-1, 42, 66-9, 134-5

INDEX OF CONTRIBUTORS

GENERAL INDEX

PICTURE CREDITS

Title page Imperial War Museum EA58566; 11 Imperial War Museum MH12850; 17 Imperial War
Museum EA48014; 22 Imperial War Museum FRA200371; 37 akg-images; 43 Imperial War Museum
EA48296; 47 Imperial War Museum HU86298; 71 Imperial War Museum EA47933; 74 Imperial War
Museum EA47966; 81 Imperial War Museum EA47962; 87 Imperial War Museum EA47947; 101
Imperial War Museum AP50915; 103 Imperial War Museum EA48892; 106 Imperial War Museum
EA48040; 116 Imperial War Museum FRA102200; 127 Imperial War Museum AP48452; 136 Imperial
War Museum FRA101888; 145 Imperial War Museum EA43216; 152 akg-images/Tony Vaccaro; 167
Imperial War Museum AP48554; 169 Imperial War Museum EA50908; 203 Imperial War Museum
EA48447; 209 Imperial War Museum EA68715; 225 Imperial War Museum FRA101883; 237 Imperial
War Museum EA49938; 245 Imperial War Museum EA69243; 253 Imperial War Museum FRA102204;
267 Imperial War Museum HU86299